Date Due

DEC 15			
Dec 29			
WA Feb90			
FO May90			
AUApr91			
JUL 06 91			
ET Sep91			
CRAFeb92			

HARD CHOICES

A LIFE OF
TOM BERGER

HARD CHOICES

A LIFE OF
TOM BERGER

CAROLYN SWAYZE

Douglas & McIntyre
Vancouver/Toronto

Douglas & McIntyre Ltd.
1615 Venables Street
Vancouver, British Columbia   V5L 2H1

Canadian Cataloguing in Publication Data

Swayze, Carolyn, 1945–
    Hard Choices

        Includes index.
        ISBN 0-88894-522-1

        1. Berger, Thomas R.   2. Politicians –
British Columbia – Biography.   3. Judges –
British Columbia – Biography.   I. Title.
FC3828.1.B47S93 1986   971.1'04'0924   C86-091256-8
F1088.B47S93 1986

Design by Barbara Hodgson
Typeset by The Typeworks
Printed and bound in Canada by John Deyell Company

To the memory of my brothers
DOUGLAS M. SWAYZE
3 November 1937 – 6 June 1986
and
HUGH E. SWAYZE
6 June 1940 – 25 December 1978
and for
C. J. MOYER,
who believed in this book
and in my hard choices.

Contents

Preface

The first though least important fact about Thomas R. Berger is the pronunciation of his name. Berger rhymes with merger. Or, as one transcript typist heard it: "Thomas, our verger."

The second and most important fact about Tom Berger is that he believes, and believes passionately, in the integrity of Canada's system of equitable justice and its attendant jurisprudence.

In late 1983, after a twelve-year sojourn on the bench of the Supreme Court of British Columbia, during which time he conducted three royal commissions for the governments of three national political parties, he also wrote a book, published articles, taught law school, served on the boards of a number of associations, gave numerous speeches, and provoked politicians and the public more often than is fitting for a judge, Tom Berger resigned. He then chaired the Alaska Native Review Commission for two years before returning to the practice of law. He continues to advocate justice at every opportunity, and even during "The Music in My Life," a CBC radio program on which he was a guest, he managed to inject his views: "How we treat minorities, says a lot about who we are. I speak as a member in good standing of the majority." His choice of music on the show suggests the dimensions of the man and his life: "Moon River," a romantic ballad that was popular during the 1950s when Tom and his wife Beverley were courting; Judy Collins singing Gordon Lightfoot's "Early Morning Rain"; songs by Indian rights activist Buffy Sainte-Marie, whom Berger met in the 1960s; Inuit throat singers, like the ones he heard on his travels in the North, and Gordon Lightfoot's "Canadian Railroad Trilogy." Of the latter he said: "It's a good song. It reminds us that it was not just Lord Strathcona who built the railway. It pays tribute to the thousands of people, known only to their families, who do the world's work. That's worth celebrating." He also chose Beethoven's *Pastoral Symphony,* because it reminded him of what man is capable, of what he can achieve, as well as imbuing him with a sense of humility. "That music is immortal. What we've been talking about is pretty limited in time and space."

Tom Berger's comments during this show serve to summarize why I chose to chronicle his career.

I first met Tom Berger in my second year of law school at the University of Victoria. Once a week he travelled by ferry from Vancouver to teach a three-hour class in civil liberties. Initially, Berger was to have taken leave from the bench so that he could serve a term as a visiting professor. But plans had gone awry. Allan McEachern, chief justice of the Supreme Court of British Columbia, had decided that the court's work load was too heavy to spare him. Berger, however, was determined to teach something of the history of human rights and dissent in Canada, so he reorganized his work load to make time to teach the class. A measure of the esteem accorded him by law students was the size of the class; upon occasion, the aisles were dotted with visitors from other faculties.

We were drawn to the class by the Honourable Thomas R. Berger's reputation as one of the few Canadian heroes of our generation. Although he was not a consistently dynamic lecturer, his reputation was tangibly evidenced by the published reports of his commission work, by his precedent-shattering cases as a lawyer, by his intellectually rigorous decisions as a judge and by his just-published book, *Fragile Freedoms,* which formed the basis of his lectures. We were aware also of his willingness to put his judge-ship on the line in order to ensure the protection of minority rights and had hopes that through him we would learn how the law could be used altruistically.

By the end of that term I had decided that the story of Tom Berger's work was a story worth telling, that an account of his career would likely make a greater contribution to legal awareness than I might accomplish as a practising lawyer. He did not, however, react enthusiastically to my idea. After I wrote to him requesting his co-operation in the project, we arranged a meeting. Sitting face to face in a vacant office, he asked the question uppermost in his mind: "Do you think I'm about to die?"

He was nearly fifty years old, his brown hair was beginning to silver, his square jaw and blue eyes were resolute. "Not yet," I told him, "not yet."

"In that case," he said, "not yet." He was far too young to have a biographer, he said, and reiterated his rejection with clearly thought out reasons why it was a bad idea. One objection was the time it would require of me: he thought that as a law student who was nearly forty, I should make articling and practice my immediate priorities. He also naturally had some concerns for his personal privacy and more for that of his family, as well as for the sensitivities of other people still living who might be hurt by my prying.

I countered with my reasons why a biography was a good idea: it was a way to show how one person could make an impact on society, an opportunity to encourage understanding of our recent history and to head off apathy on the part of the rising generation of lawyers. And besides, I persisted, I had been a writer before law school and would continue to write. I also said I doubted that readers wanted to learn only about dead Canadians.

Our dialogue continued by mail for months, and by the last term of my final year I had begun to send him draft chapters based on my law library research. He could not resist setting me straight on the law, and eventually the chapters would come back, their margins filled with scrawled comments and corrections, which I incorporated into new versions.

Tom Berger officially conceded a year later when I followed him to Alaska where he was conducting hearings in native villages. "When I saw you get out of that floatplane in the bush," he said, "I realized that you were as determined to do your work as I was mine."

The story of Tom Berger's hard choices is the result of many interviews, together with library and archival research. Some of the story I pieced together by reading articles in scholarly and popular publications, by plowing through 40,000 federal government documents obtained through the Access to Information Act and by looking over a carload of files, news clippings, transcripts and scrapbooks taken from the basement of the Berger family home. I talked for many hours with Tom Berger and members of his family and people who had worked with him, I attended his speeches and I sat at commission hearings. I also interviewed and corresponded with dozens of other people; and hundreds more, upon learning of my work, reacted with information and comments that reaffirmed my belief that Tom Berger's life is one worth chronicling.

Of course, the career is, in essence, the man. But Tom Berger has stubbornly played down his role in the social changes his work has accomplished, changes that he diligently and tenaciously pursued through education, research, legal case work, political activism, in elected office, in the classroom, from the bench, through royal commissions, on the air, in the written word and in public forums. His work and his personal example of selfless service stand as a tribute to his dedication. Consequently, Tom Berger's work shaped the format of this book, rather than chronology: Tom Berger, lawyer for oppressed native Indians, workers and accused criminals; Tom Berger, politician, federal member of parliament, leader of the New Democratic Party of British Columbia, member of the legislative assembly; the Honourable Mr. Justice R. Berger of the Supreme Court of British Columbia; Commissioner Berger, and twenty-five years later, full circle to Tom Berger, lawyer. In all these, the consequences of his hard choices speak eloquently for him.

In writing this book, I am grateful for the initial encouragement of John Pearce and Bo Hansen, and for the sustained interest and support of Bella Pomer, C. Heather Allen, Brendan Allen, Ann Knight and Val Chapman. I commend my daughter, Natalie Moyer, for her unflagging sympathy and my son, David Moyer, for never taking me seriously. Diana Priestly, Terry Wuester, Hamar Foster and Dave Godfrey of the University of Victoria assisted me in my efforts to fit the preliminary research and writing within the prescribed curriculum of the Faculty of Law. This book was also made possible by a grant from the Explorations program of the Canada Council.

Numerous people—politicians, judges, lawyers, clients, family and friends—gave freely of their time and information. The great joy of this project was the opportunity it presented to meet with so many intelligent and thoughtful people. The native people of village Alaska were consistently hospitable and generous. I regret not being able to thank everyone personally.

I am indebted to Tom Berger for his unremitting courtesy and assistance. Although both he and I experienced separate professional and personal difficulties during the course of this project, our working relationship never wavered. Beverley Berger met my requests with candour and good humour, as did other members of the Berger family and their friends.

CHAPTER 1

Beginnings

W hen Tom and Beverley Berger's daughter, Erin, commenced legal studies at the University of Calgary in 1984, she became the fourth-generation Berger to embark on a life in the law. The tradition had begun in Sweden where Tom Berger's grandfather, the original Judge Berger, presided in Göteborg. His son Theodore, Tom's father, emigrated to Canada and made a career in the law with the Royal Canadian Mounted Police. He, in turn, instilled his son Tom with a respect for the place of justice in the life of a nation and taught him that the law must uphold not only great principles but protect small people from injustice of all kinds.

When Theodore was a young boy in Sweden, his mother left the family and Judge Berger remarried, but the boy and his stepmother never got along well. Theodore was sent to a military academy, an institution at odds with his independent temperament. When he returned home, it seemed to him that his differences with the judge and his wife were profound and irreconcilable. And so in 1911, at the age of twenty, he packed his bags. Although his eldest stepsister, Malin, aged ten, cried and begged him not to go, he walked away and did not contact his family until fifty years had passed.

As two of the five or six languages that Theodore spoke were English and French, he chose to emigrate to Canada where he became Ted Berger. For the next six years this tall, strong loner worked as a fireman in Montreal, but it was not a way of life that satisfied him. It lacked the sense of purpose he had hoped to find, and Montreal was not the Canada he had envisioned. That country was in the west. At the age of twenty-seven he joined the Royal Canadian Mounted Police, which had, he thought, the potential to satisfy both of his needs. After ten years, he was assigned to the Bulkley Valley farming community of Telkwa in northwestern British Columbia. Corporal Berger thrived on his work and was a highly regarded member of the force. The conscientious way in which he fulfilled his responsibilities and brought justice to the district earned him the respect of fellow policemen and of local inhabitants, among them Tom McDonald, his wife Susanna and their four daughters.

McDonald was an immigrant homesteader, an Irish Protestant, who had left Northern Ireland in the 1880s to find a haven in Canada. When the family arrived in the remote Bulkley Valley, one of his daughters, Perle, was just thirteen. "Things were different then," she recalls. "It was a hard life, but we didn't think it was primitive. Now, I guess, you'd say it was." Perle left the valley to board with a married sister while attending the New Westminster Modern School of Business, but after earning her diploma, she returned home. Commerce in the Bulkley Valley in the 1920s was primarily in the hands of a local entrepreneur, Dick Sargent, and Perle worked for him, dividing her time between doing the bookkeeping for his store and minding the Telkwa post office.

Perle McDonald was twenty-two when the strapping Corporal Berger caught her eye. He was thirty-seven, a pipe-smoking man inclined to be taciturn and shy with women. Although Perle was quiet, she had the friendly, forthright manner of a person raised and working within a warm circle of family and friends. She was irresistible to the lonely officer, and they were married in Telkwa in 1928.

Six months after the wedding, the RCMP detachment was moved sixty miles north to Hazelton at the confluence of the Skeena and Bulkley rivers. Here Corporal Berger was in charge of a four-constable unit with jurisdiction over a scattered population, the majority of whom were Gitksan Indians.

Vivid memories of Corporal Berger are retained by James Teetzel Harvey, who in the 1930s was a young lawyer practising in nearby Smithers and Hazelton. "He was a tall, rather slim man of an erect, soldierly bearing; balding, with a long face and large eyes. I disliked what I thought was his total absence of humour, although later I realized that he either deliberately concealed it from me or I was too young to see it. Even then, I knew that for sheer capability, competence and decency, you couldn't fault Corporal Berger. I see some of his attributes in young Tom."

Perle and Ted's first son, Teddy, was born in 1930. Two years later, a promotion took the family to the provincial capital, Victoria, where a second son, Thomas Rodney, was born in 1933. Like Teddy, Tommy was good-natured and healthy, and he gave his parents no indication he would grow up to take life quite as seriously as he did. That he did may have had something to do with his father, for Ted Berger soon took a fateful step in a small matter that to him was nevertheless a fundamental issue of justice. He chose to enforce the law against a high-ranking and well-connected naval officer. The ramifications of his steadfast belief that the law should be applied equally to all people were to reverberate through the remainder of Ted Berger's working life. Although normal advancements no longer came his way, a measure of good resulted. Out of the experience emerged a visionary Tom Berger, imbued with the conviction that principles must be defended, wrongs righted and the justice system upheld, no matter what the cost.

Tommy was still a toddler when the first signal came that Sgt. Ted Berger was not to be forgiven. He was transferred from the capital to Penticton, a dusty fruit-growing town in the south Okanagan Valley, where in January 1939, a third son, Brian, was born. Then the sergeant and his family were sent farther away to Prince Albert, Saskatchewan, "where no one was born," Perle Berger says with a faint smile.

Before long the Bergers were assigned to Regina, Saskatchewan, the national headquarters and training centre for the RCMP, where the top brass abounded and there was little opportunity to make independent decisions or to take individual responsibility. Sergeant Berger was in charge of the downtown detachment and also taught recruits at the barracks on the outskirts of the city. His duties left little time for family life, but Tom was proud of his father, the policeman. "He had trophies for marksmanship and he used to clean his revolver at home."

The family's quarters on the fifth floor of the town station were somewhat grim, but the joy of the posting was the birth of a daughter, Susan, in 1940. The boys were then ten, seven and two. For the young mother, that summer was interminable and insufferably hot. Each morning they hurried to escape their stuffy, noisy rooms. The first stop was the public library where Tom, already an eager reader, would choose a book. Then, it was on to the park where the newborn Susan slept as Mrs. Berger brushed away the incessantly moving, clicking grasshoppers. After a picnic lunch, Tom walked back to the library to exchange his morning book for an afternoon read. One day, his mother remembers, he returned in a fury, empty-handed.

"That stupid woman!" he fumed. "She won't let me have another book!"

"The librarian meant well," Mrs. Berger asserts. "And I know what she was thinking. She didn't believe Tom was reading the entire book. She thought he was just making work for the library staff."

It was a cruel rein on one of Tom's greatest pleasures, and the incident embodied what would become the two great passions of his life — an intolerance of injustice and an abiding love of literature.

By 1943 it was apparent to Sergeant Berger that the force would offer him no further opportunities and that he had little choice but to retire. A second career in the public service, which might have been expected to come his way after twenty-five years with the RCMP, did not materialize. This disappointment, too, may have been a consequence of the episode in Victoria, but he never discussed it with his children. In those days there was no Canada pension plan and his RCMP retirement stipend was not sufficient to support his young family, so the Bergers left Regina for British Columbia, which they considered to be home and where they thought employment prospects would be good. Their hopes were not realized, however, as available jobs were going to men returning from the Second World War.

The family moved around the Lower Mainland, taking low

rental houses in White Rock, Richmond, Vancouver, and finally in Dollarton on the North Arm of Burrard Inlet. Jobs were scarce, but Ted Berger did not complain. He looked for work constantly, and he never expressed bitterness about the hard consequences of having done his duty, even though for four or five years during the 1950s, he was out of work altogether.

"You can't understand the degradation, the destroying of dignity, that this does to a man and his family," Tom Berger later told *Vancouver Sun* columnist Allan Fotheringham. "When he did find work, the jobs made little use of his talents. In White Rock, Dad was a security guard at the Boeing Aircraft plant on Sea Island. Later, he was a night watchman, a warehouseman, and he worked for Eaton's. In his sixties, he was employed as a bank messenger.

"For someone who'd been a sergeant in the RCMP, the jobs he held afterward might have seemed menial, but he treated them as jobs that deserved to be done," Tom said with pride. "I've always been struck by that."

To Tom Berger, his father was a rather remote figure, but kind. Ethical and stoic, Ted Berger conveyed to his son an understanding of how the tension between politics and law made an impact on everyday life. His commentaries on the times clearly made an impression on Tom, who would later struggle to protect civil liberties in Canada. "One of my earliest memories of my father and his politics was his telling me how much he admired Angus MacInnis for defending Japanese Canadians. I think it was said during the time of their expulsion, which would make it the early Forties. We often discussed current events."

Family life remained solid, despite the hardships. Ted Berger shared a love of reading with the older boys, and both parents encouraged them in their studies. "But my mother was the centre of our family. Through the good times and the difficult times, she managed the household. She took a keen interest in our school work and, like my father, always insisted that we should tell the truth and do the right thing. My mother believed, and still believes, that family members must always be loyal to one another."

It is a philosophy of life that Tom Berger embraced. He is loyal to his late father's faith in the RCMP and does not entertain any exploration of the inside politics that may have contributed to the demise of Ted Berger's career and that brought the family so many years of privation. But he also deplores the injustice that caused it, and from the time he understood what had happened, he resolved to fight such wrongs.

Because of the vagaries of rental housing and of Ted Berger's jobs, the family moved many times and Tom was in a different school every year, sometimes two in a year. Fortunately, his early reading habits paid off, and perfect report cards came effortlessly to him. But Tom lost sight of his star in high school. "He slumped," says his mother. "He only went to school for track and English rugby. I remember talking to Mr. 'Mickey' McDougall, the principal and math teacher. He said of Tom, 'There's a boy who's only doing enough to get by.' "

His tenure as a secondary school student cannot be termed distinguished, but Tom Berger did set his goals. "I decided I wanted to be a journalist, a teacher or a lawyer. I see, looking back, all three had to do with the same kind of skills. I guess, even then, I had ideas I wanted to communicate. And I was lucky. I was able to have those three careers and more. That happened, I think, because I regained Mr. McDougall's confidence. As principal, 'Mickey' often had to absent himself because of his other duties and he would have me take charge of the class for him. I became enthusiastic about school again."

As a chagrined 1950 graduate whose grades were only average, Tom told his mother, "I should have worked harder, sooner. I could have had scholarships." Because he did not, he was forced to take senior matriculation, the equivalent of first-year university, at high school where tuition costs were lower. This time he did earn scholarship money, and the following year he commenced his studies in the Faculty of Arts at the University of British Columbia (UBC). Having earned the highest first-year mark in the provincial English examination, he was invited to join a special English literature class in which all members of the faculty took turns discussing their specialties. "In addition to my regular English lectures, I had the pleasure of being taught by Earle Birney, Stanley Reed and others. Each discussed his own poetry or period. I remember Roy Daniells on Milton. I loved it."

Tom's brother Ted was attending UBC at the same time, and both were living on campus, struggling to support themselves. Tom lived in the cheapest housing, the old military barracks known as the Fort Camp huts, sharing a room with Richard D'Andrea (later a judge of the Provincial Court in Castlegar,

B.C.), and their friendship endured until D'Andrea's death in 1986.

In the 1950s UBC was the realm of a goodhearted troika: Gordon Shrum, Norman MacKenzie and the benevolent Walter Gage. "If you ran right out of money, and I did, despite the scholarship and the summer jobs," Tom recollects, "you went to Walter Gage and he took a bursary off the shelf. He really was the students' friend."

The summer he was eighteen, Tom had a job as a labourer for McKenzie Barge and Derrick in Dollarton where they built and repaired the vessels that carried hog fuel, sawdust for the now-obsolete beehive burners. The outdoor job suited his taste. Not for him a stint in a library or an insurance agency. "It was a nice summer," Berger says dreamily. "I haven't thought about it in years. I remember standing on top of an eight-inch barge wall, maybe twenty-five feet from the ground, swinging a sledge hammer to drive spikes."

The following summer he took a job at a logging camp on the Brandywine River. "We worked in a cedar swamp. We were making telephone poles. We'd cut down the trees, peel them, drag them to a railway siding, peavey them onto a flat car. We did the whole thing, just the three of us—the owner, his son and me," Tom says with satisfaction.

Every summer after that Tom worked at Norwood Sawmill in North Vancouver on the green chain. He held an International Woodworkers of America union card for five years—his first experience with the collective protection of workers' rights. "I would go to Norwood in the morning after my last exam in the spring and would leave at the end of the afternoon shift before school started again the next fall. I never took a holiday. It was out of the question. There was no real sense of sacrifice about any of this. The opportunity to go to university and to get into a profession was one I eagerly accepted. By second year, I was determined to be a lawyer."

One day Tom went home to visit his parents in Dollarton. "A surprise visit. My father was home when I arrived, which was odd since he was employed at the time. But my mother and father said that he was simply ill and had taken the day off. I turned up a few weeks later for some reason, unexpectedly, and again he was at home. I remember both of them insisting that he was still working. My brother Ted and I then realized that he had been laid off, but they had not wanted us to find out about it because they were afraid that one or both of us would give up university to go to work to support the family." As much for their parents as themselves, the boys stayed in school. When Ted graduated in engineering, his father was intensely proud.

For Tom, who was still a student, leisure and money continued to be scarce. "I had a job in the evenings working in the campus canteen. This, together with study, didn't leave an awful lot of time for anything else." Still, he found time to notice a vivacious, outgoing young woman in the cafeteria. In the spring of 1954, he had a date with her. Beverley Ann Crosby. Her home was in Powell River, an isolated upcoast milltown, so she, too, lived on campus in student housing. Tom had no car and very little money. "Our dates consisted of walking to the Varsity Theatre to see a movie or just going for a long walk."

Bev was a fun-loving, first-year arts student who could always take time away from her studies for a mean game of tennis. Just as Perle Berger's friendly manner had drawn the taciturn Ted Berger into her life, so Beverley Crosby's engaging personality enticed the younger Berger out of his narrow, work-dominated world into hers. She taught him to play tennis and did it so well that they are still tennis partners thirty years later.

Tom and Bev became engaged in the summer of 1955. Her parents had been divorced when she was younger, and her aunt who came to take care of the household had introduced her to Catholicism, so the engaged couple attended marriage preparation classes sponsored by the Catholic Church. Tom took issue with some of the tenets of the faith but persevered. Although he had been raised in the Anglican Church, he attended only sporadically and with no particular fervour. Thus, it made sense to defer to Bev's choice and to begin their new life united by one church.

Bev completed first-year university, a prerequisite for Normal School which she went on to attend, and in November of 1955, after she had been teaching primary school for three months, she and Tom were married. They could not afford a wedding photographer, but a few friends took snapshots. Bev looks young, lovely and radiant. Tom looks young, tense and his eyes are half-closed. "From the stag party," Bev explains. "They tried to kill him with alcohol the night before. I was so upset."

It was Tom's last year of law school.

"We lived in a basement suite of an old rooming house on Twelfth Avenue in Vancouver. One of the jobs I had to defray the rent was to keep the furnace stoked by shovelling coal every night. But we had such a sense of wonder and excitement. We thought, and so did our friends, that we could achieve things that our parents had been unable to."

The young couple's friends were, for the most part, people they had met at school, particularly law students who enjoyed visiting "off-campus." One law student friend was John Bruk, a Yugoslavian immigrant who, though older than Berger, was a year behind him. Bruk, now the chairman of Asia Pacific Foundation and formerly the president of Cyprus Anvil Mining Corporation, still cherishes the times as a student spent with Tom and a few others, discussing "people, nations and humankind. It was always stimulating to be exposed to those brilliant minds." Bruk worried whether the legal community would have room for a New Canadian, and he turned to Berger for advice. "I went to see him at his office, and he said, 'John, as long as you do the same good work you did at school and do your best, you'll have clients.' "

Tom Berger took what was then called a double degree. After three years in the arts faculty he went directly into law, and after three more years, emerged with two degrees: a Bachelor of Arts and a Bachelor of Law. "Isn't that remarkable?" Berger muses. "I didn't deserve a B.A. What did I know?" He received his LL.B. in the spring of 1956, standing third behind Rendina Hossie and Elaine Evans, two of the three women in his class.

Tom's father was even prouder than when Ted had graduated. "Not because he preferred me in any way, but because it was *law,*" Tom explains. "It was then that he asked me to write to his family in Sweden—to tell them after an absence of nearly fifty years where he was."

CHAPTER 2

The Young Barrister

During the last year of law school, Tom Berger had been searching for a legal firm with which to complete his articling year—an apprenticeship of sorts under the eye of a supervising principal. An articled student, if lucky, has experiences, instruction and opportunities that help to prepare him or her for a life in the law. The articled student is paid very little, works long hours and prepares for yet more exams.

Beverley Berger's stepfather, Clifford Worthington, was a business agent for the carpenters' union, which was represented by Shulman, Tupper & Southin, and he suggested that Tom apply to article with them. "They were in the old Standard Building in downtown Vancouver and in addition to representing the carpenters, they did a lot of work in the labour law field," Berger recalls. "I wasn't a particularly aware or active union member when I worked at the mill, but I had studied labour law and done well in it. The kind of work Shulman, Tupper & Southin did interested me, so I went down to see them and they took me on."

Shulman, Tupper & Southin not only took Tom Berger on, they exposed him to the grittiest kind of legal work and allowed him to carry as much responsibility as he was capable of. His ex-

perience under the tutelage of Isaac "Ike" Shulman, Harold Tupper and Mary Southin catapulted him into the branches of law that
would make him famous.

"On my first day, the partners took me down for coffee. There
was a large booth where they always sat. Tom Hurley, who had
his office in the same building, joined us for coffee that day.
Hurley was then in his mid-seventies, the doyen of the criminal
bar. Everyone was talking about the Coffin case that day."

In 1953 the bodies of three American hunters had been found in
the Gaspé woods, and Coffin, a local prospector, had been
charged with murder and convicted. Because rumours were rampant that he had not received a fair trial, the cabinet referred the
matter to the Supreme Court of Canada (SCC); but the court
upheld Coffin's conviction, and he was hanged on 10 February
1956.

The discussion over coffee that morning was based on the
court's decision, which had just been published. "They deferred
to Tom Hurley and wanted his opinion on the judgment. After he
gave it, he turned to me and said, 'Mr. Berger, what do you think
of the judgment?'

"I can't remember what answer I may have made, but what
struck me was his genuine interest in my opinion, even though it
was only my first day as an articled student. I got to know him
well after that," says Berger fondly. "Tom Hurley had an extensive law library, but in those days, you had to send the weekly
law reports back to the bindery every month to be bound, and he
never did. So he had walls full of shelves of unbound law reports.
This meant that you could never find anything in his library. Yet
he knew the cases; in the criminal field, because he had argued
many of the principal cases, and in the civil field, because he had a
remarkable knowledge of the law anyway. Often, as we were
walking into the old police court, now the provincial court, he
would draw an envelope on which he'd written a few notes out of
his jacket pocket. This would form the basis of his cross-
examination and argument."

Berger not only admired Hurley's style, he adopted it. For both
barristers, old Tom Hurley and young Tom Berger, the "envelope defence" was a practice that reflected expertise and competence rather than a lackadaisical approach. Hurley also helped
Berger with substantive and tactical preparations. "I used to go to
talk to him about cases. Many young lawyers used to do that since

he was always available. We would leave his office and walk across to the beer parlour. We spent many hours in beer parlours, having a few beer and talking about the law. I learned much from Tom Hurley during those sessions. Often, I would drive him home and there we would have another drink together and talk more about the law."

After Berger completed his year of articles in May of 1957, he was called to the bar as a full-fledged practising lawyer. Shulman, Tupper & Southin asked him to continue working for them, and life looked even more promising. Tom was in his element. Law was everything that he had hoped it would be. On one occasion he was in Quesnel, a small country town in the interior of British Columbia, defending a client on a murder charge. It was a jury trial. When he had finished his summation, Berger phoned his office. "The jury has just gone out," he told them. "They'll be back in forty minutes with a 'not guilty' verdict." That was exactly what happened.

The Bergers moved to rental housing on Kings Road near UBC after Erin was born on 5 May 1958. Bev had resigned from teaching, as Tom's working hours were far too long and demanding for the young couple to consider sharing child care responsibilities and Bev wanted to be a full-time wife and mother. Before long, however, it became apparent that Tom's propensity for representing worthy but nonpaying clients meant that the Bergers could not live on his salary alone. When Erin was nine months old, Bev resumed teaching, this time at University Hill Elementary School.

Despite the financial pinch, the Bergers were giddy with the richness of their family life and their prospects for the future. The Bergers' optimism really was unbounded, and they shared it with their friends. John Bruk recalls, "Carol and I had young children, too, and little money. Entertainment was good conversation and the television. Bev and Tom had one and that was a great treat. We could go there for 'Hockey Night in Canada.' Sometimes we even had a case of beer."

For the most part, however, Tom Berger's life was centred on the law. He truly loved it, reading law reports the way other people read newspapers, and he was always looking for and thinking about ways to use the law for the advancement of worthwhile causes. One cause that was not popularly viewed as being worthwhile was communism. "I espoused, not communism itself,"

Tom explains, "but the right of communists to freedom of expression, which included running for office and so forth." Berger knew about the McCarthy-style purges that had rid trade unions of people with communist connections during the early 1950s. Frequently, the first to be ousted were members of the Labour Progressive Party (formerly the Communist Party of Canada), whose members had been instrumental in organizing the trade union movement in British Columbia during the 1930s and 1940s.

To some extent the communism issue was a reflection of the times in British Columbia—times that showed little sympathy for people in trouble or for labourers. The province was governed by a populist Social Credit premier, W. A. C. Bennett, who had wrested power from a coalition of the Liberal and Conservative parties. His government had not implemented the "funny money" policies of prairie Socreds but had adopted a strong free-enterprise stance that emphasized traditional conservative values. Bennett's Socreds were in tune with the ideas of western voters in a way that meant virtual extermination of the Progressive Conservative and Liberal parties. The Social Credit party was in direct opposition to the Co-operative Commonwealth Federation (CCF) party with its labour support and leftist tinge. This political and social climate conspired to push Berger into the arena of labour law where his fresh approach to contentious and controversial cases shot him to prominence.

One such case involved George Gee, who had become the business agent for the International Brotherhood of Electrical Workers in 1949 and had responded to anticommunist pressure by renouncing his Labour Progressive Party membership "for the good of the union." In December of 1954, the American Federation of Labor and its Canadian counterpart, the Trades and Labour Congress, announced a drive to rid member unions of all "red-tinged leadership" and ordered Gee to fire an assistant business agent, Don Wilson. When Gee refused, the international union claimed that the reason he would not fire Wilson was because Gee himself was "a secret agent for the Communist Party" and was obliged to wait for its orders. Gee laughingly dismissed the allegation as ridiculous, but a short time later he found himself charged with violating the union's constitution by supporting a cause detrimental to the union.

During a union-conducted tribunal in which the same men acted as both witnesses and prosecutors, numerous alleged transgressions were cited. Among them were assertions that Gee had rented space to the leftist Mine, Mill and Smelter Workers' Union, that he had attended a Paul Robeson concert and that he had attempted to have his union local pass a resolution demanding freedom for the Rosenbergs, the convicted U.S. spies who were later executed.

The tribunal convicted Gee. He was dismissed as the union's business agent and, as of 11 April 1955, was expelled from the union in which he had held membership for twenty years, on the grounds that he had worked "on behalf of the communist cause." He was only one of hundreds of unionists driven from office, even from the ranks. Gee returned to his old job as a lineman for B.C. Electric, but when his employer realized he was no longer a "union member in good standing" as required under the collective bargaining agreement which, ironically, Gee himself had negotiated, he was pulled off the job. He turned immediately to Shulman, Tupper & Southin to bring suit.

"I was only a year at the bar, then," Berger says. "Ike Shulman was to act as counsel. I was assisting in the preparation of the case. In the end, Ike was too busy, and we brought in Tom Hurley as senior counsel; I was junior. But Tom, always generous, made the opening address to the court and then had me take the witnesses through their testimony. He reserved to himself only the examination of some of the key defendants.

"Hurley was unfailingly courteous, never had a bad word to say about anyone—not even judges before whom he had just lost a tough case. He never received any of the professional accolades that he should have. He was never a Queen's Counsel; never offered an appointment to the bench. Of course, he had a drinking problem and lived many years with Maisie, a woman not then his wife. I suppose that in the Fifties when I knew him those were quite dreadful things, but I remember him as a man who taught me much."

In 1958 Tom Berger and his mentor Tom Hurley told Mr. Justice J. O. Wilson of the B.C. Supreme Court that a still-unemployed George Gee had been sentenced to "industrial death" through smears and by conspiracy. Berger's cross-examination of union officials was designed to show how trivial the union's allegations against his client had been. And, Berger argued, they were not bona fide charges in the first place, because they had been laid with malicious intent to deprive Gee of his livelihood.

But Justice Wilson sided with the international union's position that Gee had demonstrated "leftist political inclinations." He said, "Some of [Gee's] subsequent acts are capable of being interpreted as showing that he maintained his loyalty to communism . . . I think I might safely say that communism is inimical to free trade unions. The known history of all communist-ruled countries clearly demonstrates that the existence of free trade unions, the practice of employer-employee bargaining, cessation of work in an attempt to obtain better wages or working conditions . . . are unknown and indeed inconceivable in those countries."

In his decision, the judge also affirmed the principle that a closed-shop collective agreement can bar a nonmember from employment. That principle was a matter of judicial interpretation, and though Berger hated to lose, the judge's reasoning was clear. Despite losing the case, Berger benefited from the front-page status the press accorded the story, as workers with problems increasingly turned to him for help.

Berger and Tom Hurley worked together on another union case the following year, but this time with the union supporting its members fully and paying for their counsel. The men were ironworkers employed by Dominion Bridge on the Second Narrows Bridge project in Vancouver.

Today, the Second Narrows Bridge arches solidly over the waters of Burrard Inlet. But at 3:40 P.M. on 17 June 1958, with less than half of the planned two-mile span built, the structure had collapsed. Men and their tools, steel and heavy equipment tumbled into chaos. Eighteen died and twenty were injured. All were members of the International Bridge, Structural and Ornamental Ironworkers Union, Local 97. In the wake of the disaster, a royal commission established that "compound human error" had caused the collapse: the weight-bearing ability of the bridge falsework had been inadequate. Although the ironworkers' faith in the engineers was "shaken to a degree," they went back to work.

A year later the union, demanding an increase over the $2.62-per-hour basic rate of their then-expired contract, called a strike. The bridge was still incomplete, with a portion of the structure resting on a falsework bent. The employer, Dominion Bridge Company, contending that it was a "serious hazard to persons and property," sought to have the men remain on the job. The company's lawyer, J. L. Jestley, appeared before Mr. Justice A. M.

Manson of the B.C. Supreme Court to obtain a back-to-work injunction, which directed the union to order their men to continue with the section until it was "rendered entirely safe in the opinion of the consulting engineers." The order was doubly contentious: the consulting engineers were Swan and Wooster, the same company that had certified the bridge's safety prior to the 1958 collapse, and the company's application to the court had been made *ex parte,* which meant that only one party, in this case Dominion Bridge, had been heard. Consequently, when the ironworkers read the press reports, they concluded that there had been a secret hearing in which the company had told the judge that the bridge was unsafe.

Union secretary Norm Eddison conceded that the injunction barred strike action, but he also said that if the engineering company statements were true, the bridge was not safe enough for his men to resume work. "I personally would rot in jail rather than withhold this information from our membership." He announced that, in compliance with the injunction, no strike existed and that refusal to work for reasons of safety could not be construed as strike action.

The men did not return to work, and the union turned to Shulman, Tupper & Southin. Berger, now into his second year of law practice, spent a weekend immersing himself in the law of injunctions. As the four-day term of the back-to-work order had lapsed, Dominion Bridge was forced to apply for a new one. This time engineer Hiram Wooster filed an affidavit that said the danger was merely typical of all structures under erection, "but to state that it is dangerous for workers is an exaggeration completely unwarranted and unjustified by the facts."

Berger accused Dominion Bridge of having misrepresented and suppressed material facts. He told Justice Manson that not only was there no evidence of an unlawful strike but the employer had not shown any infringement of its legal rights. He cited cases to support his contention that there is "no right whatever under the laws of the Province of B.C. to obtain an injunction unless you can show that a legal right has been infringed."

Justice Manson serenely replied that the legal precedents relied upon by Berger might have been relevant "when the courts were sticklers for technicalities" but were "not persuasive today."

Berger then pointed to the contradictions inherent in the engineering partners' affidavits: Wooster's assertion of safety did not square with Swan's allegation of danger. Danger did exist, Berger argued, and it arose from the placement of the support legs close to motor vehicle and railway traffic rather than from the refusal of the workers to work.

Manson would hear none of this and granted the new injunction, compelling the union to order the men to return to the job site until the span reached the permanent support of Pier 16.

Norm Eddison relayed the news by telephone to as many members as could be reached, saying, according to his affidavit:

> As many of the members know from the newspapers and the radio, Mr. Justice Manson has ordered the Union to order the employees of Dominion Bridge Company Ltd. working on the south portion of the new Second Narrows Bridge to return to work. Our solicitors have advised us that in their opinion the order granted by the Judge is contrary to the law and the order is being appealed immediately. However, we have also been advised that the order of the Judge must be obeyed. We therefore have no alternative but to order the men to return to work, and now hereby do so.

Meanwhile, Premier W. A. C. Bennett, for whose Social Credit government the bridge was to be a showcase, commissioned a panel of independent engineers to evaluate the site. Within just two days, he telegraphed the union advising that this panel had deemed the structure safe "for all normal risks." In spite of this report and the second court order, suspicions born of the earlier disaster prevailed, and the men did not return to work.

Dominion Bridge then applied for a writ to "sequester the goods, chattels, and personal estate . . . of the defendant union" for contempt of court in "wilfully disobeying" Justice Manson's second injunction. At the contempt hearing, Jestley implied that the men must have received instructions to disobey the injunction or were afraid that, under the hiring hall system, they would not be dispatched to future jobs if they returned to work as ordered by the judge.

Berger rose to protest, these "suggestions of improper pressure." He added: "Mr. Jestley has no knowledge of that and I object to that even being suggested."

But Judge Manson's reply revealed his own bias: "On that point the onus is clearly on you. Any sane individual sitting where I am would draw the inference of deliberate defiance." Affidavits which showed that the union officers had complied to the letter with his order did not dissuade his Lordship.

As Berger explained, "Your Lordship will realize that a trade union is not a military organization. Commands made by the officers of the union to its members are not something that the members are necessarily obliged to obey." The company, in Berger's view, was attempting to circumvent an old common law principle against "specific performance" of personal services, an ancient rule that says no person may be forced to work for an employer when he no longer wishes to do so.

"There is no such rule as that," Manson retorted. "The union entered into a contract to supply men and that has not been carried out."

At this point, Berger began speaking to the record rather than to Judge Manson, as he foresaw the necessity of filing an appeal. The only way left to Berger to protect the workers was to put on the record arguments that would become the means to proceed to appeal. The transcript tells the story:

MR. BERGER: Your Lordship cannot issue a Writ of Sequestration because to do so would be contrary to our whole constitutional law and I refer to the Magna Carta in support of that submission.

THE COURT: Well, now, there is much later law than Magna Carta. I am not going to hear you on Magna Carta. I heard about that fifty years ago in law school and university and need not spend any time on it.

MR. BERGER: I should like to make a submission based on Magna Carta.

THE COURT: Start with something current.

MR. BERGER: Magna Carta is current. It is as much in force in British Columbia today as it was in England in 1215. It is part of the constitution of every one of her Majesty's realms and British Columbia is one of them.

THE COURT: This is a speech for the benefit of the gallery. You don't need to direct those remarks to me.

MR. BERGER: With respect, it is not.

THE COURT: Why bother with saying that? That is wasting my time and yours.

MR. BERGER: I should like to refer to Chapter 15 of Magna Carta.

THE COURT: Well, desist. I am familiar with Chapter 15 . . . I don't want you to take my time and yours.

MR. BERGER: If your Lordship is familiar with Chapter 15 of Magna Carta, then I suggest your Lordship ought, on the basis of that chapter, to rule that no Writ of Sequestration can go because Chapter 15 says, "No free man shall be distrained to make bridges," which means you cannot distrain on the assets of the union to compel members to make bridges which is what my learned friend seeks to have your Lordship do.

THE COURT: Well, there has been a lot of statutes passed since Magna Carta.

MR. BERGER: No statute of this province can infringe the rights or liberties granted free men by Magna Carta.

THE COURT: Yes. The Sovereign acting upon the advice of the honourable members of the Senate and honourable members of the House of Commons can repeal Magna Carta so far as Canada is concerned and so can the Sovereign acting upon the advice of the Legislature within the provincial field repeal Magna Carta.

MR. BERGER: I take issue with your Lordship on that point. . . . My submission is that Chapter 15 is still in force in British Columbia today and cannot be infringed, upset, reversed or in any way put upon . . . that no justice could undo the provisions of Magna Carta . . . and I submit that your Lordship cannot order a Writ of Sequestration against the assets of Local 97 because to do so would infringe Magna Carta because your Lordship would then be allowing the plaintiff to distrain free men, through the sequestration of the Union's assets, to make bridges.

Berger reminded Manson that his order had been directed to the union, the union had complied, and that "it cannot be said, it has not been proved, it hasn't been alleged that the members of Local 97 are in contempt. . . . The men apparently have not obeyed the direction of the union but that does not by any stretch of the imagination entitle your Lordship to say there has been defiance of the order of the Court . . . the question whether they are in contempt cannot be raised and cannot be dealt with by your Lordship and your Lordship cannot order them to be brought before your Lordship."

It was a good as a dare. Manson directed the sheriff to bring before him the following morning the eighteen workmen who comprised the south pier crew. He then announced that when the men were brought into court for examination and cross-examination, he would "probably examine them" himself. This was an extraordinary plan that would make Manson both judge and prosecutor.

Throughout all of the proceedings, Manson had refused to brook any mention of the collapse of the span the year before or of the impact that the deaths and injuries to workmates might have had on survivors. He would not permit mention of the inherently dangerous nature of high-steel work or allow into evidence the findings of the royal commission on the cause of the tragedy. He also persisted in casting doubt on the workers' union—and their counsel, young Tom Berger.

"Now, in this particular case it is my opinion," Manson said, "the workmen should consult independent counsel. There is a conflict of interest between the Union and the workmen, and there is no question about that. Apart from the fact that the men are members of the Union, they are also members of society. They are citizens of our country. Their highest duty is to their country. Now, it is not for me to appoint counsel, but I would suggest this, that senior counsel be employed; a man of ripe experience in the law."

"The workers went out to get their own counsel, 'senior,' 'ripe,' 'experienced,' " Berger recalls, "and to Manson's obvious chagrin, they hired Tom Hurley."

Even so, by Monday the younger barrister's nerves were raw. Beside him, his friend Tom Hurley. Before him, the now-familiar, querulous Justice Manson. Behind him, a full gallery of angry union labourers. The sheriff informed his Lordship that he had been able to bring only seven of the subpoenaed men into court, and Jestley advised the bench that *their* appearance was due solely to Tom Hurley's suasion.

Manson called workman Eric Guttman forward. Tom Hurley quickly intervened to say, "With the greatest of respect . . . I must confess, my Lord, I am totally at a loss to know why this man is called here. For what purpose?"

"I propose to examine the eighteen men. If you have any objection to that, I am prepared to deal with it."

Berger promptly objected for the defendant, Local 97.

"You are not in this at the moment . . . your objection is overruled."

"Would your Lordship make it clear," Berger persisted, "whether your Lordship considers this to be a criminal proceeding or a civil proceeding?"

"I will determine that later."

Both Berger and Hurley understood that if the proceedings were criminal, the workmen could unwittingly give incriminating answers. It was unheard of for the nature of a proceeding to remain a mystery.

When Manson called a second workman, J. A. Phillips, Berger interjected once more: "Would your Lordship allow me to repeat my request that it be made clear what kind of proceeding this is, and against whom?"

Manson did not reply. He proceeded to grill Phillips about the phone call from the union and why he had not accepted the assurance of the premier, the engineers and others, including the Workmen's Compensation Board, that the bridge was safe. "It would not be that you were looking for an excuse to stay away from work, could it?" Manson suggested. "How would you feel if the bridge stood there for another month or so and collapsed and somebody was killed?"

"I guess I would feel a lot worse if I was on it when it went down," said Phillips.

Manson was not amused, but Phillips insisted that the sworn affidavits by the "bridge people saying the bridge is unsafe has made me think about it a little and I kind of decided that I would not like to go on it if it is hazardous like it has been brought up to be."

Undeterred, Manson plowed through the witnesses, treating men who had gone down with the bridge and those who feared doing so with equal insensitivity. His reasons for judgment, delivered on 30 July 1959, were lengthy, flawed and riddled with hostility. He fined the union $10,000 and also fined the three union business agents $3,000 each (and in default, imprisonment for one year).

The B.C. Court of Appeal made short work of Manson's judgment, saying contempt had not occurred merely because the employees, who were under no obligation to obey the union, did not report for work. As Mr. Justice H. W. Davey put it:

Appellants were obliged to comply in good faith with the mandatory order, but they were not obliged to do so gracefully, and reluctant compliance was in itself, not contempt.

I now turn to another matter. The learned judge in his reasons for judgment criticised the conduct of learned counsel [Berger] . . . on several grounds. I have read and reread the transcripts and, with respect, think the criticism was unmerited.

This vindicated Berger of any wrongdoing. The judgment also vindicated Manson, but equivocally: though theoretically entitled by law to order the men into court for questioning, his having done so, the court acknowledged, was the "cause of some indecorum in the gallery."

Berger says, remembering his nemesis: "I think he was seventy-seven at the time of the ironworkers' case and as cantankerous as can be, but do you know, in his own crazy way, he was a charming man. His conduct in the Dominion Bridge case so outraged the profession that it led to parliament passing legislation requiring superior court judges to retire at seventy-five. The act came into force when Manson was seventy-eight, and it was referred to by the profession in B.C. as 'The Manson Act.'" Berger spreads his arms in forgiveness: "We don't see many eccentrics in court these days."

Justice Manson was not the exception in his willingness to grant injunctions to employers. Well into the 1960s workplace disorder was routinely quelled in this fashion, and Berger became something of an expert in contending with employers' applications.

Berger also made his mark through his attempts to protect workers' right to picket. In one case, *Koss* v. *Konn,* he represented Hercy Konn on the issue of his informational picketing with a sign stating: "Non-union men employed on this job." Four judges of the B.C. Court of Appeal upheld the injunction granted to contractor Michael J. Koss, while only one, Mr. Justice T. G. Norris, would have set it aside. He claimed that a restraint on information pickets under provincial labour law was shackling public opinion. Berger took the case all the way to the Supreme Court of Canada, which confirmed that B.C.'s Labour Relations Act could prohibit picketing when there is no strike or lockout. Five years later, in 1966, Berger, together with his friend and associate John Laxton, fought a multitude of injunctions on behalf of the fired employees of the Lenkurt Electric Company. They were ordered to refrain from picketing at the gates of the plant. When they persisted, walking in circles with their hands in their pockets, a sheriff was forced to shove the injunctions under their arms. The documents fell to the ground and were trampled. This was judicially construed as blatant contempt for the administration of justice. It resulted in a summer-long contempt hearing, and the attendant publicity assured Berger of a thriving labour law practice.

The nature of labour relations changed markedly during the 1960s, and the impetus for that change, which was political, had its roots in the Co-operative Commonwealth Federation (CCF), a political party that had risen out of the hardships of the Depression of the 1930s. The CCF had garnered most of its support in the western provinces by advocating progressive socialism and improved welfare programs, but by the end of the 1950s, the party was divided, labour participation was dwindling and its share of the popular vote was diminishing. In an effort to salvage democratic socialism, the CCF joined with the Canadian Labour Congress to found the New Democratic Party (NDP). The year was 1961. The NDP planned to receive contributions from the unions, whose funds were derived almost entirely from membership fees deducted on their behalf by companies from employees' wages. The other political parties, particularly those holding power, were dismayed by the prospect of the NDP tapping into what had the potential to be a rich and vigorous stream of support.

The solution of the B.C. government under the Social Credit Party was to pass a Labour Relations Amendment Act that prohibited trade unions from contributing money deducted from employees' wages to a political party or candidate. The act also required that the unions produce a statutory declaration of compliance with the law. The Imperial Oil Company was the first employer to take advantage of this new law. It sent a letter to the Oil, Chemical and Atomic Workers International Union, Local 16-601, the certified bargaining agent for the employees at Imperial's Ioco refinery, advising that the company would discontinue the deduction of union dues unless it received the declaration. The union, with Berger as their counsel, issued a writ demanding that the deductions and their submission to the union, as provided for by the "check-off" clause of the collective agreement, be honoured.

The union alleged that the Labour Relations Amendment Act interfered with the growth and development of political parties in Canada and that it interfered with the freedom of trade unions by curtailing their participation in politics and elections. The key issue was whether the object of the legislation was to prevent trade union participation in the NDP specifically.

As Berger saw it, the right of workers to affiliate with groups of their choice—freedom of association, an original and fundamental freedom—was at stake. When the court ruled that political action was a "foreign" and therefore unacceptable purpose of unionism, he decided to carry the fight further. On the basis of unions' past political connections, he believed that political action *was* within their rightful sphere. He thought there were valid grounds for appeal, for he considered the act to be beyond the powers of the provincial government. It also resembled Quebec's notorious "Padlock Law," legislation that had enabled provincial authorities to padlock premises which they believed housed communist propaganda. That law had been successfully challenged in the 1957 *Switzman* v. *Elbing* case by F. R. Scott, the eminent constitutional lawyer and civil libertarian whom Berger greatly admired. The B.C. legislation, however, was well crafted and the B.C. Supreme Court and the B.C. Court of Appeal upheld the validity of the act.

The B.C. Federation of Labour asked Berger to retain Scott as senior counsel on a further appeal to the Supreme Court of Canada. Berger was excited by the prospect, and with some trepidation sent his draft *factum* —the case law, facts and arguments on which he intended to rely—to Scott. Politically and ideologically, Berger and Scott were of similar minds. By this time, Tom had run unsuccessfully as a CCF candidate and knew the esteem the party had for Scott. And, on a personal level, Tom admired the older man's poetry and legal writing.

"We had never actually been introduced," Berger recalls. "I had sat beside him at the CCF convention in Regina in 1960, but had been too shy to introduce myself.

"One day the phone rang. 'Tom Berger? This is Frank Scott. I have just read your draft. This is good work.'

"For a lawyer only a few years at the bar, to be working with F. R. Scott and to receive such praise was kind of nice. Scott suggested I come to Montreal and that we work together on the factum. I spent a week there. Frank and I went out to dinner each night—his wife was away in the country; and each day we worked on the factum. We did this in his old office, the one celebrated in his poem, 'On Leaving My Office in Chancellor Day Hall.' "

"We worked over the factum sentence by sentence and paragraph by paragraph. It was a damn good piece of work, even though we lost the case in the Supreme Court of Canada four to three."

The court decided that the legislation in actuality *protected* the civil liberties of workers by providing that they could not be compelled to "assist in the financial promotion of political causes" with which they disagreed and that the act was within the jurisdiction of the province over civil rights.

Despite the loss, Berger treasures the honour of having worked with Scott, who argued only three other cases—all of which elicited landmark judgments by the Supreme Court of Canada. In addition to the legendary *Switzman* padlock case, Scott represented Frank Roncarelli, the Montreal restaurateur whose liquor licence was suspended at the behest of Quebec Premier Duplessis, because he posted bail for Jehovah's Witnesses arrested for distributing their literature. As well, Scott went to court to fight the banning of *Lady Chatterley's Lover* in Canada.

Berger and Scott shared an admiration of the judicial prowess of Mr. Justice Ivan Rand of the Supreme Court of Canada. Berger savours the memory of a dinner with Rand who, after his retirement, was in Vancouver conducting a royal commission on labour relations. "It was such a great occasion that I made sure Bev was invited along. I think Rand was the greatest judge in the English-speaking world during the Fifties and the greatest judge in Canadian history. The intellectual sweep of his writing, the commitment to ordered liberty, and the even greater commitment to the freedom of the dissenter, are beautifully woven together. I think every first-year law student should be given Rand's judgments in the great civil liberties cases of the Fifties, and that should be *all* that they read in their first year. In fact, Frank Scott once told me that you could base an entire three-year law school curriculum on Rand's judgment in *Roncarelli* v. *Duplessis*."

With the common bond of politics and law, a dedication to civil liberties and a love of poetry and literature, it was inevitable that these two men of ideas would become friends. They often corresponded and got together when Scott was in the west or Berger in Montreal.

Berger believes that in some ways, Scott's articles in legal journals in the 1940s were the basis of Rand's judgments which made use of the criminal law power of the British North America Act to exclude provinces from invading civil liberties. This belief reinforces Berger's own multifaceted approach to the protection of civil liberties: advocacy, judgments, political forums, scholarly and popular writing—all ways to accomplish his goals.

Later in his career as a labour lawyer, Berger won a case with a creative tactic that made him something of a folk hero to railway men and the labour bar. He hornswoggled the mighty Canadian Pacific Railway. The CPR had obtained an injunction ordering members of the United Transportation Union, Local 144, back to work after they had booked off sick in what is known in the industry as the "slow wheels tactic." The railway named two hundred union members as defendants. When Berger applied to have the injunction set aside, he was accompanied to court by the two hundred union members. They were entitled to be there because they had all been named as defendants in the suit by the CPR, but in the usual course of such proceedings, a union representative appears on their behalf. Not this time. With so many workers in court, Berger's tactic meant slow wheels became stopped wheels; which was all to the good from the union's point of view, as there were problems with an unusual air-braking system.

"After Mr. Justice McIntyre set aside the injunction," Berger recounts with satisfaction, "the president of the railroad flew out from Montreal and sat down with the local union leaders to settle the safety issues."

Safety on the job and a healthy working environment became long-standing concerns of Berger. They arose out of his earliest work in the labour field and his most frustrating files, which involved the Workmen's Compensation Board (WCB).

When the Workmen's Compensation Act abolished the right of workers to sue their employers for harm caused them on the job, it set up an insurance fund to which employers contribute and against which workers claim for a percentage of their wages lost due to injuries suffered or diseases contracted on the job. The WCB was the final adjudicator of claims, but workers complained that seemingly valid ones were being rejected.

It was commonplace then, as now, to have articling students and newly called lawyers tackle problem files that stymied the more experienced and busier practitioners, as a novice's fresh perspective and energy could often lead to new solutions. This was the situation with a number of union-referred files at Shulman, Tupper & Southin. The WCB cases that came to the attention of young barrister Berger included Robert Kinnaird, a painter who had contracted occupational dermatitis; three men suffering from silicosis, the lung disease of miners; and Mary Farrell, the widow of a maintenance engineer who collapsed on the job and died.

Berger was creative and resourceful. His love of history taught him that answers to modern problems can often be found in the past, so for his disabled clients, he went back to the origins of the common law, just as he had in the Dominion Bridge case. He also sought two of the oldest legal remedies: he applied for a temporary order to show cause why a writ, which would quash the WCB's decision and move all proceedings to court, should not be issued; and he tried to obtain a second order for a writ called *mandamus,* meaning a mandatory order, which would force the board to hear and determine, according to law, the applications for compensation.

In each case, the board defended itself on the principle that, according to the Workmen's Compensation Act, all of its decisions are "final and conclusive and shall not be open to question or review in any court."

Berger argued that this stance violated Magna Carta, "that subjects of the Sovereign shall have the opportunity of having their rights, both criminal and civil, determined by the courts." In addition, he made heroic efforts to have the "record," which consisted of documents that substantiated his clients' claims, expanded. If a board does all that it is supposed to do and nothing more—that is, if it acts within its jurisdiction—a judicial rehearing of a decision will be granted only when there is an error of law, or, in some cases, of fact, on the face of the record. Because the record provided by WCB counsel Charles C. Locke, Q.C., was always meagre, the chance of Berger successfully arguing that it contained an error was slim. Thus, challenging a WCB decision was exceedingly difficult.

Tom Berger's first such client, Robert Kinnaird, was an industrial painter who had contracted dermatitis through exposure to toxic wood sealer. He had applied for and received compensation payments, but two years later, the board decided that though he still suffered skin eruptions, his disability "can not obviously be now considered to be produced by occupational contact" and terminated his claim. The board also recommended that he obtain employment "light in nature, clean and of a clerical type."

Kinnaird's state of mind was not good. Not only did his disability prevent him from returning to his trade but he also lacked the education for the office or clerical work the board recommended, and he was therefore totally without prospects for several years until the Workmen's Compensation Act was amended to provide for cases where there was a "bona fide medical dispute." The amendment provided for workers disputing a decision to be examined by a medical specialist who was to produce a certificate that "shall be conclusive as to the matters certified." The WCB was "to review the claim and notify the workman in writing of its decision regarding the matters contained in the certificate" within eighteen days of receiving it. Kinnaird had new hope.

At the end of January 1957 he was examined by a specialist, a Dr. Greenwood. At the time, there were active blisters on Kinnaird's fingers and feet, though he frequently suffered eczematous eruptions over his entire body. Two months later, without advising him of the contents of the specialist's certificate, the WCB sent him a letter saying there would be no change in the status of his claim. Kinnaird concluded that Dr. Greenwood had decided that his disability was not a result of his past employment.

When Berger took on the case he soon learned that Dr. Greenwood had reported Kinnaird's unfitness for work was indeed due to his skin having been previously sensitized as a result of his occupation. The doctor said the "skin in itself would constitute very little disability to an individual employed in clerical work. This man, however, is permanently unfit for either of his two trades [painting or baking]. He also states that his educational attainments do not fit him for any other, more suitable job."

Berger applied his best efforts and succeeded in having Dr. Greenwood's letter made part of the record in Kinnaird's case. A year later, however in a two-to-one decision, the B.C. Court of Appeal ruled against him on the main issue: the WCB's decision, it held, was beyond the reach of the court. Although the court's interpretation of the law favoured the board, it chastised the WCB for the letter of rejection that had left Kinnaird in complete ignorance of the specialist's findings. The court also made it clear that the board's behaviour left much to be desired: decisions should be based upon the real merits and justice of the case.

Thus encouraged, Berger continued the struggle on Kinnaird's behalf. However, after another year, the Supreme Court of Canada held that the fact it was "unable, on the material before us, to understand how the Board reached the decision which it did, is quite beside the point." Mr. Justice Emmett Hall, a discerning supporter of the rights of the individual and a judge who would bear heavily on Berger's career in the future, concurred with the legal correctness of the judgment, but was "impelled . . . to say, that this workman does not appear to have received the substantial justice which . . . the Workmen's Compensation Act of British Columbia contemplated." He, too, directed to the board the admonition that a decision "shall be upon the real merits and justice of the case."

The courts were saying that the power of the WCB was almost impenetrable but, spurred by the plight of Kinnaird and other disabled workers, Berger resolved to establish the board's accountability. He persevered.

His second such client was Louis Battaglia, who had come to British Columbia from Italy in 1913 to work in the coal mines. In 1953 he had begun a fight for compensation, claiming he had contracted silicosis during his forty years in the mines. His claim had been rejected in 1955, so he sought, as had Kinnaird, the impartial justice of a certificate from a specialist. This time it was a Dr. A. K. Mathisen, whose opinion it was that the "radiological lesions present in this workman are as characteristic of silicosis as any x-ray finding could possibly be," and that Battaglia was "entitled to a pension for silicosis."

Although the board had to reach a decision within eighteen days of receipt of the specialist's certificate, which was to be binding, it not only solicited opinions from other medical people but did not send the disabled miner a letter until more than eight months after his visit to Dr. Mathisen. The letter informed Battaglia that "The findings on file do not show that you are disabled by silicosis as defined by the Workmen's Compensation Act." Once again, the worker did not see the doctor's opinion.

Berger tackled the file and in 1958 received a letter from Dr. Mathisen stating he had previously diagnosed silicosis. "I still feel that my diagnosis is correct," Mathisen wrote. "However, only a biopsy or autopsy can confirm it."

Berger immediately launched legal action, and the case came before Chief Justice Sherwood Lett of the Supreme Court of British Columbia.

When Battaglia had begun his fight for silicosis compensation, he had $2,000 in savings. "I wore out my shoes walking to the board's offices," he said. When his money was gone, he asked, "What am I going to do if they don't give me something?"

Louis Battaglia was now over seventy-five years old. His disabilities had recently caused him to be moved from a nursing home to the old men's ward in the annex of Vancouver General Hospital where Ben Metcalfe, a reporter for the Vancouver *Province,* paid him a visit. After listening to the little miner's story and his laboured breathing, and seeing the expressive brown eyes and workworn hands, Metcalfe reported that Battaglia was "one of that long list of otherwise unsung men—the salt of the earth."

The WCB filed with the B.C. Supreme Court a record that consisted of only the application and the letter of rejection. This necessitated a further order that the record be supplemented with the certificate of the medical specialist. But the WCB filed an affidavit from its chairman, J. E. Eades, putting forward the argument that the disclosure of certificates would discourage "adequate, frank and complete medical reports" and mentioned doctors elsewhere who had been shot by disgruntled patients.

Berger's cross-examination made a shambles of any credible rationale behind this WCB policy. It seemed abundantly clear the public interest would be best served by disclosure, and this the chief justice ordered. Dr. Mathisen's letter to the board, which Berger alleged *was* the specialist's certificate, was finally subjected to scrutiny.

The chief justice ruled that the letter was the certificate and that it was not ambiguous, as the WCB contended it was. Had the board reviewed the claim within the prescribed eighteen days, treating the certificate as conclusive, he ruled, it could only have found that Battaglia was disabled by silicosis. He also said that the only legitimate inference he could draw from the record was that the board, fearful of opening the floodgates to all disabled miners, had based its decision on extraneous considerations. In so doing, he said, the WCB was in excess of its jurisdiction—an error of law. In such situations a statute cannot oust the authority or right of the court to review the decision of a tribunal, and the jurisdictional error can be proven by evidence outside of the record.

SILICOSIS VICTIM WINS 6-YEAR PENSION BATTLE read the four-inch-high headline emblazoned on the front page of the *Vancouver Sun*.

"Is it true? Is it true?" Battaglia asked his union representative, his old hands trembling on his cane. He had no savings, he told a reporter, and his "Mr. Berger" had been carrying on the case without charge.

"I was able to do so," explains Berger, "because Shulman, Tupper & Southin's policy was to allow and encourage that sort of thing. I could do it, using their office resources, so long as I carried my paying client caseload. Of course, I was busy."

Once more the WCB appealed, and in the spring the WCB's lawyer Charles Locke and Berger were back hammering it out before five judges of the B.C. Court of Appeal while a penniless Battaglia's health failed. After two months the court supported the ruling of Chief Justice Lett.

Within a month the WCB launched yet another appeal, this time to the court of last resort, the Supreme Court of Canada. The matter was set down to be heard on 4 October 1960, but on 1 September 1960, sixteen years after making his first claim, Louis Battaglia died.

The fight was not over. An autopsy was ordered, and a WCB spokesman told reporters that pathology reports on the cause of death would settle the matter.

"The cause of *death* was not the point," Berger later said, reliving his frustration. "At issue was the cause of the *disability*. We maintained it was silicosis."

After three contentious attempts to select a coroner's jury, the inquest broke into a fracas when the board's counsel, J. P. Berry, finally penetrated Berger's professional aplomb by demanding an apology from Berger for his suggestion that WCB doctors incorrectly diagnosed what were really silicosis cases.

Berger was incredulous. "You owe the workmen of this country an apology!" he shouted.

The inquest was adjourned while tempers cooled. Ultimately, the jury found that Battaglia had died a natural death from bronchial pneumonia. Berger dismissed as "gobbledygook" a statement from the coroner's office listing several lung diseases. Berry said the WCB "would make a complete review of the case," and the union vowed to fight on.

At this point Berger, who was handling the Farrell case as well as many others, increased his efforts to reform the WCB. Through political forums, interviews and personal contacts, he urged that the provincial government strike a royal commission to investigate the operation of the WCB. Chairman Eades, he said, should be dismissed.

The day before Battaglia's death, the B.C. Supreme Court had ruled in favour of another of Berger's silicosis clients, Charles Ursaki. Ursaki, who had been employed as a gold miner, had first claimed a silicosis pension in 1944 but had been turned down twice by the WCB during the next twelve years. Not until he submitted to a painful lung biopsy, conclusively proving that he had silicosis, did the board accept his claim. However, the WCB put forward the implausible proposition that the condition did not develop until, as the newspapers put it, "the day the doctors snipped out a piece of lung for examination," and awarded his pension of $133.50 a month from the date of diagnosis rather than from the time of disability. It was not a position towards which the judge,

Mr. Justice David Verchere, was sympathetic, and he said the board had "distinctly determined not to do what it was required to do" and ordered it to rehear the case. This meant paying Ursaki his pension from the date on which he had become disabled due to silicosis.

Berger, meanwhile, had in court the case of a third miner, Don MacLennan, whose silicosis fight had taken six years. After the Ursaki decision, the WCB abandoned its appeal on the MacLennan case and agreed to pay the $2,500 that the lower court said was owed him in back payments. Again, justice came too late. MacLennan's wife, who had worked as a waitress to support the family, was unemployed and in poor health. Their three children had quit high school to go to work. By the time the first pension cheque reached the impoverished MacLennan family, the miner of thirty years had been taken to hospital and placed in an oxygen tent.

In the Farrell case, Berger's clients were the widow and four infant daughters of a worker whose death had been attributed by a North Vancouver coroner's jury to "over-exertion at his work which aggravated a previously unsuspected heart condition." After running up and down two flights of stairs to fetch an electric drill, hospital maintenance engineer Jack Farrell had collapsed and later died.

Mary Farrell, his widow, had applied for compensation under the Workmen's Compensation Act. After three months, she had received a terse letter from the WCB stating they had been unable to approve her application: "It would appear that your husband died from natural causes and that his death was not the result of an accident arising out of his employment."

Berger knew from his own childhood experience the financial hardships the family would face, and he also knew that the WCB would make no concessions out of sympathy. The law would be the only weapon he could wield against an obdurate board.

Mary Farrell clung to the hope that someday there would be a small but regular pension. She was not young and had no marketable skills; moreover, she was needed at home to care for her four infant daughters.

When Berger and Locke appeared before Berger's old adversary, Mr. Justice A. M. Manson, Manson was quick to say: "I think it is clear beyond argument that the death of this workman [Jack Farrell] was accelerated by the work done in the course of his employment."

Before the judge released his decision, Berger received a phone call that brought terror into his heart. "Alec Manson here. I want to see you in my chambers."

That meeting was unusual, Berger recalls. "By this time the judgment of the Court of Appeal, reversing Manson and rebuking him on the Dominion Bridge matter, had been handed down." He said to me, 'I hope there are no hard feelings about the iron-workers.' "

"What could I say to that?" Berger laughs. "He said, 'You did a first-rate job on this Farrell case, and I'm going to decide in your favour. I want you to read my judgment.' This time he was biased *for* my client. He wrote a judgment on her behalf that went so far I could not successfully defend it when it went to appeal. Manson asked what I thought of it. I told him it was just fine and rushed out of there to tell Locke and M. M. McFarlane (counsel for the attorney general). I felt bound to disclose this astonishing impropriety. I thought the whole case was compromised—all our work wasted. But they only laughed. Nothing Manson did surprised them."

Mr. Justice Manson's decision officially came down on 30 May 1960. On key issues he had relied on the unanimous judgment of the Court of Appeal in Battaglia's case. He found it "utter ridiculousness" to infer that the Workmen's Compensation Act gave decisions of the WCB the same finality as those of the Supreme Court of Canada, and there was no doubt in his mind that the provincial legislature could not abrogate the sacred right of private citizens to have their rights determined by a court of law. He held that there had clearly been an "accident" within the meaning of the act; Farrell's death was accelerated by exertion in the course of his employment. He ordered the board to pay compensation, but Mrs. Farrell was not at ease for long. The board appealed, and the judgment that would have given compensation to the family was overturned six months later. Berger proceeded to the Supreme Court of Canada, but two and half years after Jack Farrell's death, seven judges upheld the B.C. Court of Appeal. "A heartbreaker," Berger says. "The family had nothing, and there was nothing more I could do."

There was nothing more he could do with the case, but he did continue with the cause, speaking out on it at every opportunity. He believed that the purpose of the WCB had been perverted, denying natural justice to workers and their survivors.

When in 1962 the government appointed a royal commission of

inquiry into the administration of the Workmen's Compensation Act, under the chairmanship of Mr. Justice Charles Tysoe, Berger appeared before it on behalf of the B.C. Federation of Labour. He told the commission that Eades, after becoming chairman of the WCB, had by his own admission tightened up. "It was tightening up with a vengeance."

For twenty years before the appointment of Eades, the average ratio of claims rejected to claims reported was about one in one hundred. From 1954 to 1958, 2.7 per cent were rejected; and from 1959 to 1963, 3.6 per cent. The best explanation, said Berger, was that during Eades's regime claims had been rejected that should have been accepted. But Mr. Justice Tysoe suggested that perhaps, on the contrary, in the earlier period people who should not have had claims granted had received them.

"It is better that someone not deserving a pension gets it, than that a person entitled to it is rejected," Berger insisted.

The commission eventually recommended that changes be made to the administration of the Workmen's Compensation Board, and some of these were implemented. The system was improved, but it was far from perfect.

Today, Berger is dismayed to discover that the attitude epitomized by Eades—not granting the benefit of the doubt to the disadvantaged—is again becoming prevalent. But he has shown the way, and young labour lawyers are now using his early cases as models and motivators for their own perseverance as they continue the struggle on behalf of a new generation of disabled workers.

CHAPTER 3

The Defender of Human Rights

Improving the system and fighting the establishment were two phrases that epitomized the 1960s and the goals of people under thirty during that decade. Tom Berger tackled the Sixties with a fervour and dedication that made the era his own. In addition to his growing expertise in labour law, he broadened his horizons and the scope of his practice to forge new frontiers in environmental law, as well as in defending the rights of people charged as habitual criminals and the rights of native people. This work, in hitherto unexplored realms, led him to question the integrity of the system itself and to move on to political action as a logical tool for social change. He managed to juggle his full personal life of family and friendships with a stellar legal career as well as numerous robust political campaigns. He did it all—and he did it all simultaneously—but it was in the law, in Tom Berger's legal accomplishments of that decade, that he made a lasting mark.

Inside prison and on the street, people called preventive detention "the bitch." Deservedly. The usual punishment for a conviction under the habitual criminal section of the Criminal Code, preventive detention was the sentence that never ends: life on the bitch.

Canada had enacted this Draconian legislation in 1947, adapting it from a 1908 English law, but the maximum sentence British offenders received was fourteen years, whereas the standard imprisonment in Canada was the remainder of a person's life. Although the purpose of the act was, ostensibly, to protect society from dangerous criminals, during its thirty-year life span it was used to confine some men and women who had in fact been nothing more than continual social nuisances. They were neither violent nor dangerous, but were street people who engaged in petty crime. Conviction on a third indictable offence could bring about habitual criminal proceedings.

In British Columbia the political climate was such that the habitual criminal legislation was enforced with greater rigour than in any other province, and Tom Berger fought it for more than a decade, beginning in 1960. He and client George McKnight endured a devastating defeat in the B.C. Supreme Court when Mr. Justice A. M. Manson found that McKnight was an habitual criminal and sentenced him to preventive detention. Manson must have recognized what a blow it was for a new lawyer to see his client go down for life, because immediately after imposing the sentence and before giving McKnight ten years on the primary offence of conspiracy to commit arson, he addressed Berger: "Perhaps it does not help much, but may I say to you, Mr. Berger, as a young man, that I was very gratified to hear such an able and orderly argument put forth. You did it in really exceptional fashion." But Berger was able to persuade the Court of Appeal that the arson conspiracy conviction was invalid, as Manson had seen McKnight's criminal record prior to the proceedings and had even commented upon it to the jury, thus negating the habitual criminal charge.

Berger next took on the case of Tony Cappello, who had been convicted in Vancouver County Court on a drug charge and had then been sentenced to preventive detention as an habitual criminal on 5 November 1958. After Cappello's unsuccessful appeal, Berger represented him before the Supreme Court of Canada on a motion for leave to appeal, and argued that as only two of the three convictions proved against his client had occurred after the enactment of the habitual criminal legislation, Cappello was being wrongfully detained. His motion was dismissed without reasons, and Berger applied to Minister of Justice E. Davie Fulton for the mercy of the Crown. "So long as Cappello remains in prison . . .

his presence there is an affront to the will of Parliament as well as the conscience of civilized humanity," Berger said, citing the UN Universal Declaration of Human Rights and emphasizing one sentence in particular: "No one shall be held guilty of a penal offence on account of any act or omission which did not constitute a penal offence at the time it was committed. *Nor shall a heavier penalty be imposed than the one that was applicable at the time the offence was committed.*" But mercy was not granted to Cappello nor was it to be extended to other men luckless enough to stumble into the tangle of that law.

On 11 May 1964 William Gilbert wrote a polite but desperate letter to Berger from the B.C. Penitentiary:

> Dear Sir:
> I was hesitant about writing this letter to you because of my complete lack of finances. However, my present situation is so serious I feel I must do so. The Attorney General is proceeding against me as an Habitual Criminal and if at all possible there is no one else I would prefer to defend me . . . I realize of course the extremely difficult task confronting you in the defence of this procedure but, regardless of the result, I would like to know I had the most competent counsel available.

At the time, Gilbert was serving three years on a narcotics charge, and his lengthy record included vagrancy, living on the avails of crime and gambling, dealing in forged documents and petty theft. The Legal Aid Committee of the Law Society assigned the case to Berger at Gilbert's request.

In July, Berger presented the case, but Gilbert was, nonetheless, sentenced to preventive detention. The morning after the ruling was handed down, Berger wrote to the Law Society to outline the reasons for an appeal: allegations at the trial about Gilbert's lifestyle, the questionable need to protect the public from a drug addict and shoplifter, and the possibility that preventive detention constituted "cruel and unusual treatment or punishment" as prohibited by the new Canadian Bill of Rights. As there were no facilities or programs at the B.C. Penitentiary for the treatment of drug addicts or habitual criminals, the Criminal Code provisions for "reformative treatment for habitual criminals are nothing more nor less than a cruel hoax," Berger asserted. He asked for compensation for appeal expenses and enclosed his account for services to Gilbert at the Legal Aid rate of $50 a day in court.

The appeal was filed in August 1964, but it was not heard until May 1965. At that time, however, Berger was able to tell Gilbert some good news. Although the three judges had upheld the finding that he was an habitual criminal, they had set aside the sentence of preventive detention. He needed to serve only the sentence for narcotics possession before being released.

Gilbert responded promptly to this good news with a heartfelt letter: "Wow . . . I'm more than delighted . . . a great relief . . . knowing how busy you are makes me all the more grateful."

The rare success sustained young barrister Berger's hope.

One man who fought the habitual criminal legislation longer than Berger was George Paton, and for much of his fight, he had Tom Berger in it with him.

Paton was a break-and-enter man who, at the age of thirty-eight, had made the mistake of doing a B & E in the Okanagan Valley town of Kelowna. On 12 December 1956, Paton had stood unrepresented by counsel before County Court Judge J. R. Archibald. Two weeks earlier, Paton had been served a notice advising that, if convicted, an application would be made to impose a sentence of preventive detention upon him as an habitual criminal. The grounds were that since the age of eighteen "on at least three separate and independent occasions previous to the conviction of the crime charged," he had been convicted of an indictable offence for which he was liable to imprisonment for five years or more, and that he was leading a persistently criminal life.

Judge Archibald had said there was no doubt in his mind about the break-and-enter charge and found Paton guilty. He also found Paton to be an habitual criminal and sentenced him to preventive detention.

In the fall of 1964 Norm Levi came to see Berger. He, like Tom, was an active member of the New Democratic Party, and they shared an interest in guarding human rights. Levi was a parole officer with the John Howard Society, which was concerned with inmate welfare, and from time to time he would put together the dossiers of three or four "hopeless cases" at the B.C. Penitentiary and take them down to Berger's office at the Inns of Court building, where Berger was by now practising on his own. On this occasion, Levi mentioned George Paton.

Paton had now served most of his eight-year break-and-enter time, all the while fighting the preventive detention sentence without success. He knew of Berger and, on a long shot, persuaded Levi to contact him, shading the facts in a calculated risk to draw Berger in. Paton was a gambler fighting for his life, and he wanted Berger fighting for it as well. But when Berger had a look at the court documents, he wrote to Paton offering little encouragement: "In my view there is nothing essentially wrong with the allegations in the Notice. If they were proved, the Court would have been justified in finding that you were an habitual criminal and in sentencing you to preventive detention. The Code has changed in the meantime, as it relates to habitual criminals, but of course you were prosecuted under the old provisions."

Paton, however, found enough meat in this seemingly negative response to reply promptly with a lengthy, laboriously typed letter that became part of a marathon correspondence, in which the two men exchanged more than a hundred letters over four years.

"Dear Sir," George began. "Received your letter and wish to thank you for looking into my case no matter how much you have been misinformed reguarding [sic] grounds." Having nabbed Berger's attention with that provocative beginning, he presented an intriguing mixture of law and facts. The nub of his complaint was that the notice said he had been *convicted* of three indictable offences previous to the Kelowna caper, but one was a charge that had gone to only a preliminary hearing. Paton had researched the common law and learned that preventive detention was to be used *after* a jail term had been served. The idea of the law, he felt, was for the court to then decide whether jail had done any good.

George Paton was a persistent man. Working with a grade eight education and the prison library's limited materials, he had set about to learn the law. He drafted his own pleadings and became in the process a competent legal researcher, and an expert on habitual criminal legislation and case law.

On 6 April 1965, Berger wrote Paton an encouraging letter: "I think you have a point that is worth arguing in that habitual proceedings were brought against you before you had an opportunity of serving your sentence on the third of the previous convictions that the Crown relied upon in your case." At last Paton, who had been in custody for eight and a half years, knew there was someone on his side.

Paton sent Berger four pages of legal research he had done on two similar cases, saying, "I hope to reimburse you in the future.

It's very hard to express gratitude for a man in my position."

Berger applied to Minister of Justice Lucien Cardin to refer the case to the B.C. Court of Appeal under Section 596 of the Criminal Code. He set out Paton's court history and submitted that it could not be shown he had not responded to the punishment imposed on three previous convictions because he had not yet served his sentence on the third conviction when charged as an habitual criminal. Common law dictated that it must be shown such punishment had been of no use, and precedents indicated that the courts, in deciding if an accused had lived a persistently criminal life, looked to the life led after sentence had been served. "In these circumstances it cannot be said that Paton had shown he could not benefit from that sentence," Berger said. He argued that the question "is one of very great importance, having regard to the large number of prosecutions being brought in the Province against persons alleged to be habitual criminals." The latter point was of increasing concern to Berger, to whom Norm Levi was bringing more cases than his workload would allow him to handle, and rumours of further applications were filtering down to him.

Berger received a reply to his application six weeks later, not from Cardin but from F. P. Miller, executive director of the National Parole Board. Miller conceded that the Notice of Application for Sentence as an Habitual Criminal might have provided insufficient grounds for sentence, but he added that Paton had "an impressionable [sic] number of other lesser offences [which] qualify him as one who is leading persistently a criminal life . . . I regret to advise that your request for the Mercy of the Crown . . . cannot be considered at this time."

Berger wrote back immediately to complain of what he thought was a blatant disregard for the protection offered any accused person under the Criminal Code of Canada:

It is astonishing that the Board, in considering this request for the mercy of the Crown, should have looked into offences that were never brought up when Paton was charged as an habitual criminal in the first place, were never adduced in evidence against him and formed no part of the adjudication at the time.

It seems to me absolutely vital, and I should have thought it would have seemed equally vital to the National Parole Board, that no one should be confined to imprisonment except according to law. . . . Yet the Board has gone completely outside the evidence against him and has brought up for the first time, four prior convictions and sentences. This is quite extraordinary.

Paton, in a brief note of thanks, commented astutely that Miller had taken on the role of judge and jury. To go around Berger's brief, he thought, would show contempt. Unfortunately, Paton's new-found reverence for the law was not shared by the National Parole Board, whose chairman, T. G. Street, wrote:

> The National Parole Board is not an appeal court and accordingly is not limited in its investigation to the evidence submitted at trial.
>
> The power given to the minister under Section 596 of the Criminal Code has been used rarely and only in instances where there appeared to be a manifest injustice. It does not seem appropriate that it should be used only to correct an alleged error of procedure.

This missive entirely offended Berger's sensibilities, and he wrote to Member of Parliament Andrew Brewin (NDP-Greenwood), explaining the case and asking him to raise the matter in the House of Commons. The closing paragraph of Berger's letter to Brewin epitomizes the tenacity that kept him embroiled in numerous cases where the only reward was the possibility of seeing justice administered equitably: "I suppose the only justification I have for bringing this case to your attention is that I have nursed it along myself for quite a while now, and do not like the way in which the Board has dealt with it. I would rather lose with a bang than a whimper." A bang can cause people to sit up and take notice.

In Ottawa, Andrew Brewin presented Berger's argument on behalf of Paton to Justice Minister Cardin as forcibly as he could. In response, he received a lengthy letter, in which the justice minister said he had canvassed the National Parole Board file and RCMP records, and discovered that Paton "appears" to have several other convictions.

Cardin's letter was a heavy blow to Paton, and a month passed before he could bring himself to write to Berger: "Document from Cardin received. I must say the man is not very intelligent."

Lawyer and client responded to this setback in the same way: with action. Despite the slim possibility of success, Berger sent an application for habeas corpus to the Supreme Court of Canada.

The court ruled that the question of not having served the requisite three sentences could not be dealt with on an application for habeas corpus; but in an extraordinary move the court did decide that it could treat Berger's application as one for leave to appeal the 1957 B.C. Court of Appeal decision, which had affirmed the sentence of preventive detention. The case was to be heard on 26 June 1967, one week hence.

"I think the longest extension ever granted prior to Paton had been two years," Berger says. "According to W. R. Burke-Robertson, the Ottawa counsel who appeared for the attorney general of B.C., Chief Justice Cartwright, who was presiding, said, 'We have decided to extend the time for applying for leave; we have decided to grant leave and we want you to urge the attorney general for British Columbia to pay Mr. Berger's fee and expenses so that he can come to Ottawa and argue the appeal on Paton's behalf.' "

The Canadian Press story was headlined: AFTER TEN YEARS B.C. THIEF STEALS INTO SUPREME COURT.

The matter of the attorney general picking up Berger's fees posed an ethical dilemma, as he was now a member of the B.C. legislature. He wrote to the Legal Aid Committee of the Law Society to inform them that he could not, as an MLA, accept remuneration from the Crown. He would, however, go to Ottawa, do all that he could on Paton's behalf and send a list of his expenses to the Law Society, leaving it to them to decide if he could be reimbursed in any way. The Law Society appointed Berger as Paton's legal aid counsel, eligible for an honorarium of $50 a day in court.

A month before the hearing, Paton's isolation and anxiety became evident in a letter to Berger that closed on a note of optimism mixed with despair. "Thanks a million. Maybe we can sue for a million, if you beat it. What a hope—the million I mean."

Berger apparently also had things on his mind. His departure for Ottawa was followed by a letter from Essa Horswill, his secretary, to the Supreme Court registrar, Ken Mathisen: "Mr. Berger left Vancouver without taking his gown, etc., and I have forwarded them to him care of yourself by yesterday's mail."

Berger presented his arguments, which he had thoroughly discussed with Paton, and Burke-Robertson stated the case for the attorney general of B.C. before a full bench of nine judges. While awaiting their judgment, Berger returned to his increasingly busy law practice, his duties as an NDP member of the legislature and to his family: Erin and David were seven and ten, and Bev was a part-time student. His life was rich and full. But for Paton there was only the emptiness of prolonged waiting, and by March a bitterness was seeping into his missives. "Do you think I have a complex, Tom?" he asked. "I've about lost everything and conspired on for the rest. They never let up."

Judgment was finally pronounced on 13 March 1968, five months after the hearing. It was an achingly close decision against Paton: four judges would have granted the appeal, but the majority of five dismissed it. Paton was angry and disappointed. He would himself appeal, he told Berger. "I shall have no trouble getting a new Appeal under the Magna Carta . . . I have no idea if you are finished with my case or not, but I can assure you that I have just begun to fight."

"I am afraid there is nothing further that can be done from a legal point of view," Berger wrote. "You still have the right to apply for parole. If there is anything that I can do to assist you in that regard, please let me know."

On 6 May, however, Paton's annual parole application was again denied. "Well, Tom," he wrote, "I wish to thank you for the four judges, I had nothing before. Now I've got a case. Thanks a million. I'll win now."

But winning was to be sixteen years away, and for Paton and the other men who had been bitched, it was a doubtful victory.

Again it was hope, not money, that sustained Berger when he represented the Hadden brothers, both of whom had been bitched.

During the Depression their father had been on relief, and the Hadden boys had done the best they could. Danny had sold newspapers after school and, later, tried to survive by pilfering such demand items as silk stockings, ladies' dresses, tools and licence plates. John had racked up a similar record of petty offences, none of them serious or violent. John was the first of the brothers to be "bitched" when he was convicted of the theft of a $2.99 can opener in August of 1963 and declared an habitual criminal.

After Berger had argued George Paton's case in the Supreme Court of Canada, he argued John Hadden's appeal before the same nine judges. "The point I argued in the SCC was that he was a nuisance, not a menace to society. I thought it was not therefore necessary for the protection of society to sentence him to preventive detention."

Berger was successful, and the Supreme Court of Canada ordered John Hadden's release.

The life of John's brother Danny had followed a more convoluted path. In 1940, after serving an eighteen-month prison sentence, he had joined the army. His wartime service was exemplary and earned him mention in the book *Action with the Seaforths,* but was given scant notice later when he faced trial on charges of robbery. In spite of a turbulent postwar life, he had managed to go straight for twenty years. Then, while working on a road crew in the Yukon, he had a longing for a "night on the town" and headed for Vancouver with a $6,000 stake. It was his undoing, he admitted: "After living high for a few months, I foolishly robbed a bank and was sent to prison for fifteen years."

He was out in six years but found parole conditions so restrictive that he "purposely got into trouble" so that he could serve his full time to regain his freedom. Shortly after his release, he was arrested and charged with the robbery of a bank in Vancouver. "I must tell you," he said to Berger, "I don't go around robbing banks because I'm one big-time bank robber. It's because I just seem to get involved."

He was awaiting trial on the bank charge when he was notified an application would be made to have him declared a habitual criminal. Recognizing the enormity of his jeopardy, he wrote with a curious fatalism that if he were found guilty, "Then that is my lot. And it is the end of my life."

Danny proved to be a fighter rather than a fatalist, however, and took action. Through the prison grapevine, he knew he could do no better than to have the man who had worked to have his brother freed. At Danny's request Legal Aid appointed Berger to handle the appeal, and through Norm Levi, Danny provided Berger with his handwritten biography. The pride of his life was his citation for bravery and investiture at Buckingham palace. He wrote: "I was so very proud that day. . . . The facts are I don't like crooks. I think they are ignorant and fools. I have the greatest respect for educated people and decent law-abiding people."

On New Year's Eve 1970, a day when few practitioners were preoccupied with their clients' problems, Berger wrote to Danny enclosing a copy of the factum. The points Berger had selected for argument were, in Danny's opinion, "real eyebrow raisers." They were:

1. The trial judge had no jurisdiction to hear the application for preventive detention, since sentence had not yet been imposed for the substantive offense, i.e. robbery.

2. The Attorney-General did not consent to the application to have you sentenced to preventive detention. The application is dated June 14, 1967. It recites as a fact that the Attorney-General had consented to the application. In fact he had not. He signed a consent dated June 3rd, 1968, but that cannot be regarded as consent to the application brought the previous year.

3. There was no satisfactory proof of age. [Evidence had been adduced at trial of Danny's prewar record but as his birth had never been recorded, it was possible that he was a juvenile of 15 or 16 when he first ran afoul of the law. The requisite three proved offences needed to be committed after the age of 18.]

4. Three previous convictions were not satisfactorily established on the evidence.

5. It was not shown that you were leading persistently a criminal life.

6. It was not shown that it was expedient for the protection of the public to sentence Hadden to preventive detention.

"I think the first and second grounds are the strongest. I will be out to see you before the appeal is heard," Berger promised.

This was Berger's great gift to all his clients. He gave them as much detail as possible about what he was doing and thinking about their case. He never forgot how critically important every scrap of information can be to a confined man who has day after day to think and turn over all that has happened, again and again. He recognized his obligation to lessen their anxiety and to share with them the nuts and bolts of their problems.

Despite the thoroughness of Berger's preparation of Danny's appeal, Justices Maclean, Robertson and Nemetz were unanimous in their rejection. Danny Hadden, like George Paton, was doomed to spend a long hard time in prison. Most people on the outside were oblivious to their fate, for it was generally believed that the Canadian justice system had provisions built in to prevent such injustices.

In 1969 the Canadian Committee on Corrections, under the chairmanship of Mr. Justice Ouimet, investigated the habitual criminal legislation and the records of eighty persons who were serving sentences under it. The committee found that while in some cases the act had served to protect the public from dangerous offenders, it had also been applied "in a substantial percentage of cases to persistent offenders who, while constituting a serious social nuisance are not dangerous." It also found that of the eighty persons sentenced, forty-five were in B.C., and of those, thirty-nine had been sentenced in Vancouver. The committee did not comment on the political or social climate that might have been factors in these statistics, but it did conclude that legislation "susceptible to such uneven application had no place in a rational system of corrections."

Eight years later, when dangerous offender legislation was passed to replace the old habitual criminal section of the Criminal Code of Canada, the Honourable Ron Basford, minister of justice, promised that the status of people sentenced under the old legislation would be reviewed by the National Parole Board "against the new formulation of what a dangerous offender is." But by 1980 the men doing life on the bitch were still in prison.

At the instigation of Michael Jackson, a law professor at the University of British Columbia, the B.C. Corrections Association approached the National Parole Board to undertake an extensive study of the habitual criminals remaining in prison. Jackson, who was a specialist in Canadian correctional law policy and administration, coincidentally had been involved with Berger in native law issues and was to work with him on the Mackenzie Valley Pipeline Inquiry. Jackson considered that he was familiar with injustice and its many variations in Canada and was intimately acquainted with penitentiaries through his work on behalf of men in solitary confinement. Still, he says, he was shocked by the plight of the forgotten habitual criminals.

George Paton, the break-and-enter man, was then sixty-four and serving his twenty-sixth year in confinement. Danny Hadden, a Canadian war hero, was sixty-seven and serving his thirteenth year. These two men had the shortest criminal records of all the men in the study. Jackson's report stated the obvious: "The length of time these men have served is greatly disproportionate to the harm or damage they have done and they have served more time than any other group of prisoners in Canada, including those convicted of murder."

Finally, on 23 May 1984, the royal prerogative of mercy was

extended to remove the habitual criminal label from seventy-one individuals. For most of them, including the now-old men George Paton and Danny Hadden, however, it was a case of too little, too late.

If habitual criminal legislation was used to keep undesirable men out of sight and out of mind, it was applied even more unjustly and arbitrarily against three women whose visible means of support did not include a wage-earning husband or an acceptable job of their own.

For Berger, success in representing the only three women ever to be prosecuted as habitual criminals in Canada was a satisfying counterbalance to the frustrations of fighting for the men. It was the summer of 1964 when among the notices of habitual criminal applications in Vancouver appeared the name of Margaret "Penny" McNeil.

McNeil's plight as the first woman ever to be charged as an habitual criminal was quickly picked up by journalists such as Simma Holt of the *Vancouver Sun*. (Holt later became a member of the National Parole Board.) Although there is no way of knowing if the publicity helped Penny McNeil in a court of law, the news did serve to alert public sympathy.

Penny McNeil was thirty-five years old. Born in Czechoslovakia in 1929, she had emigrated to Canada with her family at the age of five. Her father administered a heavy-handed kind of discipline in attempts to force her adherence to a European way of life.

"She ran away eight times in all until, at 13, she hitchhiked to Trail and got a job as a waitress," Holt wrote. She was returned to the care of her parents, but the following year her father had her charged as an "incorrigible" to teach her a lesson. She was sentenced to two years in the Girls' Industrial School in Vancouver, where she learned street smarts: how to avoid the police, how to use drugs and how to support herself through prostitution. By the time she was sixteen, she was married to her pimp, and at seventeen she was sentenced to six months for possession of drugs. Within a week of her release from jail, she was charged with prostitution. After a brief interlude of happiness with a prairie sweetheart, during which she gave birth to a daughter, Penny visited her sick mother in Vancouver.

Penny was staying with friends when the police arrived to find drugs on one of them, and she was charged with "guilty knowledge," an offence that has since been repealed. She was sentenced to six months in Oakalla, escaped to see her baby, fell into drug use again, and with convictions on vagrancy, possession of drugs, trafficking and prostitution charges, moved inexorably towards the day when she would be charged with being an habitual criminal. She had never committed a violent crime in her life.

Once again, the spectre of a wasted life and a grave injustice drew in Tom Berger, his only monetary reward being the $50 stipend that Legal Aid would pay for each day of his courtroom time. Berger stood beside Penny McNeil before Magistrate Douglas Hume and argued that "preventive detention would be cruel and unusual punishment for a drug addict-prostitute and an infringement of the Canadian Bill of Rights and the Magna Carta. I maintain her crimes were not against the public but against herself by taking drugs and prostituting herself. Preventive custody would, in fact, be a sentence of life imprisonment."

Four social workers spoke encouragingly of Penny's prospects for rehabilitation, and one of them, Dorothy Shepherd, testified that Penny had tried everything in an effort to overcome her addiction.

As Holt said: "This girl did not let society down; society let her down. She tried, but could not get proper treatment when she sought it, she could not get training, she could not get parole. This girl has been more sinned against than she has sinned."

Magistrate Hume found that she was, indeed, an habitual criminal but said, "I am not satisfied that the protection of the public is needed." He declined to sentence her to preventive detention. All that she had to face was a two-year sentence for drug possession.

Holt reported that "Penny McNeil flashed a quick smile at lawyer Berger when she heard she would not have to spend the rest of her life in prison."

Within two weeks the Law Society appointed Berger to represent Maureen Gilbert, age thirty-seven, the second woman to face the bitch. Gilbert, who sometimes used the more romantic name June Alleyson, was charged with many offences, including that she had kept a common bawdy house and that she was a "loose, idle, disorderly person or vagrant, who, being a common prostitute or night walker, wandered into the public streets."

Her other offences are a stark testimony to her life: in the early 1950s she had stolen a suit valued at more than $25; stolen a radio;

broken windows, dishes and a buffet. In 1960 she had been sentenced to one month for possession of five stolen tins of Sea-Lect Fancy Lobster. In 1964 she had received two years for possession of a narcotic as well as a $50 fine for causing a disturbance in a public place by shouting and fighting—evidence that sixteen years of living what the law called a loose, idle and disorderly life were taking their toll.

Berger wrote to her:

Dear Mrs. Gilbert:

I know you are concerned about the fact that your case will not come up for trial until October 13th.

As you know, I wanted to put if off until October so that I could devote to it the time it requires.

I feel confident that we will be successful in your case and I will do the very best I can on your behalf.

I hope that you will be able to relax now. If you wish to get in touch with me about anything, please do not hesitate to telephone me if you can get permission to do that.

P.S. Your mother has made arrangements to come to see me this afternoon to discuss your case with me.

Maureen's mother, a Mrs. Stewart, was prepared to give evidence that her daughter had stayed with her during periods of freedom and had worked very hard keeping house. In addition, Berger intended to subpoena an employee of the city social service department to testify that Gilbert had received social assistance from time to time, thus negating the allegation that she had no lawful source of income. Welfare was frowned on, but it was not a crime. Berger also contacted Dr. Guy Richmond, the senior medical officer at Oakalla Prison, who had known Maureen Gilbert since 1953 and confirmed that she, like Penny McNeil, was a victim of harsh circumstances. Her brother was in the B.C. Pen's death row awaiting execution, and she was married to William Gilbert, whose habitual criminal conviction Berger was then appealing.

When Berger appeared in Magistrates Court with Maureen on 13 October 1964, the prosecution requested a further delay because of the uncertainty about the power of a magistrate to try an habitual criminal case. Berger submitted to the court a letter of

9 October 1964 from Dr. Richmond, which he had shown to City of Vancouver Prosecutor Stewart McMorran the morning before. Dr. Richmond said of Maureen:

> At the present time we are treating her for acute anxiety and depression. She has been in a state of tension for some months, awaiting the hearing of her charge of Habitual Criminality. It is essential to prevent grave deterioration in her mental health that she should not be kept waiting longer in her present state of extreme apprehension. We had hoped that with treatment she would be able to attend her hearing on Oct. 13, but any further delay I feel will aggravate the problem considerably.

"It isn't the fault of this woman if there is legal doubt regarding the magistrate's jurisdiction," Berger told Magistrate Gordon Scott. "This woman is in the grip of psychological terror. This is a parlous state for the administration of justice. The Crown should be made to proceed—otherwise the case should be thrown out."

Magistrate Scott declined to accede to Berger's request and adjourned the case until 4 November. However, on 30 October, Maureen was brought before the court (as all remand prisoners are, every eight days, so that the court may be satisfied that they are well and may respond to any changes in plea). At this appearance, Prosecutor McMorran entered a stay of proceedings, which meant that the Crown did not intend to continue with the prosecution. On 3 November 1964, Berger wrote:

> Dear Maureen:
>   I just thought I would drop you a note to explain what happened at Court last week, although I think that you must have understood.
>   Mr. McMorran, on behalf of the Crown, entered a stay of proceedings against you.
>   Under the circumstances, you will simply have to complete your present sentence of two years (if you are not in the meantime paroled), and that will be the end of the matter.

Since the matter did not go to trial, Berger billed Legal Aid only a token amount for his preparation time. A member of the committee replied, "in all fairness, I think you should be entitled to at least one day in Court and, therefore, return the copies of your bill in the event that you may wish to include same."

Berger was not only foregoing the benefits of a more lucrative clientele, he was giving up a great deal of what would have been family time. Bev remembers the lonely weekends with Tom toiling at the office or visiting the prisons on Saturdays and working first for the CCF and later the NDP on Sundays. "It was something he had to do," she says staunchly. "Tom's work was so important, and he did it so well. Friends and relatives helped by doing things around the house or coming to the rescue in an emergency. Still," she admits wistfully, "I do remember taking Erin and David for walks on weekends and seeing families complete with a father, and I'd think, 'Gee, that must be so nice.' "

But the 1960s were a time of commitment for Tom Berger and the demands of his practice left little time for the pleasures of family life. "Bev carried the full load," he concedes, but neither Tom nor Bev begrudges the choices they made. His accomplishments in the law have rewarded them and benefited the individuals and groups on whose behalf he laboured.

With the two women spared a lifetime in prison, Berger had only time to give a sigh of relief before the Vancouver prosecutor struck again. An application of 25 January 1965 alleged that it was "expedient for the protection of the public" to sentence Roberta Mason to preventive detention.

Berger was by now distressingly familiar with the pattern of social and judicial censure. One March weekend he visited Roberta in Oakalla Prison, and from her and a counsellor, he learned that she was another of life's victims, a girl who never had a chance. She was a child of the Depression, an Indian born to alcoholic parents in 1932 at Drift Pile, Alberta. Her counsellor, Mrs. Clarice Harkley of the John Howard Society, said: "Roberta was abused beyond belief. At the age of six she was sent to a convent, but she was already an emotionally damaged child. At 12 years the family brought her home and life must have been unbearable. At 14 years, by now herself an alcoholic, she ran away from home. The only way she knew how to live was by prostitution and theft."

Beginning in 1949 at the age of sixteen, she had been convicted of breaking, entering and theft, then theft of stockings, gloves, slippers and a bracelet, and an impaired driving charge. In 1953 she had served time for "having no visible means" of maintaining herself, "living without employment" and being thereby "a loose, idle, or disorderly person or vagrant." She served two more short sentences for vagrancy in 1959 and was later convicted of possessing drugs. At the time of her first appearance on the habitual criminal charge, she was thirty-two years old and had been convicted nineteen times.

Mrs. Harkley chronicled Roberta's attempts to break the pattern of her life at the age of twenty-eight when she determined to stop drinking by switching to drugs, at which time her antisocial behaviour ceased. Mrs. Harkley concluded a lengthy letter to Berger by saying: "After working with many addicts I truly feel Roberta is not a true addict, that her other antisocial behaviour has in the last years ceased and that a habitual sentence could only add to the wrong society has already done this woman."

Berger could also show that Mason had tried to obtain employment, though the problems faced by an unskilled Indian woman with a criminal record had proven to be insurmountable. He presented her case as compellingly as he could during two days before Magistrate Jackson. The magistrate reserved his decision for nearly a month, protracting Roberta's agony until 23 June—more than six months after she had been charged. He refused to find that she was an habitual criminal and dismissed the application. Mason still had a thirty-month sentence to serve on her last drug possession charge, but she could accept that. She would keep busy with her hobbies—knitting and leather work—and she would work in the prison laundry. The time would pass.

In December 1965 Berger wrote to her at Kingston Penitentiary:

Dear Roberta:
Thank you very much for the beautiful socks which you sent me. I appreciate your kindness very much. I hope that you are getting along alright. If I can be of any assistance to you, please let me know.
Best wishes for a merry Christmas and a happy new year.

Just before her release in July 1966, Roberta Mason wrote to Berger in a graceful hand: "A message to thank you, for a great job . . . not much I could say in words, but I do want you to know that I appreciate . . . perhaps I can show or prove my gratitude in future."

But Tom Berger needed no further proof. In addition to the socks he had a special bonus: no woman in Canada was ever threatened with life on the bitch again.

CHAPTER 4

The Man for Maisie's People

The texture and shape of Tom Berger's life as a lawyer, indeed of his entire career, was moulded by Tom and Maisie Hurley. Their influence had begun that first morning over coffee when Tom Hurley asked young Berger for his opinion, and the ramifications of that influence continue today. The Hurleys brought Berger and native people together, and that alliance was responsible for helping to bring about changes in the law, in politics, in the place of Indians in society—and in the life of Tom Berger.

In the 1950s there were two kinds of law in Canada: law that applied to Indians and a justice system for everyone else. The original inhabitants of the country had been, for the most part, relegated to reserves; and their numbers were much fewer, of course, than when the first white Europeans had arrived, especially in British Columbia, where diseases such as smallpox had literally decimated them. Native people had also suffered the loss of their traditional way of life and of their religion, and the breakdown of their extended family units had been exacerbated by alcohol abuse and the government's practice of placing children in residential schools. In short, Indian people in B.C. were low on the social scale and had few rights. The Hurleys thought things should be different.

Tom Hurley was larger than life, a stereotypical, hard-drinking, Irish defence lawyer of legendary wit and charm. The legal folklore of British Columbia abounds with tales of his salty, robust courtroom repartee. He had skill, humour, compassion. And, though he practised law alone, he had Maisie.

Maisie was a rebel. She always had been. Born Maisie Amy Campbell-Johnston in Wales to aristocratic, world-travelling Scots, she felt that life had begun for her when, as a teen-ager, she moved with her family to Aspen Grove in British Columbia's Nicola Valley. Exploring this largely unsettled land with her closest friend, an Indian girl named Lena Vogt, she had become an accomplished horsewoman and grown to love the high, dry, wilderness country. She had also grown to love an unsuitable man but was thwarted in an elopement attempt on her nineteenth birthday in 1906. A few years later she eloped again—this time successfully—with an American boxing promoter named Murphy, and did not return to B.C. until 1924 with her five children in tow (she did not do anything by halves). She never returned to Murphy, and she had a reconciliation with her mother who, like Maisie, was also a great friend to many Indian people. Maisie's daughter, Kitty, once told reporters, "I've never known anybody so fearless as my mother and grandmother. Grandmother loved animals. She used to say the only damned beast she feared was man."

Not Maisie. Her love of boxing frequently took her to the Vancouver Athletic Club, where she met a special man and fellow fan, Tom Hurley. It was an electric, long and loving union. She became his secretary, a post that enabled her to learn a great deal about law from a fine practitioner.

Tom Hurley would not think of turning down a needy person who required a lawyer, and Maisie helped to expand this one-man unsubsidized legal-aid program by bringing him a number of Indian clients. When the workload became more than Hurley could handle, Maisie started to go to Magistrate's Court as the Indians' agent. "I appeared in nearly eighty cases, and never lost one," she reminisced. "I've come to the conclusion they let me win to get me out of there."

Hurley fondly called it "my wife's bootleg law" and relied on her as the ultimate paralegal secretary, confidante, clerk and agent.

In 1944 her dedication to native peoples was recognized when the Native Brotherhood of B.C. made her an associate. Two years later, with $150, she began to publish *The Native Voice,* the first Indian newspaper in Canada. The paper was the official organ of the Native Brotherhood and focussed attention on Indian grievances: not until 1948 did Indians win the right to vote in B.C. and it was 1960 before they were able to vote in a federal election. *The Voice* strove to unify Indians and to publicize their cause so that their rights could be restored. A recurring theme was that, morally and legally, the Indians still owned the province because they had never signed a treaty. "They were not conquered," Maisie often said, "just robbed."

Maisie publicized her views and harangued the government in any way she could, and particularly relished a scheme she hatched with writer Paul St. Pierre. "We served a proclamation on the government, taking the province back and giving it to the Indians," she boasted.

Tom and Maisie were married after the death of her husband Murphy in 1951. The only invited guests were Indian friends, who joined in celebrating the commencement of what Maisie called "the happiest decade of my life."

During that decade Maisie began to apprise the young Tom Berger of the advantage that B.C. had taken of Indians. "In those days," Berger recalls, "native rights meant the right of a native person to a fair trial. Maisie took it much further." True, she made her husband's talents at the bar available to Natives charged with crimes and she was frequently in court herself. But her passion was the notion of "aboriginal title." Berger became intrigued by this concept. Although newly graduated from law school in a province with a large native population, he had never encountered the idea that the first peoples retained an interest in the land on which they had subsisted from "time immemorial." And yet, and yet, Maisie's logic was impeccable.

Berger admits, "We never paid too much attention to her idea. Not then." But he gradually became increasingly certain that Maisie was right. Frequently, in the months and years to come, Berger found himself turning the idea over in his mind, looking at it from the historical perspective and the legal one; he examined the viewpoints of natives and of the white establishment. He looked, too, at the work of anthropologists, though Maisie said, that like woollen underwear "they make me scratch." Her point was that by the virtue of their age-old use and occupation of the land, recognized by the Royal Proclamation of 1763 which reserved all the land west of Quebec for the Indians, they had aboriginal title, which could be extinguished only by treaty, and B.C. had never signed a treaty with the Indians.

"Meanwhile, Tom Hurley had started to come to me to ask me to represent clients of his," says Berger. "He felt his health failing. As well he occasionally worried aloud about who would support Maisie's 'charities' when he was gone."

Maisie, for her part, persisted in doing all she could to educate Berger and to pass on the torch to him. Tom Hurley died on Christmas morning in 1961, at the age of seventy-seven. Maisie never did completely rally from the loss, but she paid one final visit to Berger's office, smacked her cane across his desk and said, "Now, Tommy, you will have to defend all the native people."

"It was a visit I should have expected," Berger concedes with a wry smile. "She was a formidable woman. The subject was not open to debate."

From that time on, Maisie's people defined Tom Berger's life.

Initially, he represented native clients facing criminal charges, but once he had proven his mettle to Maisie, she began to send him the stuff of larger issues: Native Brotherhood leaders who wanted to discuss sovereignty, as well as aboriginal hunting and fishing rights. There were no easy answers, only the knowledge that the fight would be a long and rugged one. First, Berger would have to delve deeply into Canada's past and into the history of aboriginal peoples in Canada and around the world.

To discover the answers, Berger turned to pre-Confederation correspondence, reports of royal commissions, textbooks, historical papers and journals. What had been a specialty of the Hurleys' choosing became an all-consuming dedication. The difficulty would be in convincing the white establishment, and the only way to do that, he knew, was to build the structure of aboriginal title on a strong legal foundation.

An important episode in the saga of Berger and the native people began on Vancouver Island on the first Sunday of July 1963 when Clifford White and David Bob, two members of the Nanaimo Indian band, shot several deer to feed their families. As they did not have the permit that allowed native people to take game for food, they were charged under the Game Act and were summarily convicted by Magistrate Lionel Beevor-Potts: a fine of

$100 each was imposed and their guns were impounded. They could not afford to pay their fines, so the court found them in default, and they were shipped off to Oakalla Prison on the mainland.

When Maisie Hurley heard the news, she was furious; she saw it as a classic illustration of how the system worked against native people. She paid the fines and got Berger busy on their appeal.

Thus began yet another research project of staggering proportions. Berger built up files bulging with notes, memos, letters and documents dredged out of obscurity. The material acquired during this period is dotted with the names of people who were to participate in the balance of his career. It was then that he first wrote to Wilson Duff, curator of anthropology at the B.C. Provincial Museum, who had been accumulating data, maps and theories about B.C. Indians and their lands. Duff was delighted that at last someone familiar with these topics had come to him with intelligent questions, probing questions that sent him digging even more deeply into the history of the Pacific Northwest. A similar process of discovery occurred with B.C. Provincial Archivist Willard Ireland. Through these men and others of their calibre, Berger became connected to scholars around the world. Together, they reconstructed the routes of Sir Francis Drake and other explorers; they defined patterns of native land use, systems of inheritance and territorial boundaries; they searched through government correspondence, orders in council and unreported legal decisions with respect to Indians in Ontario, the prairies and the United States. Berger was an assiduous correspondent, never failing to tell each resource person what he had learned, how it was fitting together, how he expected to use the information acquired, and asking the next question. It was a technique he would use and perfect in decades to come.

Berger drafted briefs and factums, passing them on to the Allied Tribes, Native Brotherhood and friends in the bureaucracy, as well as to academic experts on constitutional law such as Frank Scott at McGill University and Ken Lysyk at the University of British Columbia. He sought their comments and compiled historical data with an almost innocent belief that by applying his findings to the law, he could change the way Whites treat Indians. The purity of this hope made others believe with him that *White and Bob,* a seemingly inconsequential case, had the potential to be very significant.

Duff and Ireland produced evidence that in 1854 a treaty had been signed with the Nanaimo Indians, guaranteeing their right to hunt. Although it is commonly assumed that no treaties were made with Indians in British Columbia, there is an exception— Vancouver Island.

Success would depend on a virtual mountain of historical, legal and anthropological evidence. Success would also depend on the precise testimony of the two accused, so it was essential that Berger canvass with the two men every detail of the hunt and of the charges, as well as of the traditional use made of hunting grounds. He set aside Saturday, 23 November 1963, to devote to White and Bob and wrote telling them he would be in his office all day. As they had no telephones, he also sent notes to community leaders who were raising funds for their defence, asking them to remind his clients of their appointment. The day passed, and they did not appear.

On the following Monday, Bob wrote: "I'm very sorry I couldn't come. I didn't have any money. I tried as hard as I could." A similar letter came from White. He, too, had been defeated by the minor expense involved in getting to Vancouver. As intimately involved with natives as Berger was, he had overlooked the chronic impediment to their progress—poverty. There is little cash flow in a hunting and fishing economy.

Berger went to Vancouver Island to meet with White and Bob on 10 December and won an acquittal for them the next day when their appeal was heard in Nanaimo County Court by Judge A. J. Swencisky. The judge upheld their treaty rights and also ruled that the "aboriginal right of the Nanaimo Indian tribes to hunt on unoccupied land, which was confirmed to them by the Proclamation of 1763, has never been extinguished and is still in full force and effect."

Wilson Duff, writing to Berger about the trial, said, "May I once again express my admiration for the masterful way in which you represented your argument," but then chastised Berger for his limited vision. "Your conception of native title is based on usufruct, the right to use the products of the land. Mine is more than use; it is based on clear-cut Indian concepts of ownership." Duff supported his opinion with the U.S. Court of Claims decision in *Re Tlinget and Haida Indians,* which he urged Berger to read.

Berger replied that "*White and Bob* may go to a higher court and with the Indian Claims Bill in Parliament, I have a feeling that more work has to be done." He promised Duff that he would spend the Christmas holidays reading the U.S. decision and putting together an extensive outline on the subject of Indian title in B.C.

On 14 December 1963, parliament gave first reading to Bill C-130, which would establish a commission to consider Indian claims. If a band could show that the Crown had taken its land unfairly, the commission would be empowered to award compensation, but it could not order the return of the land, because the British North America Act (renamed the Constitution Act), which created Canada, allocates control over land titles and public lands generally to the provinces.

Berger examined Bill C-130 on behalf of the Native Brotherhood and found it sadly lacking. The most troublesome flaw was the limitation that claims against only the Crown federal would be heard. After the old colonies of Vancouver Island and British Columbia had united and entered Confederation in 1871, the Crown provincial had neither recognized aboriginal title nor entered into treaties. There were exceptions. On Vancouver Island, James Douglas, in his capacity as chief factor of the Hudson's Bay Company, had treated with the Nanaimo Indians and other tribes. As settlers arrived, however, they simply took the land—all of it—from the original native inhabitants.

Berger briefed everyone who would listen and put endless hours into legal research. On 22 June 1965, a revised version of Bill C-130—Bill C-123—was introduced in parliament. The new bill still did not provide for compensating native people for B.C.'s post-Confederation land grabs and nowhere did it acknowledge the aboriginal title of the Indian tribes of British Columbia. It stipulated that within three years the bands must give notice of their claims, setting out particulars in writing "with reasonable certainty and detail." Berger protested that it was "paradoxical that parliament, after waiting 97 years to establish an Indian Claims Commission" should require tribes to complete a thorough, detailed and costly process so quickly. Further, any claims were to be proved by "evidence in writing that is reasonably contemporaneous to the time when the subject matter of the claim arose." That directive meant, Berger warned, that "an Indian band to prove its claim must be able to produce a written document as old as its claim in order to prove its claim. It seems to me unlikely that there are very many cases where an Indian band would be able to produce such a document." Thus, the constitutional and ethical dilemmas posed by the idea of native claims remained unresolved. In the event, the federal government did not proceed any further with the legislation.

In the interval, Berger's comment to Duff about *White and Bob* proved to be correct, as the Crown did appeal the decision of the County Court judge. Maisie Hurley gleefully relished the prospect of that appeal, as her pet theories, her life work and the history of "her" people would be reviewed. "This is what I have lived for all my life and I am going to be there," she vowed, but sadly, when the time came, her health was too precarious to allow her to make the journey to Victoria for the hearing in the Court of Appeal.

The County Court judge had held that the document was a treaty and that, as a result, White and Bob were entitled to the benefit of the exception in the Indian Act that recognized hunting rights as contracted for by the treaty. This understanding was also the crux of Berger's argument in the B.C. Court of Appeal.

Berger argued that the treaty of 23 December 1854 between the ancestors of the accused and James Douglas of the Hudson's Bay Company established the right for Clifford White and David Bob to hunt out of season. The Crown was arguing that the 1854 treaty was not binding, so Berger also relied on the concept of aboriginal title, which included the right to hunt over the land. The Royal Proclamation of 1763 deals with Crown lands, and it is to this document that native people have looked for an affirmation of aboriginal title:

It is just and reasonable, and essential to our interest, and the security of our Colonies, that the several Nations or Tribes of Indians with whom we are connected, and who live under our Protection, should not be molested or disturbed in the Possession of such Parts of Our Dominion and Territories as, having not been ceded to or purchased by Us, are reserved to them or any of them, as their Hunting Grounds . . . which not having been ceded to or purchased by Us as aforesaid, are reserved to the said Indians, or any of them.

And We do further declare it to be Our Royal Will and Pleasure for the present as aforesaid, to reserve under our Sovereignty, Protection, and Dominion, for the use of the said Indians, all the

Lands and Territories not included within the Limits of the Lands and Territories lying to the Westward of the Sources of the Rivers which fall into the Sea from the West and North West as aforesaid.

Berger submitted that the proclamation had the effect of legislation and that it created a right superior to the Game Act. He then argued that the 1854 treaty reserved the right to hunt for food over the land in question, for as in all agreements made by James Douglas with Indian tribes, the following clause appeared: "It is also understood that we are at liberty to hunt over the unoccupied lands and to carry on our fisheries as formerly."

Berger argued that White and Bob, as native Indians, possessed the aboriginal right to hunt for food over unoccupied land lying within their ancient tribal hunting grounds.

The Crown, in response, contended that the 1854 treaty "conferred no hunting rights and if it did, that these rights have been extinguished" by the Indian Act.

Before the Court of Appeal's decision was handed down, Maisie Hurley died. She died fretting over her inability to carry the struggle for the rights of her people to its conclusion, but content that the fight was in Tom Berger's hands. At the end of her time, this rambunctious, spirited woman and the idealistic young lawyer shared a conviction that there is a rightful place in Canadian society for the first peoples and that it must always be defined in their own way. Today, this is a familiar theme, but in the 1960s it was an unusual one. In a graveside tribute to the woman who had done so much to open society to Indian values, Monsignor J. L. Bradley echoed her philosophy when he urged Natives to "Be Indians; be proud you are Indians."

They were proud, as Berger was, when the Court of Appeal upheld the County Court ruling. Mr. Justice Davey, speaking for himself and two others in dismissing the Crown's appeal, held that even if the provincial Game Act had been "sufficiently clear to show an intention to abrogate or qualify contractual rights of hunting notoriously reserved to Indians," it could not override the paramountcy of the federal Indian Act under the authority of the BNA Act." The 1854 treaty was upheld.

"This is the kind of case that opens up a lot of new country," F. R. Scott wrote in a congratulatory note to Berger.

No one was surprised that the attorney general of British Columbia applied to the Supreme Court of Canada for leave to appeal, and Berger did not oppose the application because he wanted the highest court in the land to rule, once and for all, on the issues. Still, the cost of yet another appeal was enormous, sorely taxing the resources of the native community. They took some comfort from a newspaper item that reported the federal government intended to offer assistance to White and Bob for the cost of their defence.

Berger persevered, his energies pushed to the limit. His work for habitual criminals was then at its peak, he had just subpoenaed the premier of British Columbia to attend Examination for Discovery in the *Jones* slander suit, he had been working hard on Bill C-130 on Indian claims and he was commuting between his Vancouver office and the provincial capital of Victoria on Vancouver Island to attend to his duties as an elected member of the Legislative Assembly. His wife Beverley was carrying the full load at home, tending to the needs of Erin and David, both preschool age, while trying to keep in touch with Tom, their families and friends.

Berger had taken on an associate, a law school gold medallist named Doug Sanders, who assisted with the preparation of the factum for *White and Bob*. Sanders accompanied Berger to Ottawa as his junior counsel, and together they entered the Supreme Court of Canada on 10 November 1965, to emerge shortly thereafter with a mixed victory on their hands. The Supreme Court agreed with the majority in the B.C. Court of Appeal that the 1854 treaty superseded the Game Act. The Nanaimo treaty and eleven other treaties made on Vancouver Island in the 1850s were given new life. However, the judgment was confined to the 1854 treaty and did not decide the validity of the aboriginal claim.

Berger did not limit his advocacy of native rights to casework, and newspapers of the era chronicled his growing activism. In a 1967 brief to federal Minister of Indian Affairs Art Laing, Berger charged that the ministry's obligation to protect the interests of the Ohiaht band had been breached when the B.C. government granted timber licences to MacMillan Bloedel, which allowed the forestry company to log the Ohiahts' reserves. Berger also pointed out the refusal of the judicial system to appoint Indians to jury duty, so that they were denied the opportunity to be judged by their peers, but it was 1986 before that issue was again given prominence by the media. Little wonder that he accused the government of arrogance in trying to mould Indians into the

North American way of life and that he insisted a special fund was needed to offset what he characterized as "apartheid against Indians."

"This is the only part of the English-speaking world," Berger announced, "where a government refuses to recognize aboriginal cultures."

The whole question of aboriginal title remained unresolved. Unwilling to wait for judicial rulings, native groups demanded that the laws be changed to recognize their aboriginal rights. In Vancouver, on 8 August 1968, newly elected Prime Minister Pierre Trudeau said no.

> If we think about restoring aboriginal rights to the Indians well, what about the French who were defeated at the Plains of Abraham? . . . the Acadians who were deported? . . . the Japanese Canadians who were so badly treated at the end of or during the last war? What can we do to redeem the past? I can only say as President Kennedy said when he was asked about what he would do to compensate for injustices that the Negroes had received in American society: We will be just in our time. This is all we can do. We must be just today.

Despite official rejection of the claim variously labelled Indian title, aboriginal title or native title, it continues to be a contentious issue. Berger wrote later in his book *Fragile Freedoms* that in British Columbia, "the Native protest over the loss of their lands has been more audible than elsewhere. One tribe, the Nishgas, has been in the forefront of this controversy. . . . Their story takes us back to the beginnings of European colonization of North America, and it brings us forward to the very centre of the present conflict over land claims, Indian self-determination, and the concept of Indian government."

The basis of the Nishga case was ideological and came from the supposition that they had an interest in the land. The courts had to be shown that the interest—aboriginal title—was a legitimate burden on the land, existing contemporaneously with the Crown's interest. True, native people *could* surrender their interest to the federal Crown—the Queen in the right of Canada. But the Nishga people had never done so. The provincial Crown lacked the jurisdiction to interfere with that right. To work up to and to prove those principles had taken Berger ten years of work and research.

Members of the Vancouver bar thought it was all nonsense, so Berger could not discuss the finer points of the case with other lawyers, who pegged the idea as romantic idealism. And Berger certainly is a romantic idealist: not naive, not even innocent, but always fresh, always open to new ways of seeing.

In 1968 Berger commenced an action in the B.C. Supreme Court on behalf of the Nishgas by issuing a writ that neither claimed compensation for them nor demanded settlement of their land claim. It simply sought a declaration that the Nishgas' "aboriginal title, otherwise known as the Indian Title of the Plaintiffs, has never been fully extinguished."

Berger's arguments and those of Douglas McK. Brown, Q.C., acting for the provincial attorney general, took five days. That fact leaves B.C. Supreme Court Chief Justice McEachern breathless. "Do you know what goes on in courtrooms today? An ordinary barrister would take weeks, months even, to present the same case." He goes on to complain of "those lawyers not even starting from scratch, like Tom was, but who take five times as long as they need, to present a claims case today."

Call it "from scratch" or call it "pioneering in the law," Berger did it. He canvassed native history, treaties, documents, correspondence and the statutes of colonial and post-Confederation governments throughout Canada, as well as the rights of aboriginal peoples around the world. He tendered as evidence copies of letters between Governor James Douglas and the British Colonial Office that revealed the governor's English overseers believed failure to immediately resolve native land issues presaged complex problems for the future. He showed how early treatises on constitutional law mentioned unsettled aboriginal claims and how government persistence in saying the claims were without substance had led to their being overlooked by legal writers.

Although Douglas had negotiated treaties extinguishing Indian title on Vancouver Island, there were no treaties on the mainland of British Columbia. The Nishgas lived in a remote valley in northwestern British Columbia. By 1861, however, the British Colonial Secretary had made it clear that London viewed cession of lands as a purely colonial matter and would not provide funds to assist "in extinguishing the Indian title to public lands in the colony," though he remained "fully sensible of the great importance of purchasing without loss of time the native title to the soil." Subsequently, despite this clear acknowledgement that Indian title existed, the Colony of British Columbia resolved to ignore Indian title. Upon the union of the colonies of Vancouver Island and British Columbia in 1866, Sir Joseph Trutch succeeded Douglas as land commissioner. This was a dark day for B.C. Indians. Trutch made vehement statements to the effect that Indians had no interest in the lands they claimed, and further, that they should not even be allowed to retain those they had. When British Columbia entered Confederation and became part of Canada in 1871, Trutch became the new province's lieutenant governor, and he actively discouraged Prime Minister Sir John A. Macdonald from contemplating buying out Indian titles.

The Nishgas, who had not signed treaties and had resisted being herded onto reserves or coming under the purview of the Indian Act, became engaged in a lengthy and resourceful series of manoeuvres to assert their rights. Their accomplishments, particularly in the light of those times and their geographic isolation, are remarkable. During the 1880s they brought their plight to the attention of Lord Dufferin, the governor general of Canada, who admonished British Columbia for its actions, which he said restricted or interfered with the "prescriptive rights of the Queen's Indian subjects." As a result of his comments and continued native agitation, a joint federal-provincial royal commission was appointed in 1887 to "enquire into the state and condition of the Indians of the North-West Coast of British Columbia . . . for the purpose of hearing the expression of their views, wishes, and complaints, if any."

The report of the commission included a statement by Chief David MacKay which Berger tendered as part of his evidence:

What we don't like about the Government is their saying this: "We will give you this much land." How can they give it when it is our own? We cannot understand it. They have never bought it from us or our forefathers. They have never fought and conquered our people and taken the land in that way, and yet they say now that they will give us so much land—our own land. These chiefs [of ours] do not talk foolishly, they know the land is their own; our forefathers for generations and generations past . . . had their own hunting grounds, their salmon streams, and places where they got berries; it has always been so.

One of the commissioners, J. B. Planta, had been instructed by Attorney General Alexander Davie to be impartial and "not to give undertakings or make promises" and to "be careful to discountenance, should it arise, any claim of Indian land title to Provincial lands." Not surprisingly, after the commissioners returned to Victoria and submitted their report (which recommended only moderate changes), the Nishgas were forgotten once more.

In 1906 and 1909 Nishga leaders were among those British Columbia chiefs who went to London to present their demands to the king. In 1910 and again in 1911, they met with Prime Minister Wilfrid Laurier, who considered federal action to bring the provincial government to court for its failure to acknowledge native land claims. However, there was a B.C. statute in place that precluded bringing an action against the province for an interest in the land without first obtaining an enabling document, called a *fiat*, from the province's attorney general. This meant that any party wanting to sue the provincial government on such matters had to get the government's consent. Premier Richard McBride had refused his consent, and so the Nishgas, ever tenacious, retained a firm of London solicitors to petition the king, but this tactic was not successful either. Thus, after the defeat of Laurier's Liberal government, they formed the Nishga Land Committee to embark on a further fifty years of effort, during which there was no support for their position from any level of government.

As a member of the Allied Tribes of British Columbia, the Nishgas also lobbied to reject the report of the 1915 McKenna-McBride commission, which had been struck to investigate complaints about the inadequate size of Indian reserves and to examine the aboriginal claims of non-reserve Indians. The commission had recommended that 47,000 acres of the most valuable land be "cut-off" from reserves and replaced with 87,000 acres of poorer land. (Compensation for this fiasco began in 1984.) The McKenna-McBride Report allotted the Nishgas one-half of one per cent of their former territory.

Despite the futility of participating in official hearings, the Nishgas made presentations to Special Joint Parliamentary Committees appointed by the federal government in 1926, and again in 1959, to examine aboriginal title. They were equally ineffectual.

Finally, after their long history of encountering denial by the white establishment, the Nishgas met with Tom Berger. In representing them, Berger embarked on the most significant human rights case of his career. He thought that there was a way to get around the hurdle of the fiat requirement by casting his pleadings on behalf of the Nishgas in the form of a declaratory action. The case was brought in the name of Frank Calder, president of the Nishga Tribal Council and a direct descendant of the people who had testified in 1887 before the royal commission. Calder, along with four Nishga chiefs, gave cogent evidence of a viable Nishga culture; of a language distinct from that of other tribes and of the Nishgas' occupation from time immemorial of a specific territory defined by tribal boundaries. Berger also called anthropologist Wilson Duff as an expert witness to describe the Nishgas' advanced society. Duff's opinion, which followed along the line of the argument excerpted below from his book *The Indian History of British Columbia,* was one of the few accurate sources of such information then available:

> It is not correct to say that the Indians did not own the land but only roamed over the face of it and used it. The patterns of ownership and utilization which they imposed upon the lands and waters were different from those recognized by our system of law, but were nonetheless clearly defined and mutually respected. Even if they didn't subdivide and cultivate the land they did recognize ownership of plots used for village sites, fishing places, berry and root patches, and similar purposes. Even if they didn't subject the forests to wholesale logging, they did establish ownership of tracts used for hunting, trapping, and food gathering. Even if they didn't sink mine shafts into the mountains, they did own peaks and valleys for mountain goat hunting and as sources of raw material.

Counsel for the province asserted that the two pre-Confederation colonies had, in passing a series of ordinances, effectively extinguished whatever interest the Indians may have had in the land. In closing, he warned Mr. Justice J. G. Gould of the "dangerous and staggering consequences" of granting a declaration.

Berger agreed that such a declaration might have great bearing on other Indian claims, but reminded the judge that "In the case at bar, all that is sought is a declaration that their aboriginal title was never extinguished. They seek no relief beyond the declaration. . . . This is not an action for compensation."

Mr. Justice Gould thanked the lawyers for their "most interesting" arguments and reserved his decision. In due course, he ruled that he was persuaded of the correctness of the province's position. He stated that he favoured the opinion of County Court Judge Schultz in *Discon and Baker* and of Mr. Justice Sheppard in *White and Bob* that the Royal Proclamation of 1763 did not apply to the lands in question because they were *terra incognita,* that is, they were not then officially known to the Crown. He concluded his judgment with the comment: "One would have to be self-blinded to the events and attitudes of the day to ignore the fact that this litigation is of great concern, and this judgment a deep distress, to the Indian peoples of British Columbia." He acknowledged that the cost of the inevitable appeal would be high, due to the historical research germane to the issues, and suggested it was a cost that could more easily be borne by the provincial treasury than by the Nishgas.

Berger was immersed in his campaign for the leadership of the New Democratic Party when he took time to argue the Calder case in the B.C. Court of Appeal. Here the Nishgas lost again. Chief Justice H. W. Davey held that he could "find no prerogative or legislative acts ensuring to the Nishga Nation any aboriginal rights in their territory." Both he and Mr. Justice Tysoe said that if they were wrong on this point, then the historical and legislative material offered by counsel for the attorney general demonstrated that any rights acquired had been extinguished.

Unfortunately, the chief justice was unable to comprehend the complexity of Nishga society. Although Duff had detailed the Nishga matrilineal system of succession to land and demonstrated their sophisticated concepts of land ownership, Davey said: "They were undoubtedly at the time of settlement a very primitive people with few of the institutions of civilized society, and none at all of our notions of private property."

Berger's response to this opinion a decade later was the epitome of tolerance. In his book on human rights, *Fragile Freedoms,* he wrote that Davey was "one of British Columbia's finest judges: he was patient, scholarly and upright," but that he viewed the Nishgas across an "ethnographic gulf" he could not transcend, despite the weight of the evidence. Davey was not to be faulted for this, Berger said, as it typified the perspective held by Canadians for centuries, but Berger went on to vigorously refute Davey's view:

The culture of Native peoples amounts to more than crafts and carvings, dancing and drinking. Their tradition of decision-making by consensus, their respect for the wisdom of their elders, their concept of the extended family, their belief in a special relationship with the land, their respect for the environment, their willingness to share—all of these values persist in one way or another among them today, despite unremitting pressure to abandon them.

Thus Indian culture is not moribund. Indian ideas about their relationship with the land are the foundation of aboriginal title.

For Berger and the Nishgas there was only one hope left. a final hearing in the Supreme Court of Canada. In this they received a stroke of good fortune when Emmett Hall delayed his retirement so that he could sit on the case, which was set for November 1971.

The Nishgas wanted the federal government to intervene on their behalf in the Supreme Court. "I had written to Jean Chrétien, then the minister of the Department of Indian Affairs and Northern Development," Berger recalls, "and urged that the federal government intervene in the scc on the side of the Nishgas. We met in Ottawa and had a good discussion, at which time he made it clear that he would like to intervene, but Trudeau was against it. They did not intervene."

In the Nishga case, the court looked, as do all Canadian inquiries into the nature of Indian title, to the *St. Catharines Milling Co.* case, which is familiar to every student of constitutional law. In 1883 the federal government, believing that it owned the lands and resources in a particular area with respect to which it had entered a treaty, granted a timber-cutting licence to the milling company. The Province of Ontario, however, claimed that the British North America Act gave it the land and negated any Indian interest there might have been on it. The then-final arbiter, the Judicial Committee of the Privy Council in England, held that after the treaty, the entire interest in the land and legislative jurisdiction over it fell to the province. In effect, this was a circuitous way of recognizing Indian title, for it recognized that the Crown's interest had existed concurrently with aboriginal title, which was something tangible and capable of extinguishment and which had originated with the Royal Proclamation.

In *Calder,* the court looked at two questions raised by Berger: Is Indian use and occupation of the land, prior to the arrival of the Europeans, sufficient to establish Indian title? Berger argued that it is sufficient. Does the Royal Proclamation of 1763 apply to the Nishgas' territory and entitle them to its protection? To assist with these questions, the court had before it all of the historical documents and evidence presented at trial.

Fourteen months after the appeal was heard, members of the court handed down their decision with lengthy written reasons, but newspapers condensed it thus:

COURT REJECTS INDIAN LAND CLAIM
NISHGAS DENIED 'ABORIGINAL TITLE'

It seemed at first that the Nishgas were defeated. Mr. Justice Judson, with whom Mr. Justice Martland and Mr. Justice Ritchie concurred, said that the Royal Proclamation of 1763 had no bearing upon the problem of Indian title in British Columbia because of the geographical limits implicit in the proclamation and by looking at "the history of the discovery, settlement and establishment of what is now British Columbia." Although he was emphatic that Indian title in the province could not owe its origin to the proclamation, he acknowledged that when the settlers came, the Indians were there, occupying the land in an organized societal system, and that their ancestors had been doing so for centuries. That, he said, is what Indian title means. This meant the fact that the Indians had used and occupied the land was a sufficient basis for aboriginal title. Indian title gave the Nishgas the right to continue to live on their lands as their forefathers had lived. But, said the three, in B.C. this right had been extinguished.

Speaking for the three, Mr. Justice Judson said that they accepted the opinion of the judge at trial, Mr. Justice Gould, who had found that the nineteenth-century legislative documents tendered in evidence "reveal a unity of intention to exercise, and the legislative exercising, of absolute sovereignty over all the lands of British Columbia, a sovereignty inconsistent with any conflicting interest, including one as to 'aboriginal title' otherwise known as the 'Indian title.' " Thus, they concluded, aboriginal title had been extinguished, the action failed and the appeal should be dismissed.

Mr. Justice Emmett Hall had spent the summer writing his opinion, a lengthy and wide-ranging decision delivered on behalf of himself and his brother judges Mr. Justice Spence and Mr. Justice Laskin (later chief justice of Canada). Hall also considered *St. Catharines Milling* and paid particular attention to the words of Lord Watson in that case who, after acknowledging that the Crown held the land in question at pleasure "for the present" use of the Indians, added that there was a "great deal of learned discussion at the Bar with respect to the precise quality of the Indian right, but their Lordships do not consider it necessary to express any opinion upon the point." Relying on Lord Watson's words, Justices Hall, Spence and Laskin did not think they were obligated to consider themselves bound by *St. Catharines Milling*. Accordingly, they decided that: "In respect of this Proclamation, it can be said that when other exploring nations were showing a ruthless disregard for native rights England adopted a remarkably enlightened attitude towards the Indians of North America. The Proclamation must be regarded as a fundamental document upon which any just determination of original rights rest." But the Royal Proclamation was not necessarily the source of aboriginal title. Hall mentioned a basic principle of property law: "Possession is of itself at common law proof of ownership. Unchallenged possession is admitted here." The proclamation affirmed a pre-existing aboriginal title. Had it been extinguished? Hall said no.

So, while all six judges agreed on the issue of aboriginal title, they were evenly divided on the issue of extinguishment, and the seventh judge, Mr. Justice Louis-Philippe Pigeon, did not decide it. Taking refuge in a technicality, he ruled that the Nishgas' action must fail because they had not obtained a fiat. So the Nishgas lost again, four to three.

After his initial disappointment, Berger realized that though the declaration they sought had not been granted, six judges in the highest court of the land *had* identified aboriginal title as an interest in the land recognized under Canadian law: the Nishgas, they said, held this possessory interest at the time of the coming of the white man. And three judges held that their title had never been extinguished and could be asserted today.

Since the decision on the Nishga case, there has been much progress in native claims, and for the source of that momentum, Berger looks to Emmett Hall's judgment to illustrate what he calls "that sense of humanity—that stretch of the mind and heart—that enabled him to look at the idea of aboriginal rights and to see it as the Indian people see it."

The federal government was cognizant from the beginning that the Supreme Court's decision would be critical. Employees of the Prime Minister's Office and the Department of Indian Affairs and Northern Development drafted anticipatory statements for the three possible judgments: *for* the Nishgas, *against* the Nishgas, and one to address an ambiguous decision. When the ruling came down, a DIAND spokesman read a statement on behalf of the prime minister:

> I have just been informed about the Supreme Court decision. This is an important case and it will require close study by both the Indian people and the Government. I will, of course, be discussing it with the Minister of Indian Affairs and Northern Development. I know he will want to examine the judgments carefully before commenting upon them . . .
>
> The government is anxious that the right course be followed. The matter is complex. It seems clear that further research in historical and other records may be required to provide a clearer understanding of the position of the Native people of Canada.
>
> We must also remember that the decision is a legal one which in no way alters the responsibility of the federal government to support and encourage activities so that the Indians may achieve their cultural, economic and social aspirations within Canadian society.

For a short time, there was confusion about exactly what the judgments meant and how the government would seek to implement them. Gradually, it became clear that Berger's solid work, accepted and confirmed in Justice Hall's lucid dissent, had achieved the breakthrough dreamed of for so long. This was confirmed when Prime Minister Trudeau later spoke to an assembly of native groups and said, wryly, "Well, it looks like you've got more rights than I thought."

That concession is synonymous with Berger's crusade to bring native people to the bargaining table as equals, just as Maisie Hurley had advocated in numerous *Native Voice* editorials. Trudeau's words signalled that negotiations to effect settlement of aboriginal claims had begun. In August 1973, only six months after the Nishga decision, Minister of Indian Affairs Jean Chrétien announced a change of government policy and the intention to settle aboriginal claims across Canada. This was the event for which those Indians, Métis and Inuit who had never entered into treaties had been waiting and working for more than a century. Berger insists that government policy was overthrown not by his efforts but by the determination of the native peoples to reject it and keep on rejecting it, until it was rejected. In fact, nowhere in the chapter on "The Nishga Indians and Aboriginal Rights" in *Fragile Freedoms* does he mention his role in helping the Nishgas finally attain federal recognition of their claim. His position is that the Nishga clung tenaciously to their culture, steadfastly maintaining that there was a critical issue as yet unresolved, and took every intelligent approach towards having that issue resolved. That they utilized his expertise and dedication to find the nugget of decency they had so long been seeking from white society was, according to Berger's version of the events, merely an incidental tactic.

Today, twenty-five years after Maisie Hurley planted the concept of aboriginal rights in Berger's fertile mind, the story is not yet over. The first few federal-provincial First Ministers Conferences on aboriginal rights have been marked by acrimony, and federal negotiations with the Nishgas have been painfully slow.

The official position in British Columbia continues to be confrontational. Late in 1985, Attorney General Brian Smith insisted that land claims would financially ruin the province and would never reach the bargaining table as long as he was in a position to stop it.

"How can there be a settlement," Berger asked in a feature article commissioned by the Vancouver *Province* on 24 November 1985, "when one of the parties refuses to come to the bargaining table?"

"If we believe in a democracy in B.C.," he said, "it is only a question of time . . . under this administration or another, before all parties sit down and make a settlement."

Smith flatly dismissed a broad interpretation of the Supreme Court decision in the Nishga case. "The court ruled they no longer held aboriginal title to the land in question," he said, without acknowledging that in the 1984 *Guerin* case, Mr. Justice Brian Dickson of the Supreme Court of Canada relied on *Calder* to rule that the nature of Indian interest in the land is best characterized by its "inalienability," when he stated that a B.C. band's aboriginal title to the land was a "pre-existing right" predating Canadian and British colonial law.

Although the road to redress for the Nishgas is still strewn with obstacles, they are people who know everything about persistence.

Jean Chrétien tempers the praise and credit accorded Berger for progress in native rights and land claims. "It was not just because of what the judges said, that we changed government policy when we did," he protests. "It was time to do that because that was what the native people wanted us to do then."

Verna Kirkness, a prominent Indian educator, actively in touch with native leaders across the country, says that Berger's case work is the least of his worth to them. "The law isn't what makes Tom so special," she laughs. "He has always worked for us. He has always been our friend, our helper, our consultant. All across the country, Indian people want him—to speak or to work for them—because he has always been the leading advocate of native rights. He has been the one who has come forward on the big issues. There is no one else with nearly his stature coming forward. Who?" she asks almost despairingly, "who will take over when he's gone? No one else, Native or White, has ever worked for us with such sheer commitment. He has been able to hold himself above native politics and to help us achieve native autonomy. He is loved because he doesn't speak *for* native people. He speaks and works in support of them. That's the difference."

Beverley Berger has also earned the respect of the native community. For her master's degree in education, which she completed at the University of British Columbia, she spent a year working on a thesis that examined how art could be used to develop cultural awareness. She then tried out her ideas for four months at Spirit Rising, an alternate urban Native Indian school. She wanted to illustrate, she says, "that art doesn't take place in a vacuum but comes out of cultural experience." In this she succeeded. The students made their own tools—"art with a practical purpose." She also took the children on field trips to the beaches, forests and mountains. "I'm so proud of her work with those children," Tom says. Beverley also served as a counsellor with the University of British Columbia's Native Indian Teacher Education Program.

In the spring of 1986 the Nishga Tribal Council's annual convention took place in the Nass Valley. Bev and Tom Berger flew to Terrace where they were met for the three-hour drive along a gravel road to Canyon City, a Nishga village accessible only by a swinging foot bridge over the Nass River. The closest white community is Hazelton, where Ted and Perle Berger lived from 1929 to 1932. Tom and Bev attended the blessing of the lava beds (where, according to a Nishga legend, their ancestors were buried when a volcano erupted), and witnessed traditional dancing and a procession of people wearing ceremonial button blankets. Then it was back to the meeting hall where Frank Calder officially introduced Tom Berger to the Nishga people. The standing ovation was long and sincere.

CHAPTER 5

The Politician

"Yes, I'm a bleeding-heart liberal and proud of it."

Tom Berger

In British Columbia during the 1960s, opportunity was not limited to a network of people within an elite establishment, for it was a fractious, potentially rich province with room in politics, business and the professions for the able, articulate and ambitious. At first Berger aspired to professional prestige and economic stability—reasonable expectations for a lawyer and not surprising goals for any young man. With the legal territory, however, came political prospects, and party membership could help young lawyers further their ambitions.

Tom Berger's political attributes had been noticed while he was still attending university. He was earnest and steady, near the top of his class, and he was aware of the history of the country as well as of its current political machinations. "I was persuaded by friends to join the Liberal Party," Berger said. When the media reported what he, as vice president of the Young Liberals, said at a Co-operative Commonwealth Federation (CCF) Open Forum, he became aware that politics meant ready access to the public. On that occasion, he told the audience that Liberal Minister of External Affairs Lester Pearson had brought Canada "closer to the centre of world affairs." In the ensuing debate, he ably defended

Pearson (the future prime minister) and the party against attacks by CCFers, but not out of any deep-seated commitment. For Berger at that time, the partisan aspects of politics were almost superficial considerations; he was more interested in the exchange of ideas and the actions of people of principle. "I greatly admired Lester Pearson, of course. He'd won the Nobel Peace Prize and he was a great man, a fine man." But Berger was to be only a temporary member of the Liberals.

After graduating from university, Berger's law practice and legal reputation got their start in the field of labour and employment law. He successfully represented unionists, strikers, picketers and disabled workers, and his exposure to injustices sanctioned by the law piqued a social conscience that was beginning to mature. People in the trade union movement began to tell him, "You should be in the CCF." The CCFers remembered him from his student days and courted him.

Berger's father had told Tom how Angus MacInnis of the CCF had been the only elected member of parliament in Canada to speak out in an attempt to prevent the wartime persecution and internment of Japanese Canadians. "And I *had* always admired J. S. Woodsworth, M. J. Coldwell, Tommy Douglas, David Lewis and Stanley Knowles," says Berger. "They were people who, in the crunch, always said what needed to be said, and were prepared to take the heat. In the end, the Liberals, despite favouring the true, the good and the beautiful, always seemed to be running for cover, and it would be Woodsworth, Angus MacInnis or one of those people who would be standing in the breach. These CCFers had always been the stoutest defenders of minority rights. So, I decided that while the Liberals were all good people, my true home was in the CCF." But then he waves the certitude away. "Look, I don't think anyone reasons these things out that precisely. Looking back on it, it's too easy to sound self-righteous. I *think* that's how I must have felt at the time."

Beverley Berger has learned this about her husband: "Tom is predictable. Once he sees a problem, and that's usually some kind of injustice, he studies it until he has a solution."

"There are two ways to sink a battleship," Berger says, expounding on his philosophy. "Fill it with concrete, or drill a hole in it. I prefer to drill that hole."

It is a slow business sinking a ship by drilling small holes in it, but eventually, it *will* go down. Berger, who worked for aboriginal rights for a decade before they were recognized, has used this tactic many times. But for most people entangled in the justice system, the problems are more immediate, and the law is the law, even if it causes injustice. In realizing this, Berger was ready for bolder, wider action. The small increments gained through legal casework no longer satisfied him. The best way to drill a hole in entrenched injustice, he decided, would be to hold political power.

He joined the CCF in 1960. "Not to be a foot soldier. By nature I don't particularly enjoy group activities. I wanted to be elected. I thought provincial issues were most pressing and agreed to run for the 12 September election in Vancouver Centre." Vancouver Centre was a two-seat riding, and Berger's running mate was Bill Dennison, a World War II veteran and construction worker. The Communist, Liberal, Progressive Conservative and Social Credit parties also fielded two candidates each.

"W. A. C. Bennett was very much in power and I thought there were abuses," Berger says. People like to categorize that era between 1955 and 1963 or so as placid, but I don't remember it that way. I thought they were exciting times."

In his campaign, Berger advocated compulsory car insurance to compensate victims regardless of any findings of fault, a system that "would eliminate a great deal of the costly litigation in the courts, the hallmark of the present system of private insurance." He decried the Social Credit election advertising, which he said was paid for by big business. Big business, he warned, would control the province if Bennett's Socreds were returned to power. He admonished Attorney General Robert Bonner for sitting on an RCMP report for two years before prosecuting Lands Minister Robert Sommers on bribery and conspiracy charges, and he berated Premier Bennett for "giving Swedish industrialist Axel Wenner-Gren 40,000 square miles of B.C.'s wealth in return for dubious promises of development." This was in reference to a grandiose scheme to build a monorail from the foot of the Rocky Mountain Trench to the Alaska boundary. Wenner-Gren and the plans were both phonies, Berger pronounced. He was twenty-seven years old.

Electioneering in those days was rowdy and freewheeling, depending more on personal initiative than it did on party organization. Candidates, especially for the money-short CCF, got their audiences where they found them. Berger was helped in this by Percy Hubbard, who had been an active socialist in Britain. "He was a big man, a former English bobby. He'd brought his socialist zeal to Canada and would say, 'C'mon, Tom, let's go and beat up a crowd.' "

The two hit Berger's riding whenever he could slip away from Shulman, Tupper & Southin. Percy had a booming voice, and once he had attracted the attention of passers-by, Berger would step in to explain how the CCF would take over B.C. Electric or improve education. One day he mounted the steps of the courthouse to enlighten the noon-hour crowd, and a court clerk appeared to advise him that the edifice of the law could not be besmirched by politics.

"The weather was wonderful that year," Berger recalls, drifting back to the days of his youthful, exuberant idealism. "We campaigned outdoors. I remember speaking in all the parks and in Victory Square. One day Percy beat up a crowd at Pioneer Square across from the Carrall Street Station and I launched into my spiel. Well. A drunken logger took exception to my words and climbed the fence to straighten me out. I was glad I had Percy. He wrestled him to the ground with a full nelson. That impressed the audience," Berger says with a burst of laughter. "Then Percy announced, 'We in the CCF are opposed to violence.' "

What impressed one *Vancouver Sun* reporter was that Berger, upon seeing a crowd around Pioneer Square, "had easily vaulted the 4½-foot fence and addressed the constituents from the centre of the tiny park. Candidates over 30 don't jump fences—they mostly sit on them."

Percy Hubbard still remembers that day and especially remembers Tom's boots. "He wore big honest brown boots. They were firmly planted high on the fence while he spoke. You can trust a man with boots like that. I thought he was going to be prime minister of Canada. I still think so."

Mrs. Hubbard also recalls their work with Tom Berger with pride and affection. "I like to think of the times Percy and I, and Tom and Bev, hiked around Stanley Park, with Tom telling anyone who would listen how things could be changed for the better in B.C. He believed it could happen. That's what kept us all going. Bev was so good—such a trouper. She had one of the children with her and she was so friendly and outgoing. I think she enjoyed it more than he did. She always gave her best to support Tom."

There is no doubt it was a frugal campaign. After a day of beating up a crowd, the group went back to the Hubbards' for a dinner of sardine sandwiches.

The newspapers predicted that the CCF's chances were hopeless, and the Vancouver *Daily Province* bolstered the veracity of the prediction by warning voters of the "flight of capital" that would ensue should the socialists be elected. In response Berger wrote an appropriately irate Letter to the Editor, in which he said it was "ridiculous to stampede the voters into voting Social Credit by raising bogus issues and ephemeral fears."

The Socreds easily maintained their grip on the province, however, and Berger discovered that politics was not the surest way to accomplish change. Undaunted, he resolved to do better the next time.

The CCF, recognizing that to compete with the other parties they had to establish a much larger financial and membership base, entered into a formalized union with organized labour and was reborn as the New Democratic Party (NDP). The new party's members were imbued with excitement and purpose, and Dave Barrett, whose political career would develop in tandem with Berger's, announced at the first Vancouver convention of the new party: "There is no place in the NDP for those with faint hearts and weak knees."

Berger was recognized as one of the party's new, stout-hearted men when he was elected their provincial president; and, though he had reached the advanced age of twenty-eight, he was proclaimed honorary president of the NDP Youth. The newspapers said he was accorded these positions because he was a "straight middle-of-the-roader . . . the one man good-natured enough to bring both the trade unionists and the oldline CCFers together."

Art Laing, perhaps one of the first prominent B.C. Liberals to regret that they had let Berger slip from their midst, sent him a singularly nonpartisan letter of congratulation:

Dear Tom

I am full of regret that the progressive elements in our Canadian political spectrum appear destined to overlap or be in open conflict.

This is not going to prevent me from congratulating you upon

your election to the Presidency last week. This is a very great
honour and came to you out of the implicit trust the New Party
members have in you.

I have always thought the CCF made a real contribution to
Canadian public life and am certain the New Party will keep its
standards high. My best wishes to you!

Bev Berger was pleased that her husband had taken a position in
the party executive, because she thought it meant he would not
run for election to parliament. But by the following spring a
federal election had been called, and Berger had strong feelings
about Canada's place in the world, particularly with respect to
nuclear weapons. There was a movement afoot to allow U.S.
weapons into the country, and Berger thought it essential that
Canada play a non-nuclear role.

Bev, realizing how strongly he believed in the issue, consented
to his running for parliament; and despite outspoken advice from
friends who told him he would be harming his promising legal
career by being a "lowly Ottawa backbencher," he tackled
another campaign. He ran in Vancouver-Burrard, where he was
pitted against a former law school classmate, Liberal Ron Basford.
Berger eked out a 556-vote victory over Basford. But for Berger
and nine other NDP candidates elected from British Columbia, the
pleasure was marred by the defeat of the party's national leader,
Tommy Douglas.

The 1962 federal election sent to Ottawa new faces that would
remain on the scene for many years, and *Time* magazine called it
"The Able 25th Parliament," noting the presence of young,
talented Liberals Walter Gordon, Edgar Benson, Donald
MacDonald, Jack Davis and John Turner. The NDPers to watch,
said the magazine, were Stanley Knowles, Andrew Brewin,
David Lewis and 29-year-old Tom Berger, who "is expected to
make a good impression in the House as a dependable, logical,
fluent speaker."

He did just that. In his maiden address, he urged government
action with respect to the growing number of unemployed, and
true to his reputation as a "young man in a hurry," he introduced
private member's bills at breakneck speed. None of them passed
into legislation, but they were publicized and raised the social
issues that were on his mind. There was the Civil Servants' Bill of
Rights Act, to allow government employees to engage in political

activity and to freely associate; the Control of Consumer Credit Act, to limit high interest rates and finance charges; the Hours of Work Act, to hold down the work week to forty hours; the Senior Citizens Act, to give them free public transit, and an act to amend the Criminal Code, to give trade unions the right to picket peacefully. The proposal that received the most publicity was the one to establish a Canadian Youth Service; Berger put this forward in his maiden speech, the full text of which was run by the Toronto *Globe and Mail*. Berger likes to think his proposal influenced Pearson's Liberals to respond with their Company of Young Canadians but concedes, "Perhaps this is claiming too much."

Whatever the measure of his success, Berger was trying to make his mark and thriving on it. His secretary was not. "She was used to typing two or three letters a day. After a week with me, she told me she was going to take a job at the Senate." Fortunately, Beverley Berger had befriended Essa Warrener Horswill, who lived in the same apartment block and was looking for a job. Tom and Essa recognized competence in each other and decided to give it a try. "I knew very little about Canadian government, having been educated in England, but it was exciting," Essa recalls. "There was a sense of purpose and Tom was so dedicated and idealistic that I was caught up in his enthusiasm."

It was all cut short when an election was called for the spring of 1963. What was a major upheaval for Tom, Bev, and toddlers Erin and David, was an event that entirely altered Essa's life. She went to Vancouver with the Bergers and was astonished by the spirit of camaraderie that made her feel welcome and among friends right from the start. She also fell in love with the sea, the mountains and Vancouver, and decided that she had found her Canadian home.

The big issue in the 1963 campaign was one on which Tom Berger had previously expressed his opposition: the presence of nuclear arms in Canada. Pearson advocated accepting U.S. nuclear weapons in Canada. Conservative Prime Minister John Diefenbaker waffled. Tommy Douglas, in spite of knowing that it would cost the NDP votes, insisted on strong party opposition, and his party's members fell in behind him with a resounding no to nuclear weapons.

One local issue caused Berger and the NDP some embarrassment. The Communist Party, which was not running a candidate, urged CP support for Tom Berger in Vancouver-Burrard, but he told communist supporters that "the NDP have rejected the Communist Party in the past and we don't want it today. We believe it is not working in the best interests of the people of Canada." He placed some of the blame at the feet of Lester Pearson, for having accused the NDP of following the Kremlin line, a notion that Berger dismissed as "McCarthyism in a bow tie . . . Canada should not be dictated to by Moscow or any other capital."

The political parties were by that time streamlining the haphazard approach to election campaigns and were getting massive turnouts to hear the leaders. In April, when more than 10,000 people came to a forum in Vancouver to listen to Tommy Douglas, Berger optimistically told the crowd that Pearson and Diefenbaker were "empty drums whose sound will not be heard much longer."

But on election day, 10 April 1963, Liberal Ron Basford polled 11,685 votes to Berger's 9,887. News photos portray a stricken young man, stunned by defeat. He decided that he was finished with federal politics. "We were literally broke."

Money was not the only consideration. Berger missed the practice of law, and the entire family missed British Columbia. Although it was open to him to rejoin Shulman, Tupper & Southin or to approach other law firms, he had matured and become an independent spirit who rejected the idea of accounting for his time in terms of "billable hours and minutes." A man who loved to research and study the law, he was back to his original dream; despite the financial uncertainty, Bev supported him in his decision to open his own office.

Berger asked Essa to assist him with the new venture. "I knew even less about law than I had about government or politics," she laughs. "I suppose that's why I said yes."

They took space across from the courthouse in the dingy old Inns of Court on Howe Street and set up shop. "It was not so much a suite of offices as two cubicles partitioned off," Essa recalls. "We didn't know how to do anything practical. At Shulman, Tupper & Southin there had been solicitors, conveyancing secretaries and other useful people who did things Tom had no interest in. He would ask me to do a statement of claim or to file a document and it would take forever. That's how I got to know the people in this city and how I learned to do this job—by phoning around, asking for help and picking brains. Tom wanted to do civil liberties work, but of course that didn't pay the rent, so when a union member or some other luckless client came in for real estate or family law work, we had to try to do some of it."

Mercifully, those days were brief. Berger's reputation, built on his courtroom excellence, his civil libertarian stance and his political exposure brought in the kind of work he cared about. He still had no high-paying clients, but office overhead was very low and the Berger family did not live a flashy life. His law school friend, John Bruk, remembers that during this time, while Tom was trying to rebuild his law practice, he was also preoccupied with his political future. Despite being wounded by his federal defeat, he still wanted to help bring about change and still thought politics was the way.

Berger's return to practice was increasingly reminding him that inequities were rampant in British Columbia. In his view social services were being neglected while the exploitation of primary resources was stunting the growth of secondary industries. He supported the provincial NDP position that the government should intervene in the private sector by expropriating chronic care hospitals and placing them under the hospital insurance service. This and other solutions to social ills would not become reality, he thought, unless he and other New Democrats were elected. When a provincial election was called for 30 September 1963, less than six months after the federal campaign, he accepted the nomination in Vancouver-Burrard, a two-seat constituency.

Tom and his running mate Patrick "Paddy" Neale were narrowly defeated by Socreds Eric Martin and Bert Price, and Berger confessed that he was tired of the fight. "A man can only take so much," he declared, happy that there would not be another election for a few years.

Meanwhile Berger received a call from law professor Leon Getz of the University of British Columbia. Getz had a student, Don Rosenbloom, nearly ready to article, and he thought Berger should talk to him. Rosenbloom was an easterner who had paid his way through a Canadian Studies degree at Carleton University by working as a newspaper reporter. He had intended to get his law degree and return to Ontario for a career with the CBC but decided to get his "ticket"—his call to the bar—first. He asked Getz, "Look, if you were in my boots, who would you be applying to for articles?"

"He gave me three names and Berger's was at the top. Of

course I'd heard about Tom because during law school we studied his cases. All of his reported work was new and important. In fact, in every area of law that had a political complexion to it, there was Tom Berger's name."

The problem was that Berger was a loner and did not want a student, the more so as he was grappling with the question of running for the leadership of the NDP. "He was a much more formal man than he is now," Rosenbloom says. "The interview was strained and stilted, but what he spoke about, and this is what matters, was 'pioneering in the law.' He always used that term. 'There's so much pioneering to do,' he'd say."

For months Rosenbloom waited for a decision, checking in regularly with Tom, until one day Berger pulled out a stack of Appeal Books and said, "I'm taking this case to the Supreme Court of Canada. Take these home tonight. Come back tomorrow and tell me how you would argue the case."

Rosenbloom was traumatized. "I had visitors from Ontario, just for the night, and we had planned to party. I didn't tell Tom. And I have no idea what I told him the next day."

Don Rosenbloom was hired.

By then, Berger was involved in a case that thrust him into the headlines, *Jones* v. *Bennett,* a highly publicized tragicomedy that spanned more than four years of court hearings.

G. E. P. "call me Jeep" Jones was a burly, bellicose, cigar-smoking man. Bennett was W. A. C. Bennett, the premier of British Columbia.

The drama had begun on the morning of 2 October 1964, when two members of the Royal Canadian Mounted Police entered the British Columbia Purchasing Commission building in Victoria where Jeep Jones presided as chairman and placed him under arrest on charges of accepting a benefit in his capacity as a public official.

At the trial in County Court, Jones's counsel, Hugh McGivern, Q.C., called for dismissal, saying: "For the first time in Canada we have a trial founded on hope. The Crown has adduced no evidence to prove Jones was guilty and all the evidence produced by the Crown was *for* the defence." This was not hyperbole, for it was a peculiar case. One Crown witness testified that he had offered Jones no benefit and that Jones had requested no benefit. Equally peculiar were Crown endeavours to have three of its own witnesses declared hostile. Judge Montague L. Tyrwhitt-Drake acquitted Jones.

Exonerated, Jones returned to his office expecting to be

reinstated. He was not, and in February the Crown appealed against his acquittal, while Jones filed a writ claiming five months' salary. Yet another element was added to the brouhaha when Premier Bennett, in the midst of a speech to the Victoria Social Credit Association, said: "I am not going to talk about the Jones boy. I could say a lot, but let me assure you of this; the position taken by the government is the right position." These words were widely reported and, according to Jones, they damaged his reputation and exposed him to "public contempt, odium and ridicule."

Also in February, Provincial Secretary Wesley Black introduced "An Act to Provide for the Retirement of George Ernest Pascoe Jones." Black told the House that Jones's retirement was necessary because the government no longer had confidence in him. When the bill came up for debate, bedlam erupted, culminating in the entire NDP opposition stalking out of the House, but the bill passed, and Jones was fired.

Jones announced that his new lawyer, Donald A. Thompson, would serve the premier with a Writ for Slander. But no member of the legislature can be served a writ within twenty days of a session, so the premier's lawyer, George L. Murray, accepted the writ. Lawyer Thompson withdrew from the case as suddenly as he had entered.

A once-powerful administrator, Jones was now broke and demoralized, a "little guy" in need of a champion, a counsel who was willing to fight the Socred establishment and who did not fear losing government business. He turned to Tom Berger.

Berger was deeply engrossed in legal work for native Indians as well as a number of political and professional activities, but he agreed to help Jones. Jones's situation was oddly parallel to that faced long ago by Tom's father, Ted Berger: invidious forces within government had deprived both men of employment for reasons that were not articulated and could not therefore be challenged.

"Jones's cause was certainly worthwhile, but I marvel that I found time to represent him," Berger says, without admitting that he was vicariously vindicating his father.

Berger caused shock waves when he subpoenaed the premier to attend Examination for Discovery, a private session under oath that enables lawyers to explore the evidence by questioning the witnesses for the other side. At the trial, discovery transcripts may be read into the record or used to challenge the parties' veracity.

At 10:30 on the morning of 26 November 1965, W. A. C. Bennett's black, chauffeur-driven limousine glided up to the entrance of the Victoria Law Courts. Over the next three hours and 209 questions, Berger probed the imperturbable premier, but it was a futile assault on an adamant foe. Premier Bennett admitted to no knowledge. If Jones had been charged and acquitted of criminal wrongdoing, if the attorney general had appealed, if Jones had been dismissed or refused to surrender his position, if he had faults, if there had been debates either in or out of the legislature, if the bills had been passed, if he himself had spoken the troublesome words, noticed reporters, or if the media had reported any of it, he could not be sure. Everything or nothing may or may not have happened.

"Well, do you read the papers, Mr. Bennett?" Berger asked.

"Not very often, because I am too busy," replied the premier serenely. "I make the news, I don't read the news."

The trial began on 20 December before Mr. Justice McInnes and an all-male jury of eight. Berger presented Jones's case with direct simplicity. Speaking from a few notes scrawled on an envelope, he related the tangled events of the past year leading up to the bill retiring Jones and the slander suit:

> Now, Mr. Bennett, according to the evidence, said, "I'm not going to say anything about the Jones boy but I could say a lot." Now he has had a chance to say a lot. . . . If somebody sues you for slander you can say, "Well, it's the truth. The man is unfit for office." But Mr. Bennett didn't do that. He has not pleaded that what he said was true.
>
> There is only one other thing I am going to say to you before I call the evidence for the plaintiff, and that is this: Mr. Jones happens to be suing a man who is Premier of the Province, and we are not here to decide, and you are not here to decide — you are the judges of the facts in this case — whether Mr. Bennett's Government is a good Government or a bad Government. That's what we have elections for. All that you are here to decide is whether Mr. Bennett slandered Mr. Jones.

Judge McInnes ruled that the premier's comments contained no slander of Jones, either in the natural ordinary meaning of the words or through innuendo. He dismissed the case, without allowing the jury to bring in a verdict.

Berger successfully appealed the judgment, and a new slander trial went on before Mr. Justice Ruttan sitting as judge and jury in January of 1967. In his judgment released on 2 March 1967, he concluded that Bennett's words were slanderous and calculated to disparage the plaintiff in his office as chairman of the Purchasing Commission. He awarded Jones $15,000 damages, at that time the largest non-jury award in a defamation case in British Columbia.

Berger was not surprised when this decision was taken to appeal, but he was dismayed by the unanimous ruling of the Court of Appeal that while the words were defamatory, they were spoken on an occasion of qualified privilege, and as they were not actuated by malice, were not slanderous. Jones was confused and "visibly shaken" by this pronouncement. Worse, being controversial was not making him employable.

Berger geared up for one last fight on Jones's behalf, as he felt the principle at stake was important enough to be brought before the Supreme Court of Canada. Bennett retained a new lawyer; he knew he needed the best, and he secured the dean of Canadian lawyers, John J. Robinette. Robinette's factum relied on qualified privilege. Berger's arguments for Jones were as before: that the premier had been "neither fair nor frank, and that is evidence of malice."

Robinette's arguments on qualified privilege did not hold up. The Supreme Court held that since Premier Bennett had uttered the words complained of at a public meeting, in the presence of newspaper reporters, the privilege was lost.

"In fairness to Robinette, remember that my factum contained the discovery transcripts. While I was presenting my case," Berger chuckles, "I could see that the judges were reading ahead to the lines where Premier Bennett said, 'I don't read the news, I make the news.' One judge would show the next, and when I saw them smiling, I knew they would decide for us. Bennett had done the work for me."

The Supreme Court of Canada unanimously reinstated Justice Ruttan's award and the $15,000 damages. For Berger the decision was a significant victory; proof that he ranked with the best and that good law, ably argued and tenaciously pursued, could ensure justice regardless of the unequal stature of the adversaries.

Berger's pioneering in the law had not been enough for Jeep Jones, however. "My name is anathema," Jones said. "I've been vindicated of wrongdoing, but the egg was thrown against the wall and the stain remains."

"He came to Vancouver a few years later to take me to lunch," Tom Berger recalls with a sigh. "Though obviously dying of cancer, he was trying mightily to be his usual irrepressible self."

The cloud continued to hover over Jones. He was able to pay only an occasional $25 on his account, and was, at the time of his death, unemployed.

When the time for another provincial election came in September of 1966, Berger's legal work had him deeply engaged in the struggle for aboriginal rights and in extricating people from harsh habitual criminal prosecutions—both of which he thought reflected the prevailing mentality of the government in Victoria and were good reasons to rally. He announced he was ready to give it another try in Vancouver-Burrard. Berger and his running mate Ray Parkinson faced Bert Price, a powerful Socred, and Tom Alsbury, a former mayor of Vancouver. This time around the issues were both bigger and smaller: the Bennett government's "Two River Policy" for dams on the Columbia and Peace—Berger called the dams "latter-day pyramids"—and the means test for the provincial old-age supplement of $30 a month.

The Socreds were returned to power, but Berger and Parkinson won their contests handily, and so did Dave Barrett. As members of the opposition in the twenty-seventh Legislative Assembly, they followed their leader Robert Strachan to Victoria. Strachan, a Vancouver Island carpenter, had proven unable over the course of ten years and four elections to significantly change the NDP's fortunes. During that session Berger became convinced that Strachan was virtually ineffectual in eroding the Socred power base, and he quickly assumed a more active role himself.

Strachan did have a tough job, however, for Premier Bennett ruled supreme over a notoriously unparliamentary legislature. Events in the House were reported by a small press gallery, there was no *Hansard* for clarification of the record, no question period, and the debates were a far cry from the occasional civility and intelligence Berger had enjoyed in Ottawa. In Victoria, name-calling was a not-unusual style of discussion, and the sessions frequently lapsed into free-for-alls that continued all night. Premier W. A. C. Bennett liked to pretend he did not know Berger's name and habitually referred to him as "that city-slicker lawyer." Bennett also kept warning Strachan that the city-slicker lawyer was "put there by the labour bosses to kick Strachan out," but he was merely repeating public gossip, not private machinations.

The press had, since the birth of the NDP, speculated that Berger was slated for federal or provincial party leadership.

On 29 October 1966, George MacFarlane wrote in the *Globe Magazine:* "Tom Berger seems well-endowed with those attributes . . . youth, energy, enthusiasm, education, responsibility, courage, personality and the fragile intangible voter appeal that swings elections . . . he offers socialism in a more attractive package, ribboned with respectability and reason and right. He also carries with him the sweet smell of success."

Powerful trade unionists did want Tom Berger at the helm of the NDP. They were led by Berger's close friend, E. P. "Pat" O'Neal, secretary of the B.C. Federation of Labour. Another close friend, political scientist Walter Young, led a group of NDP intelligentsia in prodding him to seek the leadership.

When the Berger and the Bruk families went to Crystal Mountain for a weekend of skiing, Bruk advised Berger not to try for the leadership then. "When the time is right it will be handed to you on a platter." But at a 14 April 1967 meeting of the NDP party executive, Berger announced he would seek the leadership.

Berger harboured no grudge against the leader, but he thought that he could do a better job and that the issues were too pressing to wait until Strachan stepped down. Yvonne Cocke, considered one of the most powerful women in the NDP, says, "I don't think he would have done it on his own. Tom has a lot of self-confidence, but he does not have a big ego." Insiders say that Berger was used, for pragmatic reasons. They say that the party needed to sell itself to the public and that Berger was the best they had to offer. Be that as it may, Berger accepts responsibility for what happened. "I was ambitious," he says. "And I was impatient."

The New Democratic Party was divided on both the question of the leadership and the timing of the assault on Strachan, and traces of that rift remain today. Strachan retained the leadership by a vote of 278 to 177 on 3 June 1967. The majority of the delegates had decided that Berger was a young man in too much of a hurry. Berger expected the outcome but thought that if he had had another month to campaign, the tally would have been different. He openly admitted that he would be trying again, and he did not expect to wait long. The party was sharply divided, despite Strachan's assurances that unity would prevail. Walter Young said of Strachan's win, "That was no victory. That was a stay of execution."

Dave Barrett had all along supported Strachan, not because he was the best leader imaginable, he said, but because Strachan was doing the job and deserved the support of his troops and the dignity of leaving on his own terms. Barrett's loyalty won him the support of some of the more powerful MLAS, who urged him to accept nomination for the post.

By the time Strachan officially yielded the leadership in the spring of 1969, there were four contenders for the post: Tom Berger, Dave Barrett, Bob Williams and John Conway. For a fight like this, Berger needed help, and he got it in Yvonne and Dennis Cocke, and Yvonne's sister Marge Cragg.

Bev Berger worked for her husband again, and this time they toiled harder than ever before. Tom's legal practice was also at a critical stage, and he spent the week prior to the April 1969 NDP convention arguing for the Nishga Indians, the most important legal case of his career, in the Court of Appeal.

The NDP continued to be deeply divided. To some insiders, Berger was too ambitious, too much the newcomer who had raced to the fore without regard for established niceties. To outsiders, he was that "city-slicker lawyer, not a working person." His critics said that the Bennett-imposed label typified Berger's lack of political savvy, that he should have wittily dismissed it as the nonsense it was, instead of trying to argue it down with reason.

Barrett, on the other hand, knew how to move within the party structure, honoured its traditions and had bided his time. He had spent his first few years as an MLA writing policy papers in Victoria. When he realized a politician had to appeal to the public, he changed his political persona and became Jolly Dave, relieving tension, getting press coverage and making friends by poking fun at himself and, sometimes, at the issues. "I admire Tom Berger," he insists, "for the brilliant, dedicated man he is. But he's too serious. I don't think he's ever had a belly-laugh at his own expense."

Berger was very earnest in those days, and so were his supporters. When the last edition of the *Berger Booster* was packaged and bundled, Anita Hagen noticed that on the front page their man Tom was lauded for his devotion, not to public affairs, but to pubic affairs. His horrified workers did not laugh. "We destroyed every copy," admits Yvonne Cocke ruefully. "Now, I'd love to have one. But then, we were paranoid about Tom's opponents seeing it."

This competitiveness was not imagined. In the Cockes' New Westminster riding, they did not win a single Berger delegate to the convention. Tom was philosophical about this. Politics, he had come to realize, was a nasty business.

The 1969 NDP convention was notable for being one of the first instances of "big-scale on-the-spot news coverage" with CTV and CBC crews interviewing and filming in black and white. It was one A.M. Sunday before the final ballots were tallied. Although there were nearly 1,000 delegates, Berger took it over Barrett by a mere thirty-six votes. Barrett leapt to the platform to hail the new leader and said, "This is the greatest night in the history of the socialist movement in B.C." He was followed by Berger, who shouted: "The years of neglect must end. We must rid our province of the injustices and inequality that disfigure the face of society today."

The crowd went wild, and Bev Berger, who was for the first time sharing the stage with Tom, found it was an exhilarating moment after the weeks of slogging. Beginning the next day, they were deluged with requests for interviews and photo sessions. The press, in anticipation of Tom becoming a major political force in the province, stretched Berger family trivia into news stories. Their habits, household, pets, children and routines were duly noted. Tom, they said was pudgy or tall and lean. He ran for a half-mile as fast as he could alone every morning, or he jogged with Bev wearing old shorts and a rumpled T-shirt. He read *Playboy* or Shakespeare. He was variously reported as being a teetotaller, quaffing scotch, sipping dry vermouth, drinking gin and tonic, and as being a nonsmoker or chain-smoking cigarellos. He was quiet, friendly and almost shy in private conversations, while in the House he was tenacious, cold, with more than a touch of ruthlessness. It was all in the minds of the reporters. He had, in short, become public property.

What drove Tom Berger? He had endured five election campaigns, two leadership bids, and had a thriving law practice that fought contentious labour issues as well as championed habitual criminals, impoverished Indians and opponents of pollution. He had directly challenged the government on environmental issues both publicly and in the courts, and he had confronted the premier and subpoenaed him over the government's firing of its purchasing agent. He was thirty-six years old, and his typical answer to the question of his motivational drive was this: "Observers say Berger is in too much of a hurry. I've been in a hurry all of my life. I think that you have to speak up and speak out and if that thrusts you into a position of leadership, then you've got to offer leadership."

If Berger was a young man in a hurry, the more thoughtful journalists saw that in Bev he had an equal and ideal helpmate. She was an energetic campaigner; she skied, swam, played tennis and, because she did not want her husband to get too far ahead of her, had returned to university. She was earning an advanced degree in education, was pursuing her interest in and talent for art, and had completed a paper on the history of the CCF for her Canadian history course. She often served the role of both parents to ten-year-old Erin and eight-year-old David when Tom's schedule kept him away from home.

With an election imminent, Premier Bennett resorted to aggressive and expensive action. Armed with a $500,000 propaganda-style file titled *The Good Life* (which Berger dubbed *Cecil in Wonderland*), W. A. C. Bennett embarked on a 10,000-mile grandstanding tour of the province.

The public and the press were excited by the prospect of a new government under an idealistic new leader, and the NDP was touted as strong enough, and Berger moderate enough, to win. But they were not as strong or as well organized as the Socreds, and clear-cut issues proved to be elusive. At first there were minor skirmishes: the need for an auditor general, dam deficits, modernized drinking legislation, expropriation laws and sewage treatment plants. Berger got good press on a plank that could be slipped neatly into a contemporary election platform when he urged that no more raw logs be exported from the province until every B.C. mill was running at full capacity. He had working with him his articling student, Don Rosenbloom, who had interrupted his articles to assist with the campaign and to develop policy issues.

When Berger announced that the NDP would take over the B.C. Telephone Company, Bennett decreed that Berger was a proponent of Marxian socialism. "Our program so far as nationalization is concerned begins with the telephone company and ends with the telephone company," Berger assured repeatedly, but he could not say it loud enough to muffle the echoes of the old Bennett scare tactics that socialism was a bridge to communism. The Socred posters and advertisements said it neatly: "Don't take the turn to the left," and kept the issue alive.

On 27 August 1969 Berger was soundly defeated; he lost even in his own riding to Harold Merrilees. Although the NDP retained 34 per cent of the popular vote, they lost seats due to the way the vote was distributed. Many people blamed the issue of telephone company takeover for the loss, but Berger, when questioned, stated firmly: "We didn't get enough votes." He was devastated by the loss, his dreams of accomplishment shattered. Dennis Cocke offered him his newly won seat, but Berger declined. "Your career in politics is just beginning," he said. "I am just one man and I am not indispensable."

The fact was, he still had his ideals and he was still a young man in a hurry. Politics had proven to be too slow, and he could not spare the time waiting for things to change. On 22 September 1969, Tom Berger called a press conference to announce he was resigning from the position he had fought for so vigorously and dubbed Dave Barrett the "de facto leader of the party."

Disciples, believers and others who had hoped for a new era in British Columbia politics were downhearted. And Allan Fotheringham, who was then building a reputation as a tough, cynical reporter, was noticed standing quietly at the back of the room, shedding a tear or two. He was not alone.

CHAPTER 6

The Judge

In 1971 the sun was shining on Tom Berger's professional life. He was free of political ambition and responsibility, his work for the Nishgas had attracted national attention, he was practising what his friend Liberal lawyer Nancy Morrison calls "people law," a line of work much different from "money law," and he was thriving on it. His associate in that circle of people lawyers, Don Rosenbloom, asserts that Berger's career progressed as it did because he always made time to read law reports and to think about new directions in jurisprudence. Consequently, he rarely saw clients as ordinary clients with routine difficulties to be sorted out. "He had that rare quality of being able to recognize people whose problems could be used to test the law and move it forward," Rosenbloom recalls. Berger's fresh perspective and alertness to infringed rights or ambiguous laws ensured that his work was rich with flavour and potential.

As often as not, the habitual criminal, prostitute, discharged worker or special interest group had little money to pay for Berger's services, but his exemplary work on their behalf enhanced his reputation and attracted paying clients to the firm. His forte was in presenting the law concisely, stripped of all peripheral issues and hyperbole. He respected his clients and represented them with dignity and care, and like his father who had also treated every job as worth doing well, his manner was always gentlemanly.

"If there's anything he taught me," Rosenbloom says, "it was this: keep to the high road. Don't get excited."

In addition Berger had a rare attitude towards the law, harbouring a love for its promises, intricacies and truths. "A love of the law," says Rosenbloom, "and I know that expression is overused. But he has. A commitment to law that goes beyond anyone's expectations." Rosenbloom spreads his arms, trying to encompass Berger's passion. "He used to love reading decisions. He had a subscription to the *All England Reports,* and he read them. He took them home to read. He was the kind of man who probably read them in the bathroom. How many lawyers in this country are reading the *All E.R.*'s on a regular basis? They might subscribe for their law libraries or use them for research, but Tom," and here he pauses for emphasis, "Tom loved reading, working, living law.

"We used to have office hours on Saturday. He'd see clients then, and he expected me to. And he went out to prisons on weekends to see clients. He was a man so devoted that everything else but law seemed secondary. Now for that commitment, there must have been some great sacrifices," he concedes, "But he made them because he loved the law. To this day, I have never met anyone with his determination to fulfill a lawyer's mandate and to commit himself to the law. It was almost an obsession, it was so strong. I loved to watch him."

Berger also conveyed this approach to the profession of law to John Baigent, a student who was articling with a nearby firm and who chose to use his off hours helping Tom in order that he might learn "law for the underdog" from the best in the field. By 1971, Berger & Co. also had on staff Harry Boyle, a former journalist with a wry wit who was destined to become a judge frequently commended for his fine judicial skills and ethics. And there was Essa Horswill, who made the transition from politics to running a law office with her own style of energetic capability. "I loved it," she says. "Sometimes the volume of work Tom turned out was so punishing that I'd break down and cry. I was young and foolish and refused to ask for more help. I thought, if he can work that hard, then damn it, so can I."

Berger's pattern was to breeze in early and to go through the mail, immediately dictating pleadings, file notes and correspondence; even if Essa left a clear desk at night she returned to one stacked with work. During the course of a day, paralegals and lawyers around the city called on her for help because if she did not know how to do something, she could always find out.

"Essa has class," says Rosenbloom. "She knows how to approach the gruffest senior partner, court official, politician or bureaucrat to glean information. She was the major special ingredient that made Tom's unique practice possible."

When Essa was on holidays, or when she finally asked for help, Allison Burnett came in to lend a hand. She held a double degree in commerce and law from the University of British Columbia, and she had articled at Shulman, Tupper & Southin the year after Tom and the year before his good friend John Laxton. Mrs. Perle Berger worked as the firm's bookkeeper.

"The office was informal, but not slack or disorganized," Rosenbloom reminisces. "I loved hearing Tom call, 'Mom?' every once in a while. It was comfortable and homey." Life at 198 West Hastings was, in a word, copesetic.

Allan McEachern, now chief justice of the Supreme Court of British Columbia and then a colleague and a Liberal activist practising law uptown at the prestigious firm of Russell and DuMoulin, concedes that, because of the nature of law and politics in the province, he too, was cognizant in those days that Berger was special. McEachern, smiling in remembrance of a secret, admits that he had "something to do with Tom's appointment to the bench," but he will not divulge the story. "Tom should be the one to tell," he says.

Preoccupied with preparations for the *Calder* (Nishga) appeal late in 1971, Berger was surprised to receive a call from Michael Hunter, John Turner's executive assistant. Turner, who in 1984 would serve a brief term as prime minister, was then minister of justice. Through Hunter, Turner asked Berger if he would accept an appointment to the Supreme Court of British Columbia—if it were offered. The call was unexpected. "Of course I was very flattered. I was only thirty-eight," Berger says.

The call raised many questions, none of which made a decision simple. Although Berger was practising the kind of law that was satisfying professionally and personally, he had to work gruelling hours. Money was never a major consideration, but he could not afford to be entirely altruistic. His participation in the political arena had been expensive. "We were, quite literally, broke," says Tom.

"Don't forget," Hunter comments, "judges have a good salary and no overhead." Berger was reputed to be earning $75,000 per year at a time when a judge's annual salary was $35,000. But as Berger was later to say in an interview with Eve Rockett of the *Vancouver Sun*, paraphrasing Mark Twain, "The reports of my earnings have been greatly exaggerated."

Berger was also very sensitive to the need to spend more time with Bev and their two children. He felt the need to talk the proposal over with people whose opinion he valued, "but the protocol in this situation, of course, is that you don't do anything until you're formally asked by the justice minister." This meant he had to be most circumspect in discussing the possibility of an appointment with anyone other than Bev. "She wanted me to accept; primarily for family reasons, but she also genuinely felt that the life of a judge would be good for me."

Berger also felt that he owed the New Democratic Party the courtesy of consultation out of respect for what the party had contributed to his career. He and Bev invited Dennis and Yvonne Cocke to the house one evening, and they argued the merits and disadvantages until the wee hours, with Dennis taking the hard-line position that Tom should grab the brass ring as it passed. Yvonne was strongly opposed. "I thought Tom hadn't exhausted his role in politics," she explains. "And he was obviously hesitant."

Berger's reluctance pivoted around the potential of the job. He thought that, for him, politics had proven to be the least effective tool for accomplishing social change. His followers perceived him as a man destined for greatness but were divided on the vehicle he should use to achieve it. As a civil liberties activist and human rights lawyer, he was a man to be heeded. Was he prematurely veering from success at the bar, as many believed he had veered from success in politics, to explore yet another tack? Would his contribution from the bench be more valuable? Ultimately, the advantages seemed to outweigh the disadvantages, and he said yes to Michael Hunter. He immediately had second thoughts.

"Tom Hurley used to say, 'You shouldn't be appointed to the bench unless you've been thrown out of a beer parlour.' I agree."

Once Berger gave his acceptance, nothing appeared to happen.

Rumours abounded and late in November, *Vancouver Sun* columnist Allan Fotheringham published tidbits of gossip: federal Liberals, "suitably nervous, as befits their trade," had approached him with "much bemoaning and bewailing of the fact that the glad news had seeped out." Party loyalists, he suggested, were pressuring Turner to withdraw the offer, despite Turner's vow to make judicial appointments according to merit. Fotheringham also alleged that Liberals wanted patronage to prevail over principles.

Meanwhile, Berger, accompanied by Baigent and Rosenbloom, was on his way to Ottawa to argue *Calder* in the Supreme Court of Canada when he was intercepted en route by a message to call John Turner's office. This alerted his young associates to the truth of the rumour. "We were dismayed," Baigent recollects. "We told him, 'No, don't even consider it. You'll be bored. Lots of people can be judges but there is only one Tom Berger.'" When Tom waved away that high praise, they took another approach. "We told him that our personal injury work and other litigation was reaching the point where it would support his civil libertarian law," says Baigent. "This was true and fair. His high profile attracted to us clients with more lucrative problems."

Berger continued to concentrate on the Nishga case, which he was later to say was "a vast undertaking, a labour of love. I think I put more of myself into that case than any other." His efforts to persuade the high court to render a historic judgment were being reported nightly on the CBC-TV national news.

John Turner telephoned while Berger was in the courtroom arguing the Nishga case, but Berger, whose doubts were still unresolved and who wanted to devote his entire attention to the matter at hand, declined the call. Turner was at that time introducing a new policy in parliament, establishing the Canadian Judicial Council under the Judges Act. The council, which was to consist of all the chief justices and associate chief justices of the superior courts, with the chief justice of Canada as chairman, would be empowered to "supervise judicial conduct." Ironically, the council would later bear heavily on the termination of Berger's career on the bench.

The calls from John Turner came sporadically until, finally, one came from Turner's wife Geills. Tom relented and returned the call: "He said he was going to be talking to the chief justices and that he'd like to tell them he was appointing me."

"Do you accept?" Turner asked.

"I said that I did. It was the hardest choice I've ever made. I questioned the life, the worth of it, the implications. A major decision which affects a person's way of life is harder than any other. All of the other hard choices of my life were of a different sort. They were hard, but I knew exactly where I stood on the issues and would ask myself if I were prepared to accept the consequences. But on this issue I had grave doubts."

Despite Berger's own doubts, his appointment was greeted with expressions of surprise and congratulations. Someone called it the "most political nonpolitical appointment ever," and the Liberals were lauded by friends and enemies alike. Nancy Morrison was the first off the mark with congratulations:

Dear Tom:

Every now and then, the Liberals do a Good Thing, and I decided that perhaps I will stay in the party a while longer. Your recent appointment has just re-affirmed my somewhat flagging faith in my party, and when I heard the news, I was proud to say that I was a Liberal.

Please accept my sincere congratulations. As you must know by now, your appointment has been greeted with unanimous approval, regardless of professional or party affiliations.

Frank Scott wrote summarizing both the dilemma and the decision:

Congratulations to you—and to John Turner as well. Your appointment, besides being a well deserved tribute to your own abilities, will do much to restore faith in a judicial process much under attack these days. I am a little sorry you are not available for more political battles, but the judicial combat is no less decisive and often more lasting. Maybe some day you will have a crack at the true relationship between trade unions and political parties.

By the time Berger returned to Vancouver from Ottawa, it was apparent that Scott had been right about public sentiment. Letters and editorials rejoiced in the "recognition by the government of ability, integrity and experience, regardless of partisan political point of view."

Elena Stelmaszczuk, the wife of a client whom Berger had

unsuccessfully represented before the Workmen's Compensation Board, wrote to congratulate him and to describe how she and her five children had managed to survive in the interval. "Somehow, you fit in with all of this. Because you believed in Mike's case. And gave us Faith and Hope."

Friend and lawyer Cecil Branson of the Victoria Unitarian Congregation wrote that before the announcement, he had prepared a sermon entitled "The Judges of What?" and had dedicated it to Tom because he felt he epitomized the qualities necessary for a legal practitioner and for a judge.

Tom was assured of the importance of his future duties by letters such as the one from retired Judge T. W. "Tommy" Brown, who disclosed that in 1955 he had been told repeatedly at the Commonwealth Bar Convention in London that the B.C. bench was, "as far as labour relations were concerned, the worst in Canada and among the worst in the Commonwealth."

Mr. Justice A. T. Robertson of the B.C. Court of Appeal also encouraged him: "If your judgments are as lucid as the arguments that I've had the pleasure of listening to, you'll do splendidly."

Leon Getz, the law professor who had sent Rosenbloom to article with Berger, admitted to "mixed feelings": on one hand "delight at the tribute to you that is implied in the appointment and at the improvement in judicial credibility," but on the other hand "sadness that a potential home for some of my more sensitive students has been torn down."

Despite the optimistic tone of most of these missives, some contained niggling allusions to the possibility that Berger had been co-opted. What else could one make of the note from the compensation consultant for the provincial government who wrote, perhaps with sly humour or relief: "You will be an ornament on the bench."

The comments from a retired RCMP staff sergeant, who had known Tom's father in Regina, were refreshingly direct. W. R. Morgan said that when he first saw the item about the expected appointment, he thought, "I bet Tom Berger will not accept it because the Federal and Provincial governments are just trying to put him on the Bench to get him out of the way, because he has been so successful as a lawyer in winning cases against them. But then I reasoned, the appointment is such a well warranted one that you would be foolish not to accept. In later years you can always go on to greater things."

Mr. Morgan was not alone in his initial response. A number of people expressed the view that the Liberals wanted to neutralize Berger politically.

With such mixed greetings flowing in daily, Berger attended to his clients' most pressing needs and went through the wrenching business of winding up his practice. As Don Rosenbloom had noted, the old place was home. When *Vancouver Sun* reporter Eve Rockett came to see Berger on his last day as a lawyer, he admitted he would miss the office and miss, as well, the "heart-starting conflict of court." He told her:

> My work as a lawyer meant I was an antagonist of the federal government in the courts, and my political background certainly would not have endeared me to the federal government.
>
> I suppose every lawyer's ambition is to be a judge someday . . . but I didn't think about it because I never thought it was an appointment that would be offered to me.
>
> Of course, every lawyer envisions himself as a judge. Every lawyer who has been in court, if he's any good at all, has thought how much better he could handle the case than the presiding judge. Every time you lose a case you think of something to say about the judge . . . although you usually keep it to yourself if you have any sense. Of course, the judges who decide in your favour are the heavyweights. The ones who decide against you are the light-weights.

With that, Tom Berger walked away from his calling.

At a farewell party at their home, Tom and Bev Berger marked the end of an era with their closest friends and associates. There was a hint of sadness in the air. No longer would they be able to argue law and politics together with unfettered abandon, for judges must leave behind the camaraderie of the bar, of political gatherings, of shared biases.

"For people-lawyers and people-oriented politicians, law and politics are endlessly fascinating," says Nancy Morrison, explaining why in their circle of friends there were "so many journalists and other verbal people. The dynamics of society captivate them and they crave an audience for their opinion." She remembers that there were no "money-lawyers" at the party.

Rosenbloom, the man who had planned a post-law school career with the CBC, took the opportunity to tell Berger, the man who had chosen law over both journalism and politics, that he was ready to return to Toronto. He reminded Tom that he had never meant to practise and only Berger's presence had kept him at it that long.

"No, no," exclaimed Berger. "You have to stay. *Especially* because I'm leaving. There's pioneering yet to be done." And almost wistfully, he repeated his credo, "So much pioneering in the law still to be done."

Rosenbloom stayed. Essa Horswill stayed. And together they took over Tom's practice.

After the party, and much to the astonishment of the others, Tom and Bev took a Mexican holiday. "Very unlike Tom to do this," they all agreed. But he did do it. He rested, read a bag full of books, including one he had not had time for when he was doing the *Jones* v. *Bennett* case: *Their Good Names,* a collection of libel and slander suits involving the famous. He and Bev relaxed, and indulged in their favourite pastimes, long walks and talks. These pursuits, coupled with the therapeutic sunshine, cast an illuminating shaft of light on his life and what he wanted to do with it. By the time they returned to Vancouver, it was perfectly clear that Aristotle had been correct when he said: "It is hard at times to decide what sort of things one should choose and harder still to abide by one's decisions."

Tom Berger decided he did not want to be a judge. "I remember waking at two one morning, very worried about it. I went downtown and walked through the east end, down Cambie Street, turning it over and over in my mind. By eight o'clock I was at the office and no closer to an answer.

"I phoned Arthur Maloney, a wonderful, upstanding man whom I greatly admired. I said, 'Arthur, I can't go through with this.' He said, 'Listen, if you don't like it, you can quit after a year or two.' That seemed a reasonable approach. After all, it wasn't a death sentence. So, I left it at that, but didn't really feel any happier. Came the morning of the day I was to be sworn in [5 February 1972], I didn't feel one bit better. If anything I felt worse."

He went through the motions of getting ready for the ceremony and left the house. Before long, a taxi pulled up, and Bev watched in dismay as Tom emerged from it, ran up the stairs to their bedroom and shut the door without saying a word. He was on the phone. "I tried to call Turner. I couldn't reach him, but I spoke to

Michael Hunter. I said, 'I'm terribly sorry, but I can't go through with this. I've changed my mind.' "

When he told this story, he was abashed by the very ridiculousness of it. He had mentally reviewed all of his reasons for having accepted the judgeship. At thirty-eight, he would be the youngest Canadian to hold a high court seat. An early apogee in a distinguished career, it was an honour that would allow him to shape the law in new and progressive directions. He would have as many years to do that as he had lived to date. It was a numbing prospect, but his father, who had died during the earliest days of Tom's career, would have been so proud of him. And yet the choice had not been entirely his. A man who was ruled by reason and rational thinking, he had consulted others; and once he had a consensus, he had bowed to it. Unaccustomed as he was to trusting his feelings, he stoically ignored the truth of the cold heaviness in his heart until he stood at the edge of the abyss, devastated at the prospect of leaving behind his first love, the practice of law.

The way Michael Hunter remembers it, Tom called that morning "sounding for all the world like a man who'd been up all night worrying. He said, 'I'm too young to die.' I tried to buck him up, but I was even younger than Berger. When he insisted that he couldn't go through with it and hung up, I knew I had to ask a heavyweight intermediary to lean on him."

Berger remembers that twenty minutes after calling Hunter, the phone rang. "It was Allan McEachern. He said, 'Listen, if you don't like it, you can quit after a year or two.' The same words!"

Bev, dressed and ready to attend the ceremony, was poised in trepidation at the bottom of the stairs with Erin and David. Berger expels a heavy sigh as he says, "I thought, well, my mother is already on her way to the courthouse to see me sworn in. So, off I went."

Off he went. And promptly at 9:55 A.M., as directed by the Order of Proceedings, he donned the elaborate black-and-red robes, white collar and tabs of a judge, and took the oath of office before a packed gallery of family, friends and members of the legal profession. One of three men appointed to relieve the backlog of trials, he was sworn in along with Harry McKay, former Liberal MLA for Fernie, who was being elevated from the County Court of Nanaimo, and with Richard P. Anderson, president of the Point

Grey Liberal Association. They were welcomed to the bench by Chief Justice J. O. Wilson, and the ceremony was covered by *Vancouver Province* reporter Jim Fairley. Wilson said he had always liked a bit of writing by Edmund Burke. This quotation from the man whose philosophy formed the basis of the Conservative party did nothing to lift Berger's spirits, although the passage was relatively innocuous: "A judge is not placed in that high situation merely as a passive instrument of the parties. He has a duty of his own independent of them, and that duty is to investigate the truth." The chief justice continued: "To my young brother Berger, I say that I have followed and admired his work for many years and know that he brings not only a good mind, but a good heart to this bench.

"Since he is about half my age," Wilson quipped, "it will not be unreasonable for me to expect him to do twice as much work as I do."

The photograph published on the front page of the papers that day shows the men of the bench laughing. Sitting closest to the camera is Berger, his hands folded decorously. He is smiling, smiling hard. Paddy Sherman of the *Vancouver Province* wrote:

> Justice Minister John Turner deserves a medal for having the courage to make such an appointment. . . . Certainly Tom Berger is a socialist. He is concerned with the excesses he sees around him in society . . . he has always had some healthy ideas on how to improve the climate between labour and management.
>
> Add to this a very bright legal mind, a deeply aware social conscience and you have an appointment that could bring us, years from now, a judge nearer great than good.

In the same picture at the opposite end is Mr. Justice Thomas A. Dohm, who was resigning to accept the presidency of the Vancouver Stock Exchange. Before long, Dohm resigned from that job to resume the practice of law. A resignation from the bench was a rare event, and a return to practice was rarer still. Dohm's doing so was to have repercussions on Berger's career. The benchers, somewhat nettled, took the matter under review, fearing that the return of a judge to the bar could bring the appearance of justice into disrepute. Consequently, the Law Society of British Columbia, a self-governing body, passed a new regulation precluding a former judge from appearing before his old court or a lower one, where he might seem to have undue influence.

This meant that if the new Mr. Justice Thomas R. Berger did not like being a judge, he could quit, as Allan McEachern and Arthur Maloney had said. But he would not be able to return easily to the practice of law.

"I continued to have grave doubts about this choice," Berger says. "I wish I could say there was a turning point. There wasn't. In time the doubts dissipated and being a judge became simply what I did. My brother Brian was a truck driver, Ted an engineer, Susan a secretary. I was a judge."

What he had been was a superb trial lawyer and what he became was a superb trial judge. "My charges to juries were never struck down," he states with pride. "Of course my decisions were overturned on appeal occasionally, but my instructions to jurors on points of law in civil and criminal trials were always upheld."

While the bench was not the intellectual death Berger had feared, he was obliged to hear his fair share of dry, routine applications. But he had an attribute that he honed to a fine edge on the bench and that was to serve him well later on royal commissions. "My attitude as a judge was that it was my job to listen. That may seem obvious; that anyone can listen or at least pay attention to what's important, but a judge should do much more than that. I realized that there was something to be learned from every person who appeared before me. And, do you know, most often I did learn something."

This new role of assessing pain, suffering and financial loss, as well as of dispensing punishment, justice and orders, carried its own satisfaction, but it did not equal the rewards of his earlier advocacy work. He valued those years, however, for what he learned by listening and for the experiences offered to him by virtue of his position. One of the fields in which he gained an education that he would never have undertaken of his own volition was in mining development. Curiously enough, it was there in the world of treasury shares, options and corporate battles that Mr. Justice Berger first made his mark and established his reputation as a competent jurist whose decisions could change the law and move it forward.

The case was *Teck* v. *Millar*. Within a year, a test articulated by Berger in that case, the "best interest" test, had been cited with approval by England's Privy Council. His decision in *Teck* stands for the principle that boards of directors are empowered to act in what they perceive to be the best interest of the company, not-withstanding the objections of shareholders. "Until *Teck,* I'd never even seen a debenture," Berger admits, by way of illustrating the intellectual challenge of the bench. "By the time we finished with that one, I knew quite a bit about mining exploration and development, as well as how the stock market responds."

Afton Mines Ltd., a junior exploration company, had in 1964 acquired copper claims near Kamloops in the southwestern interior of the province. After years of perseverance, company president Chester Millar and his associates, Douglas L. Price and John Haramboure, issued a press release: "Highly favourable results from recent drilling of the new discovery zone of the Afton Mines Ltd.'s property near Kamloops, has caused the company to initiate an immediate program of both percussion and diamond drilling." The announcement triggered a boom, and Afton shares rose from 30 cents to a high of $15.50; major mining conglomerates invested heavily in Afton, and small outfits easily raised exploration funds in the marketplace. As Tom Dohm, president of the Vancouver Stock Exchange said, $10 million was raised through the facilities of the stock exchange as a result of the boom.

Placer Developments Ltd. then announced that it had agreed to buy 100,000 Afton treasury shares and that its subsidiary, Canadian Explorations Ltd. (Canex), had the right of first refusal to place the Afton property into production. Placer/Canex was one of the world's largest mining concerns—a major. "In mining parlance, a deal with a 'major,' by which the major takes over possession, exploration and development of the property in return for an equity interest by way of shares in the junior, is termed an 'ultimate deal,' " Berger wrote.

A second major, Teck Corporation Ltd., also sought the ultimate deal with Afton, but Chester Millar rejected Teck's proposal because he thought Placer had the better track record. Teck turned to the market and within a few months, Norman B. Keevil, Jr., executive vice-president of Teck, announced his company had gained "effective control" of Afton with more than half of the 2.6 million outstanding shares, at a cost of some $16 million. Teck claimed its controlling position entitled it to veto the ultimate deal proposed between Placer/Canex and Afton; but days later, Afton announced it had signed the ultimate deal with Canex.

Teck immediately sought an injunction to prevent Afton from issuing treasury shares to the Placer unit. Millar went to see Afton's lawyer, who was Berger's old friend John Bruk, of the firm Lawrence and Shaw; after the initial consultation, Bruk turned the case over to the firm's counsel, Brian McLaughlin. After eleven days of argument, an injunction was granted pending the resolution of the issue in a future civil trial. Afton made a number of unsuccessful attempts to have the injunction set aside, and Mr. Justice R. P. Anderson ruled that all work on the mine had to stop until after the trial.

Teck v. *Millar* commenced on 24 August 1972, in the B.C. Supreme Court before Mr. Justice Thomas R. Berger, with thirteen lawyers in attendance. When the trial ended two months later, Berger reserved judgment until 8 December. His untangling of the months of discord over the right of directors to act in the best interest of the company received a full-page story in the *Vancouver Province*.

In his judgment Berger was quick to point out that Teck had accused the Afton directors of a "crass desire merely to retain their directorships and their control of the company." Teck had relied upon a 1967 English case, *Hogg* v. *Cramphorn,* asserting that it elaborated on the rule that directors may not issue shares for an improper purpose, such as merely retaining control. In his ruling, Berger said:

> Impropriety depends upon proof that the directors were actuated by a collateral purpose, it does not depend upon the nature of any shareholders' rights that may be affected by the exercise of the directors' powers. . . . By what standards are the shareholders' interests to be measured?
>
> In defining the fiduciary duties of directors, the law ought to take into account the fact that the corporation provides the legal framework for the development of resources and the generation of wealth in the private sector of the Canadian economy.

The godless socialist, as Premier W. A. C. Bennett had dubbed him, then cited an American tax case, in which the judge had said:

> The corporation has become almost the unit of our economic life. Whether for good or ill, the stubborn fact is that in our present system the corporation carries on the bulk of production and trans-

portation, is the chief employer of both labour and capital, pays a large part of our taxes, and is an economic unit of such magnitude and importance that there is no present substitute for it except the State itself.

Berger rejected the textbook view of directors' powers and duties, to say that they would not breach their fiduciary duty if they "observe a decent respect for other interests lying beyond those of the company's shareholders in the strict sense." He said:

My own view is that the directors ought to be allowed to consider who is seeking control and why. If they believe that there will be substantial damage to the company's interests if the company is taken over, then the exercise of their powers to defeat those seeking a majority will not necessarily be categorized as improper . . . I think the Courts should apply the general rule in this way: The directors must act in good faith. Then there must be reasonable grounds for their belief . . . I am not prepared therefore to follow *Hogg* v. *Cramphorn*. I think that the directors are entitled to consider the reputation, experience and politics of anyone seeking to take over the company. If they decide, on reasonable grounds, a take-over will cause substantial damage to the company's interests, they are entitled to use their powers to protect the company."

The Teck action failed.

Norman Keevil had been planning a victory party for Teck. "Now it's a wake," he announced glumly when he received a copy of Berger's 54-page decision. The traditional court view that directors' motives were irrelevant and that the "proper purpose" test must be applied was now restricted with the "best interest" test of *Teck*. Teck Corporation's shareholder control of Afton Mines was largely illusory; if Canex proceeded to develop the mine, it could receive the proposed equity bonus and the issuance of those shares would dilute Teck's majority.

Berger's handling of the case has sustained subsequent legal challenges and now stands as a guiding principle of corporate behaviour. It is a mainstay of company law courses in law schools across the country. Erin Berger was both proud and embarrassed at the University of Calgary to have her professors hold up her father's ruling as a model of lucid, progressive judicial thinking.

While Teck and a few other seminal cases shaped law and policy in narrow areas, it is debatable whether Judge Berger had the impact of barrister Berger, or even the influence of Tom Berger, elected member. At least one member of the bar—Leon Getz—is of the opinion that he did not. "I hold the perhaps heretical view that he would have been more influential than he was (and who am I to say?) if he had been a better judicial craftsman. I happen to think that a large part of the trick in incorporating policy considerations into judicial reasoning is to dress them up as legal considerations," Getz says, implying that Berger was not adroit enough in disguising his social philosophy. He believes that as a consequence Berger's judgments were too often overturned on appeal. In support of this contention, he points to Berger's reasoning in *McCrae* v. *City of White Rock*.

The case of McCrae against White Rock reached the B.C. Supreme Court late in 1972. It was brought by the owners of a grocery business conducted in a building that had collapsed. The plaintiffs were suing the building inspector, claiming he had negligently failed to inspect roof repairs and renovations.

Judge Berger heard the case. He was of the opinion that there was no precedent for imposing liability and decided to assert that, as a matter of policy, the building department had a positive duty to inspect. As three inspections had been made on call, he said this was not an instance of a failure to exercise the power to inspect. This was a bold statement, rather than a legal principle, for the collapse had been caused by improperly installed and never inspected roof trusses. The mode of construction was unsafe, not carried out according to plan and concealed from the building inspector.

Berger accepted as applicable the reasoning of Lord Denning, in an action against a municipality in England, that negligent inspection was an act of misfeasance. So, too, in White Rock, ruled Berger. He found the inspector liable in negligence and awarded damages to the plaintiff. There were important policy implications in his ruling and the case was appealed.

The appeal court judges were unanimous in their rejection of Berger's position that there was no legal basis for liability or precedent in law, adding that "if it could be said that the building inspector was at fault at all, his fault was one of nonfeasance at worst, rather than misfeasance." The judges would allow the appeal and dismiss the action against the building inspector.

Getz repeats, "My sense is that Tom was relatively impatient with my view that a judge could reach unconventional results by conventional judicial means . . . and that as a result he left himself more exposed to being attacked and overruled than he need have been."

This opinion is echoed by Berger's good friend John Bruk. His sense is that although Tom was originally happy enough with the work, the challenge did not continue at its initial intensity. "He was too young. He needed an outlet to express his inner drive. He is far more creative than that job allows," says Bruk. "I think a judge can be creative, but it is woven slowly into the fabric of our legal system and Tom wanted to use bold brush strokes."

If Judge Berger was not content, it was not evident to Amber Halliday, who cherishes her time as his secretary at the courthouse. "He was the most marvellous man to work for," she says. "He was a workaholic, but not in a frenetic way. He was never hurried or harried; he was always totally calm." When asked if this was because Tom was a well-organized judge, she said, "No. He was that way because he loved the work. The more work he had to do, the better he liked it. Do you know, he can keep at least twenty-nine things in his head, and never, ever, get them muddled. And the best thing about Tom Berger is his lovely, warm sense of humour. That's essential when the workload is as heavy as it often was."

As a lawyer, Berger had appeared in the Supreme Court of Canada before Emmett Hall many times and Hall had often ruled in his favour, particularly in criminal cases. Berger's work in *Calder* had bolstered Hall's belief that Tom would be an appropriate replacement for him on the high court, and he did what he could to accomplish this. Tom's youth and brief time as a judge on the lower court apparently were not impediments to his elevation and, in fact, one reason he had accepted the judicial appointment was the prospect of early elevation to a higher court where the real law is made. Support for his promotion came from many quarters, including the B.C. bench and bar, but as the time came for a definite decision, the opinion that the position ought not to be filled by a B.C. judge emerged and Manitoba got the call. The man chosen was Brian Dickson. Berger wrote to Hall in the spring of 1973 to express his disappointment and to thank him for his efforts, which, he was certain, "had a lot to do with my being considered at all."

Hall consoled him with "there is always a next time and when that time comes, British Columbia cannot be denied." Hall also said, "I think Dickson was an excellent choice and I am sure that he and Laskin will work together extremely well." He was correct to a certain extent; when the time came it was a British Columbian, though it was not Tom Berger but W. R. "Bill" McIntyre who was appointed. And Brian Dickson, whom Berger calls a jewel, succeeded Bora Laskin as chief justice of the Supreme Court of Canada. This is the position that might have been, and many people once thought would be, the zenith of Tom Berger's career. But hard choices and circumstances took him in another direction; in fact to the nadir of his professional life.

While on the bench Berger continued to keep his finger on the pulse of new law and to read widely. John Baigent tells the story of appearing before his old mentor. It was a labour arbitration on a question of jurisdiction: Could the employer or collective agreement dictate how many firemen had to attend certain tasks? There was an obscure Ontario decision that favoured Baigent's client. "It was no more than one and a half pages long and it dealt with two guys in a police car," Baigent says. "The lawyer for the other side hands over his factum. Tom runs his finger down the Index, frowns and says, 'Wasn't there a case in Ontario which addressed this issue?' Well, the guy gulped. His list would have enabled him to argue from every angle but the right one. Who else but Tom would have known the law so well? I had only to say a few words. He rarely had to have cases explained to him; he'd read them."

He read them so that he could do the job in the best possible way and to make his work more interesting, Berger admits. Something else that helped was the presence of Chief Justice J. O. Wilson, one of the most redeeming aspects of the early bench years. "We all revered him. He was well read, intelligent and compassionate. And he was a true British Columbian. He was born in the Kootenays and practised in the Cariboo for many years with his father. He understood our province and its people. I could always turn to him for advice and I did.

"Every job is boring at times," he shrugs, pauses and then concedes, "of course, I had no impact on social policy or legislation as a judge. A handful of cases—that's the legacy of all my listening. The cocaine case was engrossing and would interest most people, but the others—well, *Teck* is pretty esoteric stuff. My daughter Erin tells me they've studied *Bowlay Logging* at law school, but in real life it may be of interest only to a few diligent lawyers. That's about it, whereas when I was at the bar, I was creating new law. Remember, when I was a student there was no such course as environmental law, no such thing as native rights. Of course I was excited by and even proud of my legal casework. So, yes, by comparison, the bench was not quite as exciting."

During his early years on the bench, the judges' rota was arranged so that Berger did not hear cases that parallelled his previous work, as he and the chief justice were aware that it might be thought his political and advocacy background would cause him to favour a certain type of litigant or defendant in his court. Later, when the fair allocation of the workload made it necessary for him to hear matters similar to ones he had argued at the bar himself, his judgments were scrupulously researched and presented with reasoned analyses rooted in faithful adherence to law. For example, in the 1981 case *Re O'Brien and the Queen,* the applicant sought release from a life sentence imposed in 1953 under the old habitual criminal legislation. Counsel for the petitioner, no doubt thinking he had great luck in appearing before Judge Berger, argued there were fatal flaws in the notice advising O'Brien that an application would be made to have him sentenced to preventive detention: that the prosecutor did not have the authority to proceed against the accused and did not have the authority to lodge the process.

Judge Berger held to the letter of the law and ruled that the incarceration of the petitioner had all along been lawful. He refrained from making a single comment on social policy and did not refer to his own work in defence of habitual criminals or to subsequent changes to the Criminal Code which would have precluded the sentence. The following year O'Brien was released from prison by the solicitor general of Canada after Michael Jackson, whose legal career has frequently been intertwined with Berger's, cited the National Parole Board's opinion that "he is his own worst enemy and is not really dangerous . . . we either warehouse him til pensionable age or burn out or try to preserve what little this man has despite his weakness."

The cocaine case, which captured the public imagination and which during 1978–79 offered Judge Berger a measure of satisfaction in the realm of criminal law, was the epic trial of *Regina* v. *Bengert,* known around the province as the "Fats" Robertson case.

After what the Crown alleged was "the largest seizure of cocaine ever made in Canada"—19.6 pounds with a street value of up to $3.5 million—charges of conspiracy to import narcotics were laid against Richard Henry Bengert, William Faulder "Fats" Robertson and twelve others. When they appeared for trial before Berger, most of the defendants had separate counsel. There were also 21 unindicted conspirators, 185 witnesses, 41 tape recordings, 13 affidavits and 316 exhibits attesting to a cocaine-trafficking conspiracy on an unprecedented scale. The trial lasted some seven months and covered events spanning two continents.

Besides the public interest generated by the main case, there were several reported *voir dires* (trials within the trial) on the admissibility of such exotica as: intercepted private communications (disallowed), opinions on whether the quantity of cocaine purchased indicated "organized" trafficking (not admitted, and "perilously close to the very issue the jury has to decide . . . superogatory and prejudicial"), and whether it was permissible for the jury to take notes of the closing submissions and for the Crown to provide them with a typed chronology of dates and events (admissible, "The trial is now in its seventh month. . . . To refuse would be to consign them [the jury] to a never-never land").

Once the jury returned verdicts of guilty, Berger faced the dilemma of sentencing. Under the Narcotics Control Act, a person convicted of trafficking is liable to as much as life in prison. Berger, in his pursuit of truth, and being wary about sentencing on the basis of general or unsubstantiated information, thought it "important that the court be informed regarding the extent [that] use of cocaine may represent a danger to society now and in the future." Current medical literature on the topic did not square with the earlier opinions of experts that cocaine was a serious evil.

The prosecution, which was seeking life sentences for the six executive-level conspirators, responded to Berger's request for more information by calling medical professionals to provide expert evidence on the properties of cocaine: addiction, use and properties. The court was told that cocaine created no physical dependency but rather a high degree of psychological dependency. Unlike heroin, coke did not pose a serious danger, the experts claimed, to the user or to society.

The defence argued that as cocaine is similar to amphetamines, trafficking in which brings a maximum of ten years under the Food and Drug Act, the accused should be sentenced as if the maximum for dealing in cocaine were also ten years.

Berger conceded the anomaly, but said it was a matter for parliament to address. With reasoning such as he had heard, he wryly told defence counsel, parliament might well decide otherwise: that as amphetamines were similar to cocaine, they, too, should draw a life sentence. He noted, farsightedly, that since the experts of the day did not agree with what had been said about cocaine in the mid-1970s, "it is very likely that with the advent of further knowledge, judges sitting in the mid-1980s will have to consider if a description of cocaine found in these reasons any longer suffices."

Berger proved to be right, for the damage cocaine does to the mind and body, say the experts now, is far worse than once believed.

When Judge Berger delivered sentence, he acknowledged that while a conspiracy charge is a formidable weapon in the armoury of the prosecutor, it is a necessary one when it comes to organized crime, and he spoke of the conspiracy as an "assault on the fabric of the law . . . a network of lawlessness." He said, too, that the coke traffickers' world was one of private justice where people were prepared to kill. In order to deter such people, he reasoned that it was important to confiscate the profits and proceeded to not only mete out sentences ranging from four to twenty years but also to impose two $50,000 fines, dispelling once and for all the rumours that he was a bleeding-heart judge and thus concluding the longest trial in B.C.'s history.

There is a school of thought, widely accepted within legal, academic and lay circles, that believes the best judge is the unknown judge, that there should be no philosophical differences discernible in rulings, nor should there be the expectation that a particular judge will be sympathetic to a certain kind of litigant or issue.

The exception that comes to mind is the colourful and well-known English judge Lord Denning. During a trip to England in 1973, Berger paid a courtesy call on Denning and upon returning to his hotel after a day trip with Bev and the children, learned that Denning had repaid the compliment by inviting him to lunch. "That was quite a welcome for a mere judge from a remote Canadian province," Berger says, pleased.

Denning was a jurist who laced his judgments with a stout dollop of social reform and frequently revealed his sympathy for small victims of large interests. Allan McEachern had in mind Denning's ability to make law when he recommended that Berger go to the bench. Denning's innovative approach, though it made him the darling of law students, journalists and the public, also attracted criticism. Unfortunately, the outspokenness of both judges ended their judicial careers on a sour note. Ironically, Denning spoke out against an ethnic and religious minority. Tom Berger spoke out in defence of minorities. But that was in the future.

Berger, who like Denning was often in demand as a speaker, also fell victim to his own popularity. He was known and admired by the public, and this led to an uneasiness among his brother judges. Some of the reasons are obvious. He was well known for his work on the progressive side of many issues, and it was with reference to these that he was asked to speak. Secondly, the simple fact that he was thirty-eight when the average member of the bench was perhaps ten or twenty years his senior did not help him. The other judges shared professional relationships going back decades while Berger was, at first, the only one of his vintage.

It can be no easy thing for men who have spent at least a quarter-century attaining the pinnacle of their careers to see a mere stripling, with apparent ease and popularity and with prospects of advancing to a higher court, take his place beside them after a relatively brief career at the bar. One would have to be naive to suppose that all of those elements were not obstacles, however small, to Berger receiving the wholehearted support and enthusiasm of the other members of the bench.

Berger's fellow judges soon learned, however, that despite the public aspects of his career, the bench was enriched by his presence. They developed an admiration for his capabilities and frequently relied on his assistance in working through troublesome legal tangles, for each judge has a particular judicial strength, and Berger's was a facility for abstract cerebral puzzles. Nonetheless, within a few years, a trace of his benchmates' initial reservations about the boy wonder in their midst reappeared, provoked by Judge Berger's recurring role as an inquiry commissioner.

Proof that the bench had purged Berger of a partisan political taint can be seen in his commission appointments made by governments formed by three different political parties. But the conduct of the inquiries while Berger was still a judge shot him into a national prominence surpassing that which he had achieved as a civil liberties lawyer or a socialist politician, and each commission opened wider the cloak of anonymity. Berger was no longer an unknown judge, hidden by the reasoned impartiality of his decisions.

His love of the law and his dedication to social justice, along with his acquired listening and organizational skills and his innate ability to assimilate a mass of information, all contributed to making him a fine judge. As well, these talents contributed to his becoming the most innovative inquiry commissioner Canada has ever known.

"That's why I can't regret the judgeship," he says. "As a Vancouver lawyer, I'd never have been chosen to head royal commissions."

CHAPTER 7

The Commissioner

There is no protection of children from the people who are often their greatest enemies —their parents.

Thomas R. Berger

"Tom's abilities were wasted as a trial court judge," the Honourable Allan McEachern states unequivocally from behind his red leather-topped desk. The chief justice was a lawyer when he did his bit to see that Tom Berger was offered a judgeship. "I urged him to take the bench. I thought that he of all people was most likely to be a Canadian Lord Denning. Don't forget, this was 1972 when Denning was writing exciting, forceful and brilliant judgments. I meant it as a compliment. I believed that if he dived into legal research, he'd carve out a Denning-like path.

"Without that, there was no challenge for him on the bench; the issues are too narrow. Being there would allow him the scope and opportunity to fulfill his potential. But those damn commissions, they diverted him.

"Perhaps Tom was too young when he went to the bench. Still, I'm convinced that it was those damned commissions," he sighs. "*Post hoc ergo propter hoc,*" he says, savouring the cadence of the Latin words. Post hoc ergo propter hoc is a logical fallacy. It translates to 'after that, therefore, because of that,' or in other words, we can't know what would have happened if something else hadn't happened."

The history of royal commissions goes back into antiquity, with Britain's Domesday Report being perhaps the oldest and most famous. Since then, Britain and the Commonwealth countries have had a policy of striking a commission of inquiry when a crisis looms. Or, as one cynic called the practice, "anything but action."

No single English word exists to describe a person who listens, observes, reports and recommends, but the Inuit do have such a word: *ekoktoegee*. It is a name they bestowed upon another legal pioneer, Mr. Justice Jack Sissons. Sissons took the Northwest Territorial Court on circuit to the native people who, until then, had been forced to go south for their justice. Ekoktoegee, which means "the one who listens to things" or "the one to whom people tell things," is particularly applicable to a royal commissioner. Not infrequently, because of their fact-finding experience and public respect for their objectivity, judges are chosen to be commissioners.

By dint of assiduous observance of the rules of judicial protocol, Berger was earning just such a reputation. Because his political activities prior to being appointed to the bench were so well known, he believed that for justice to be seen to be done by him, he had to be scrupulously apolitical. He watched the excitement of the 1972 B.C. election campaign from the confines of the bench. "It was frustrating for the entire family," says daughter Erin. "He wouldn't let us have bumper stickers. And we couldn't have a lawn sign. The neighbours had their Social Credit signs and we had to look like we weren't interested."

That year the New Democratic Party, under Berger's successor Dave Barrett, swept to victory, and the mood of the province was charged with optimism. After twenty years of W. A. C. Bennett's Social Credit rule, anything seemed possible, and the NDP made reform a priority.

One area that desperately needed reform was family law, an entangled topic of legal, social, political and ethical import. Legislation with respect to the protection of children had changed little since the end of the nineteenth century; children of unmarried parents were stigmatized by bastardy laws; the law of marriage property was confused, and the proceedings concerning marriage and family breakdown were held in both Family Court and the B.C. Supreme Court. Berger was particularly troubled by the government practice of apprehending children. When children are taken from their parents, he wondered, "Whose standard is it that ought to prevail? The Children's Aid Society's? The Department of Human Resources? The community's? The judge's?

"I think it is important to bear in mind that we do not have a monolithic culture. We have diverse classes and their standards ought to be taken into account," he was heard to say to family law practitioners.

On 6 December 1973, the new government passed an order in council establishing the British Columbia Royal Commission on Family and Children's Law: Chairman, the Honourable Thomas Rodney Berger.

Most commissions of inquiry share structural similarities. At the first stage the scope of the subject matter is identified, and once the extent of the problem is known, the likely sources of information are pinpointed. Next comes the hearing stage, in which information is either voluntarily provided to the inquiry or elicited by the commissioners. "This commission will be one that works in public. We will be thinking out loud," Berger promised. The final stage involves assembling the gathered information, developing recommendations from it and reporting on the work of the commission in a way that will either deflect or heighten public and political interest.

Berger organized his commission team by filling it with a clutch of energetic and dedicated people. He was assisted by the Honourable Ross Douglas Collver, a Provincial Court judge who had a history of fair-mindedness on family law cases; pediatrician Dr. Sydney Segal, and social workers Rita T. MacDonald and Mish Vadasz. Lawyers Allison Burnett and Ian Waddell served as executive director and consultant, respectively.

Under Berger's direction, best described as encouragement and freedom to do one's best, the team surveyed the province and its family law problems. Family Court counsellor Gordon Birrell admired Berger's style. "He was a model of tact and diplomacy," Birrell says, "and yet a bugger to work for. He didn't suffer fools gladly. One time the naiveté in my approach showed that I didn't understand the machinations of the real world. Tom tore a strip off me very quietly and thoroughly. I was devastated but after I recovered from my humiliation I recognized that he was absolutely right. It was a lesson I've never forgotten."

The family law commission team members remember it all as a good time: hard, frustrating, but ultimately satisfying, as Berger's competence always attracted competence and they drew on his strengths. "Good God, when he came down the hall at seven every morning there were always at least eight or nine people waiting, bursting with ideas and problems. He could allow himself to entertain ridiculous ideas. He imparted his ability to remain open and fresh to other people. It is a great gift."

Berger and his team described the tangle of family law as "a bundle of legal and social situations which ought properly to come before the same tribunal . . . [causing] a multiplicity of proceedings to arise out of what may essentially be one marital dispute."

The commission was concerned by the problems caused by the fragmentation of judicial jurisdiction with respect to disputes involving families and the rights of children. In a speech to the B.C. Bar Association, Berger said, "I reject the notion that juveniles violating the law should be hived off and dealt with as if there were no connection between the events that occur in child-hood and the behaviour of adolescents . . . the Child really is father of the Man. . . . The causes often lie within the family, and the remedy often lies within the family."

With the issues identified, the team moved on to the second stage. Over a period of nineteen months, the commission conducted twenty-five hearings and produced thirteen detailed, multidisciplinary reports and a draft children's statute. Additionally, it created a pilot project: an operational Unified Family Court, a first for the province. "We've thrown all our eggs in the Berger basket," boasted Deputy Attorney General Dave Vickers. The pilot project, serving a population of 282,000 in the South Fraser Judicial District, put judges of the B.C. Supreme Court, the County Court and the Provincial Court under one roof, along with support services pertinent to families in crisis.

The philosophy inherent in all thirteen of the commission's reports is that legal sanctions should, in many cases, be a last resort, and to this end recommendations focussed on the effective use of human rather than legislated solutions. For Berger, the commission was an opportunity to reach beyond the political process and the courts, and for this reason it proposed such innovations as having lay people sit with the Family Court judge and ethnic community involvement on Children's Panels, when decisions were to be made regarding the protection of children —their custody, foster home placement or adoption.

The commission's tenth report, *Native Families and the Law*, reflected Berger's ongoing commitment to Maisie's people. After consultation with native people, the commission recognized that acceptable family life practices and standards varied according to economic situation, culture and geographic location. Custom adoptions, for example, in which a family adopts the child of a friend or relative who is unable to care for it, had no place in the establishment's legal system, and the report suggested that these be legalized. The report also suggested an examination of the prevalent practice of white social workers apprehending native children and, without consultation with native people, placing them in white foster or adoptive homes. "It's not enough merely to recommend that decisions be made in the 'best interests' of the child," Berger said, "since standards differ according to culture. Almost 40 per cent of cases arising under the Protection of Children Act involve native children, although Natives comprise only 5 per cent of the population." Today, many reserves and native communities have their own foster and group homes, and native people are active participants in decisions regarding their children.

The other reports covered such diverse topics as matrimonial property, family maintenance, adoptions, preparation for marriage, artificial insemination and change of name. Everywhere that the commission met with the public, it fostered understanding, ideas for reform and creative thinking. From all of this brainstorming came the commission's most important piece of work, one that fell within the legal and legislative framework: the Protection of Children Act. This act went beyond mere rules of child custody and provided for experts and lay people to become involved. As Berger said, "They are our children, the courts are there to administer the laws enacted to protect all of us and it is up to all of us to make our community a place where everyone understands that the cause of rehabilitation and the cause of public safety are the same."

Just two days after the second of the thirteen reports was submitted, the federal government appointed Tom Berger to head the Mackenzie Valley Pipeline Inquiry. Although he would not leave for the North to begin his investigations until the following year, it meant less of his time was available for the Commission on Family and Children's Law. The momentum of his spirit and philosophy sustained it to some extent, however, and the early groundwork, the brainstorming and community participation paid off. "He wasn't always there physically," says one commission member, "but he gave us the chance to do it." All those who were involved speak with wonderment about the Berger process, which stretched them a little further than they thought possible, into new phases of professional excellence. Team member and family lawyer Gary Somers says, however, that the troops needed their general. "When he left, there was no rudder. We were finished."

On 12 December 1975, the NDP was ousted from power by the reborn Social Credit Party under Bill Bennett, son of W. A. C. Bennett. The new government's handling of the Berger reports was devious. Bill 69, which introduced the Family Relations Act and the Family and Child Services Act, 1980, was accompanied by explanatory notes and comments claiming that sections of the act were in furtherance of the Berger commission recommendations, but this was deceptive as none of the preventive and support services proposed was included, though there was an option for the Superintendant of Child Welfare to use discretion in providing them.

David Cruickshank, research director of the family law commission, later wrote: "In retrospect, one could make a strong case for the 'big lie' by government. It began with the very title of the Family and Child Services Act. . . . Thus we have in B.C. the illusion of legislatively mandated services followed with the reality of cutting virtually all child welfare preventive services."

This was a neat twist. The elected Socred policy-makers appeared to validate the role of the commissioner while seizing the opportunity to implement their own policies, which were directly contrary to those of the previous NDP government and to the commission's recommendations.

From the vantage of hindsight, the Protection of Children Act proposed by the commission comes into poignant focus. Developed over nineteen months, the act embodies in more than one hundred closely typed legal-sized pages the wisdom, concerns and aspirations of countless individuals. But its fate also stands as a testimony to the proposition that judges, as commissioners, may be thwarted by politicians; as a warning that ignoring commission reports undermines the judiciary and makes judges appear impotent, and as ammunition for those who want to limit judges to doing their judging from the bench.

The Reports of the Commission on Family and Children's Law Commission, the Protection of Children Act and the Unified Family Court Project are tributes to a compassionate chairman and an extraordinary team. The demise of the recommendations demonstrates the fragility of idealism. The pilot program never reached the rest of the province, and the Social Credit government, which remained in power during the 1980s, implemented a harsh program of fiscal restraint at a time when the demand on limited social services for families and children was increasing.

On 30 June 1985 the Unified Family Court adjourned for the last time when Chief Justice McEachern, facing longer dockets in Vancouver, could no longer spare judges to attend the unified court in Richmond. Now, as before, applications made under the Divorce Act must be heard by a B.C. Supreme Court judge in Vancouver, while decisions about maintenance and children are heard by Provincial Court judges sitting in different locations. The family in trouble pays the price in terms of time, money and misunderstandings.

Many people believe that the unified court project was doomed from the start because of its NDP connotations. "With Tom Berger as chairman," says Gary Somers, "no other government would ever implement the reports. But without Tom Berger, the commission would never have happened at all."

Tom Berger's fears that the bench would isolate him from public affairs and political and social issues had proven wrong. The Commission on Family and Children's Law gave him meaty problems to tackle with respect to provincial policy, and the Mackenzie Valley Pipeline Inquiry placed him in an international arena that contained everything his temperament, education and experience had been preparing him for: the problems and claims of native people, environmental issues, law, politics, government policies, the concerns of ordinary people and the financial interests of giant corporations.

When Berger had begun writing his first judgments in early 1972, Canada was floating on a seemingly inexhaustible sea of gas and oil. Liberal cabinet ministers urged the export of the surplus to a decreasing number of markets before solar technology could render the fuels obsolete. Accordingly, the government granted natural gas export permits for a staggering 6.3 trillion cubic feet.

Within two years, the story changed dramatically. Projections had been based on "potential" reserves, Canadians were told, and recoverable reserves would fill domestic needs only until the late 1980s. In a televised address to the nation, Prime Minister Pierre Trudeau spoke of "shopping for new supplies . . . racing against the onset of winter." Although his solemn pledge that "under no circumstances will the government permit fuel to be diverted from those who need it most, to those who can pay the most" was meant to reassure, it fostered a sense of uncertainty. Canadians wanted a solution.

Trudeau presented it on 2 December 1973. The National Energy Policy (NEP) was to be equivalent to John A. Macdonald's national dream of the previous century: a grandiose scheme in which vast expenditures of land, money and labour would transcend huge geographic and economic problems. This time the solution would not be a railway line but a pipeline. As the National Energy Policy was fleshed out, it became apparent that the government favoured the removal of regulatory barriers to allow early construction of a natural gas pipeline up the Mackenzie Valley. This was the dream of Canadian Arctic Gas Pipeline Limited (Arctic Gas), a consortium which, despite its name, was dominated by American-owned and American-controlled firms.

Arctic Gas's goal was to transport gas from the mammoth Prudhoe Bay fields on Alaska's North Slope to the energy-starved "Lower 48" American states. Their plan was to swing a 48-inch diameter pipeline from Prudhoe Bay east across the Yukon to the Mackenzie Delta and south through the Northwest Territories to the Alberta-Saskatchewan border. Tom Berger later put the situation succinctly: "The risk is in Canada. The urgency in the U.S."

Two federal statutes are pertinent to northern energy projects: the National Energy Board Act and the Territorial Lands Act. Both acts allow for concerns about such projects to be raised, for information to be provided and for questions to be asked and answered in public hearings. The Territorial Lands Act falls within the jurisdiction of the Department of Indian Affairs and Northern Development (DIAND), and DIAND Minister Jean Chrétien wrote to Arctic Gas President Bill Wilder on 3 March 1973 to explain the government's policy. Construction, if approved, he said, must operate within the ambit of the social and environmental considerations set out in *The Expanded Guidelines for Northern Pipelines* of 28 June 1972. Chrétien did not favour the delay and expense his ministry would incur by striking a commission of inquiry; his initial response to Arctic Gas's plan was the creation of a Pipeline Application Assessment Group comprised of government specialists whose job it was to see if Arctic Gas's proposed application measured up to the *Expanded Guidelines*. It did not.

It was well known that Arctic Gas would prefer for economic reasons to build a western link along the coast of the Beaufort Sea, though controversy was rising over the potential for damage to an exceedingly fragile wilderness and thought was being given to a costlier southern route through the interior of the Yukon. In either case the projected cost was so great that it was imperative the line operate at full capacity. If an NEB certificate and a DIAND Crown land right of way were granted, the ensuing energy corridor would open up the Beaufort Sea and the Mackenzie Delta to increased energy exploration. And if the projections of huge reserves proved out, the oil companies would be back in business, exporting Canadian energy resources to the U.S. In fact there never had been an interruption: Canada expected to ship more oil to the U.S. in 1972 than the year before. The so-called "energy-crisis" had merely cast doubt on her ability to honour supply contracts.

Governments and industry on both sides of the border were amenable to the immediate approval of an acceptable route and a speedy start on construction. Chrétien's letter to Wilder discussed the *Expanded Guidelines* in the face of "inevitable development" and, though Arctic Gas had not yet made formal application, a public servant drafted a memo on the costs pertaining to the right-of-way land. The value of the land, which at the time was the subject of aboriginal land claims negotiations, was calculated by another employee this way: 40 square miles × 640 acres × $3.10 per acre. This meant that the largest project ever undertaken by private enterprise—in terms of capital expenditure and engineering challenge—could be sold to the only bidder for $80,000 a year (reviewable after five years). Federal bureaucrats did not anticipate recovering any of the expense of studies or land claims settlements from the pipeline company. Officials were pleased, northern natives were not.

Chief Elijah Smith, chairman of the Council for Yukon Indians, raised immediate objections. First, ownership of the Yukon land that Arctic Gas proposed to cross was in dispute as their aboriginal claim was still being negotiated, and Smith advised the government he would view it as a breach of faith if an Arctic Gas application were considered prior to resolution of the land claim.

Besides the conflict over the title to the land and the obvious engineering challenge inherent in burying thousands of kilometres of pipe in continuous and discontinuous permafrost during dark winter months, there were other complications. The socio-economic impact that the construction would have on Canada's last frontier was complex, and the environmental questions raised were novel and legion. Two questions feeding doubt were: was the pipeline urgently needed, and was it wise to vest so much power in Arctic Gas?

In a book called *Bob Blair's Pipeline,* François Bregha, an astute observer of the North, wrote that the creation of the Arctic Gas consortium "carried profound political consequences. By eliminating competition, it reduced the number of policy options to one, thereby sharply curtailing the government's control over northern development."

As opposition from groups representing northern natives and the protection of their homelands increased, the project—which had no key answers in place—was placed in jeopardy. Although Chrétien maintained that it was his responsibility to assess the effect of the pipeline on the North, his department lacked the manpower to do so, and pressure for action escalated. Finally, in January 1974, cabinet resolved that DIAND would order an inquiry pursuant to the Territorial Lands Act. Chrétien remembers that he started with a list of about ten candidates to head the inquiry: "I won't tell you who they were." When Tom Berger's name came up, he says, "I discussed it with some of my colleagues and eventually I decided he might be a good commissioner."

But first, Chrétien candidly admits, he met with Berger, "to tell him what his mandate was to be. His mandate was to find a way to build a pipeline, not to stop the pipeline. I'm telling you what happened there; what I wanted. And I said to Berger, 'The companies don't want to invest the money that they should invest for the social betterment of the people. What the natives want is dignity,' I said. So I gave him examples. I said, 'The people of Fort Good Hope want to operate their sawmills. You should tell the companies: buy every god-damn piece of wood they produce.

Do whatever you want, but let the Indians, the people of Fort Good Hope, process the wood and sell it, like any other business-man. If there is no market, if you lose on the sale, that's your problem.' I had ideas like that; or, where people were to get jobs on a permanent basis on the pipeline. But not jobs that look like welfare. Not jobs like sweeping the floor where there is no floor to be swept."

Chrétien thought that the Indians had a powerful bargaining chip, and he entrusted it and their future to Tom Berger.

"Chrétien phoned me," Berger recalls, "to say that he, Trudeau and Minister of Energy Donald MacDonald, whom I had known when we were freshmen MPs, had decided that I should be asked to do the job."

The appointment of a westerner so admired by the native people was a singularly apt and popular move; so much so that everyone jumped to take credit for it. Members of the NDP immediately claimed, and many still do, that because the party held the balance of power to the ruling minority Liberals, the government acceded to their request that Berger be named commissioner.

Berger, however, believes it was the Liberals' idea. "I don't think there is any evidence that it was a concession to the NDP. I don't know for certain what the truth is about this. David Lewis, who was NDP leader at that time, is dead. He never did suggest to me that any deal was made in this regard."

Liberal Senator Len Marchand, an Okanagan Indian, also rejects the NDP connection out of hand. "The NDP don't have the monopoly on good ideas," he says testily. He claims that the responsibility fell to the B.C. caucus and takes credit for the appointment himself. Marchand had been parliamentary assistant to DIAND Minister Arthur Laing, who had often extolled Berger's virtues and said that "Berger's intelligence and commitment to his ideals mark him as a man with the potential to make a great contribution to Canadian life."

"But now," says Marchand peevishly, "there are lots of Bergers. He's nothing special." Still, he takes the time to describe a flight he made on a government JetStar from Ottawa. By the time the plane arrived in Vancouver, he says, he had Chrétien convinced that he should place the new national dream in Tom Berger's hands.

Perhaps numerous people and conversations influenced the

choice. It is safe to say that the appointment of 21 March 1974 transcended party politics for the sake of the common good—the essence of liberalism.

Berger was, at the time, engrossed in the B.C. Commission on Family and Children's Law. His research and that of his team members reinforced what he had learned through his political and legal work—that native people had not been received into white society as equals. "They are not simply another immigrant minority group. They are Canada's original people," Berger reminds us. "And in the North they are the majority." Chrétien's offer gave him an unprecedented opportunity to guide Canadians to an understanding of the North before industrial exploitation could irrevocably alter it. It would be a huge undertaking that meant travel and being away from home, not to mention another hiatus from the bench.

Once more, Tom and Bev Berger pondered the difficulties. The questions centred on how: how to hear from people whose lives would be affected by the pipeline, how to bring all of the relevant information forward, how to balance his own obligations. The last concern was crucial, for though Bev was a dedicated mother willing to shoulder the greater load of parenting, there were problems, and Tom knew that time not spent with his family would be lost forever. Erin was seventeen and David was fifteen. Tom wanted to spend more time with them, but as wrenching as it was, it was not a question of deciding if he should do it, but how. In the end, he did what he could and placed great confidence in the strength of the family unit: the children's great-grandmother and two grandmothers lived in Vancouver and, in addition, they were in frequent contact with their aunts, uncles and cousins.

Berger was appointed to head the commission of inquiry on the very day that Arctic Gas finally made its official application for the Crown land right of way that would allow construction of a pipeline up the Mackenzie Valley. He was directed to "enquire and report upon terms and conditions that should be imposed in respect of any right of way" that might be granted, and also to consider "any proposals to meet the specific environmental and social concerns set out in *The Expanded Guidelines for Northern Pipelines*." The breadth of the guidelines was not widely recognized at first, but proved to be most significant. The guidelines politicized Berger and the North.

Environmentalists, cognizant of the government's blatant

desire to see the project proceed, doubted that Berger could divert the strong industrial and political forces from their tantalizing goal.

Bureaucrats, on the other hand, presumed that Berger was adequately fettered by his terms of reference and that he would expedite the process so they could get on with the action. Don Gamble, an engineer, the DIAND officer assigned to follow and report on Berger, recalls the government's mood in those heady days. His own title was senior liaison officer, Pipeline Co-ordination and Development Section, Policy and Planning Division. "Not only was there no junior liaison," he says with a disarming smile, "there was no other liaison officer. And no one could explain what Policy and Planning meant." All of Ottawa, he says, was mesmerized by the pipeline project. It was a bureaucrat's delight, it meant extra staff, it was press-worthy: "people build their careers on this stuff."

Berger, who was accustomed to the independence of the judiciary and indifferent to political machinations, began to plan with no other objective than to do a thorough and totally fair inquiry. He and Bev spent most of the summer of 1974 travelling in the North, meeting informally with people who would later offer their testimony to his commission. The Bergers canoed and explored, ate the country food and attended the Northern Games at Tuktoyaktuk. With his vision fixed on the big picture as he struggled to understand what the North required of him, Tom was grateful for Bev's observations and easy friendliness. Her cheery social nature and her inquisitive mind balanced his quiet manner. Tom became a familiar sight, sauntering through villages in baggy pants, bulky sweater and cord jacket. He talked, he watched and was sometimes invited into homes for tea. "I didn't have 'judge' stamped on my forehead. 'I'll listen' I told them, 'as long as it takes.' "

He did listen. "I had a beer in just about every town we visited," he claims.

The pipeline project was a rich prize for which industry had spent $50 million up-front to win. The massive scale of the endeavour meant that thousands of workers would be required to build wharves, warehouses, storage sites and airstrips. Berger was later to report:

The capacity of the fleet of tugs and barges on the Mackenzie will have to be doubled. There will be 6000 construction workers re-

quired north of 60 to build the pipeline, and 1,200 more to build gas
plants and gathering systems in the Mackenzie Delta. There will be
about 130 gravel mining operations. There will be 600 river and
stream crossings. There will be inumerable aircraft, tractors,
earthmovers, trucks and trailers.

The pipeline had the potential to change forever the way of life
for people in and around thirty-five northern communities, for it
was to traverse the northern homeland of Inuit, Métis, Indians and
Whites, a region where seven languages are spoken. This was a
land where, as events would show, native people were fiercely opposed to any pipeline. The future of this last frontier was, in some
measure, in Tom Berger's hands. In attempting to explain how
his inquiry was going to achieve its monumental mandate, he
came up with one of his classic understatements: "I only venture
to tell you something of what we are doing, because we may be
doing things a little differently from the way they have been done
in the past."

Berger went to see the land and the people. During his travels
he saw fish being dried or smoked in every home, stacks of musk-
rat pelts ready for sale and families going out to hunting and fishing camps. Everywhere, people were eating country food: caribou, moose, arctic char, whitefish, trout, muktuk (dried whale
meat) and sometimes muskox. And yet, he had in hand a report,
commissioned by Arctic Gas, that attributed little value to country food in the Mackenzie Valley and Delta. The report, prepared
by Gemini North, a consulting firm owned by Pat Carney (later a
federal Progressive Conservative cabinet minister), pegged the
impact of country food at less than five per cent. What the report
told Berger was that all people who would be affected by the project should realize the assumptions upon which Arctic Gas's application was made, and to this end he decided to issue a series of
Preliminary Rulings that were *his* terms of reference: first, he embraced *The Expanded Guidelines for Northern Pipelines* and said that
he felt "bound to consider the economic and social impact" of the
construction of both oil and gas pipelines; then he said he wanted
all existing pertinent studies (no matter who had paid for them) to
be submitted to the inquiry, and he announced he would conduct
both formal technical hearings and informal community hearings.

For this commission he assembled an extraordinary staff,
among whom were Ian Waddell, Michael Jackson, Ian Scott, John
Fyles, Steve Goudge and Diana Crosbie.

Ian Waddell (later an NDP member of parliament and energy critic), vividly recalls his introduction to the Mackenzie commission. "Berger is nothing if not clear and direct. He told me the prime minister had asked him to head a new commission. 'I'm going to do it and I'd like you to be my assistant,' he said.

"And Tom had the great good fortune to have his secretary, Pat Hutchison, come along. A self-effacing Englishwoman, she did all the money stuff and planning. She ran the inquiry. Another good move was to bring in Diana Crosbie as press officer. She'd been an editor for *Time,* I think. She was also Tom's tennis partner. And then we added Toronto lawyers Ian Scott, later the attorney general for the Liberal government in Ontario, and Steve Goudge.

"Special counsel, that was my fancy title," Ian continues. "I'll never forget that day. . . . Tom said, 'We've got an application from Canadian Arctic Gas. It's three feet high. I don't understand it. The only thing I understand is a map of Canada with a picture of a pipeline.' We stared down at the rainy streets. At last Tom said, 'Well, we didn't know much about family law, either, did we? I want you to go up to Yellowknife tomorrow to check it out.'

"It was wonderful that first summer and exciting to be with Tom. . . . We flew to Inuvik on a beautiful June day. There a helicopter pilot met us and took us up the Arctic Coast, up the Mackenzie Delta to Demarcation Point on the border of the Yukon and Northwest Territories. Then we went right across the ice to Herschel Island, up the Firth River, over the British Mountains, and down the Pelly River; right down the Alaska border parallel to the coast. When we got over the mountains we saw migrating caribou, three grizzlies, several wolves and dozens of seals on the sea ice.

"As tired as Tom was when we got to Old Crow, he accepted the chief's invitation to go to his home for caribou. And there was no darkness, remember. It was hard to sleep.

"The next day he said to me, 'Do you realize the magnificence of what we've seen? It's the last of North America, the eighth wonder of the world.'

"I was a young lawyer then. I thought I was a real wheeler-dealer. My time with Berger gave me a vision of Canada. I came to understand the religious notion of being one with the land."

Michael Jackson, with shoulder-length hair that makes him

RCMP Corporal Ted Berger (*centre*) and his detachment, including T. A. Harris (*left*) at Hazelton, B.C., in 1929 or 1930. *Photograph courtesy Christie Harris.*

RIGHT: RCMP Constable Ted Berger and his bride-to-be, Perle McDonald, in Telkwa, B.C., 1926.

ABOVE: The Berger children (*left to right*): Ted (16), Brian (8), Tom (13), Susan (6), in Dollarton, B.C., 1946.

RIGHT: Teddy and Tommy Berger sharing a book, Penticton, B.C., in 1937.

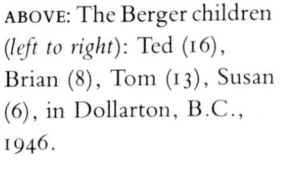

Tom and Bev Berger on their wedding day. *Left to right:*
Frank Elkins, best man; Tom and Bev; Marilyn Crosby,
Bev's sister and attendant, in Vancouver, B.C.,
5 November 1955.

Barrister Tom Berger in
1959. *Photograph by Schiffer.*

Beverley Crosby, a portrait
she had taken for Tom in
1954.

Tom and his team at the Inns of Court offices on Howe
Street in Vancouver, 1966. Tom's mother, Perle Berger
(*seated, centre*) was the firm's bookkeeper, Doug Sanders
was his associate, and Essa Horswill, who began working
for Tom in Ottawa in 1962, is still with the firm.
Photograph by Schiffer.

Tom Berger leaving the Vancouver courthouse in 1969,
probably after the appeal on the Nishga case.

ABOVE: In the midst of the campaign for leadership of the provincial NDP party, Tom, Bev, Erin and David take time to play in Vancouver, 1969.

FACING PAGE: Tom Berger, member of parliament, with his family in 1963.

LEFT: NDP Caucus members in the Provincial Legislative Buildings, Victoria, 1966. *Back, left to right:* Frank Calder, Fred Vulliamy, Dave Stupich, Tom Berger, Ray Parkinson, Dave Barrett, Bob Williams, Ernest Hall, Alex Macdonald, Rae Eddie. *Front, left to right:* Ron Harding, Bob Strachan, Eileen Dailly, Bill Hartley and Leo Nimsick.

BELOW: Dave Barrett pours a celebratory drink for Tom Berger, the winner of the leadership of the New Democratic Party of British Columbia, Vancouver, 13 April 1969. Barrett and onlookers Bob Williams (*left*) and John Conway (*right*) were all contenders for the helm.

The Hon. Mr. Justice Thomas R. Berger of the Supreme
Court of British Columbia, Vancouver, 1971.

Native children of Fort Liard, Northwest Territories, look on as Judge Thomas Berger conducts the Mackenzie Valley Pipeline Inquiry hearings in 1975.

The Hon. Thomas R. Berger (*centre*), just before receiving an honorary degree from the University of Saskatchewan, with the Hon. Emmett Hall, chancellor (*right*) and Dr. Leo Kristjanson, president, in Saskatoon, 1985. *Photograph by AK Photos.*

Berger (*centre*) and sound
man Jim Sykes (*right*) visit
with the people of Holy
Cross, Alaska, in 1984,
during the Alaska Native
Review Commission.
Photograph by Bill Hess.

Tom Berger at a village
hearing during the Alaska
Native Review
Commission, Emmonak,
Alaska, in 1985. *Photograph
by Bill Hess.*

Tom Berger in Alaska, 1985. *Photograph by Bill Hess.*

look more like a northern outdoorsman than the English-born academic that he is, was teaching the first native rights course in Canada at the University of British Columbia's law faculty, a course built around the Nishga case and Berger's early work, when Berger asked him to take charge of the community hearings in the Mackenzie. Jackson says the native people were adamant that it was necessary to have the judge in their villages, hearing the people where they lived. Native organizations also wanted time and money to prepare. They did not want any hearings to be held for a year, but the pipeline companies, which had been engaged in preliminaries for a couple of years, wanted to proceed in six weeks. "They became irate when the Dene people raised their land claims," Jackson recalls.

A turning point in the inquiry came at a preliminary hearing in Ottawa. Chief George Kodakin of Fort Franklin, a village on the shore of Great Bear Lake, made a speech in which he told Berger, "If you want to understand what the pipeline will do to our people, you need to come to live with us for six months. Then, and only then, will you understand why we don't want the pipeline."

At the close of the morning's proceedings, Berger called Jackson over and said, "I want you to go over and talk to the chief. Tell him I can't go and live in the village for six months, but that you can."

Jackson, his wife and infant son spent three months in Chief Kodakin's village, Fort Franklin, but living among these reticent, private people did not make him privy to their lives, until he showed them the Gemini North study and explained its implications. "The chief was enraged by the report. The people recalled that Pat Carney had been there once, for a day or so, but they'd never seen the study. It became clear to them just how much they'd have to do to challenge the application."

From that time on, Jackson began to learn about the importance of the land to the people. But the most important thing he learned and passed on to Berger was the way in which decisions were made. The government usually flew in to "have a meeting" at which they told villagers how things would be, and then flew out again, without having spent a night under a native's roof. When Jackson was finally allowed to attend band council meetings, he saw that native people preferred to move towards a community consensus in very subtle ways.

Berger, meanwhile, was tapping into the Pipeline Application Assessment Group's know-how by seconding them to his commission. These public servants had spent eight months reviewing 15,000 pages of technical information filed by Arctic Gas. He also had at his disposal the Environmental Protection Board's lengthy independent report that criticized the plan as unacceptable. This was extraordinary because the $3.5 million study had been entirely funded by the oil and gas industry, which had not attempted to interfere with the work of the EPB or with its final report.

In addition to these studies, the Government of Canada had funded a multitude of research projects over the years, and Berger ruled that an itemized list of all these reports and a bibliography be drawn up and made available to all participants, despite government resistance, both overt and covert. He pointed out that recent government and industry studies had cost in the neighbourhood of $65 million and, in addition, government-funded universities had been researching northern problems and conditions for a long time. "Now, it is no good to let all these studies and reports just sit on shelves," he said reasonably. Who could argue with that?

The next step was to acquire government funding for intervenors, or public interest groups. As Berger said, "they don't represent the public interest in general, they represent special interests which the public believes ought to be considered before a decision is made. . . . The pipeline companies will not take it amiss if I say that I do not want to rely upon them to represent the environment totally." A dozen environmental groups wanted to participate in the inquiry. He chose to rely on Canadian Arctic Resources Committee (CARC), an Ottawa-based nonprofit environmental group, and asked them to establish a steering committee that could represent the environmentalists' interests under one budget. Although this umbrella concept is often used today, it was a pioneering step then, for the first time allowing smaller voices to be heard through a professional, well-organized approach.

These divergent interests would have their day at the formal hearings in Yellowknife, but Berger feared that the inquiry, being as dependent as it was on experts, might become a "private, clubby kind of proceeding." He wanted to know what ordinary people were thinking. What worries or misunderstandings did they have about the big scheme? What was their northern life like? How had it been changed by advancing technology, and how did they want to live in the future?

To find answers to these questions, Berger entered the second or fact-finding stage of commission work by taking the inquiry to thirty-five communities where he heard from more than a thousand witnesses who spoke not only in English but in Loucheux, Slavey, Dogrib, Chipewyan and Inuktituk. They did not, Berger was pleased to note, offer him "thoughts filtered through a screen of jargon." It became an "inquiry without walls." This phase of the inquiry captivated the nation and made Berger famous.

Hearings were attended by the press, radio, television and even the National Film Board. Journalist Allan Fotheringham admired the technique of Berger's staff: "They cajoled the press with one hand and held the federal government at bay with the other."

The most vital and innovative coverage was the work of CBC radio's Northern Service, which served the North as it never had before, broadcasting highlights of the day's testimony in English, four Indian languages and Inuktituk. There were also daily television programs in all of these languages.

The proceedings of the inquiry were a spontaneous media event, a daily unfolding of a human-interest saga, a teach-in that engrossed people in every part of Canada and began to involve them in the decision-making process. One question persisted: Should the character of the North be determined by the South?

By 1975 the pipeline issue was becoming something much larger, more elemental and philosophical, and in July of that year, Don Gamble tried desperately to alert DIAND to the turn the inquiry was taking. He told people in the ministry that:

> It is possible that a recommendation could be forthcoming stating that no pipeline be built until the land claims issue is resolved. . . . The EPB and CARC have also backed the native view. . . . The argument that land claims recommendations, direct or indirect, are beyond the Judge's terms of reference is now academic and wishful thinking. It is my opinion that we are overstepping ourselves somewhat when we dwell on details of the pipeline application and implementation without first ensuring that the land claims issue is being actively pursued as first priority for the construction of a pipeline.

But the Ottawa mind-set was not receptive to this, and Gamble realized that his efforts were being wasted. He sincerely believed in what Berger often said about the government wanting "the views, attitudes and opinion of Northern people to be fully exposed," but it seemed to Gamble that his supervisors did not agree. "I was frustrated and angry, ashamed that taxpayers were supporting it all . . . I couldn't carry on."

Disillusioned, Gamble left DIAND and joined the commission. From the beginning, Gamble had been intrigued by Berger's total dedication to the notion of taking the time to do everything right, despite the relentless pressures to wind up the commission quickly. "Tom is very unbureaucratic—sometimes to a fault, but it's also his great strength because he just will not get immersed in the kind of paperwork dipsy-doodle that goes on . . . but I had no idea that he would go so far."

Berger often referred to the North in the words of his friend F. R. Scott, the noted lawyer who was also a socialist, philosopher and poet:

> An arena
>   Large as Europe
>   Silent
>   Waiting the contest.

"Well, the contest has begun," announced Berger. "It is our responsibility to make sure the native people are not the losers."

In addition to the inquiry, there was another contest in progress. Energy analyst and author François Bregha notes that during the course of the inquiry, the commission occasionally faced the "thinly-disguised hostility of the government that created it," a hostility that stemmed from the government's intention that Berger's role was to identify conditions under which the pipeline should be built, not to conclude whether or not it should be.

Deputy Prime Minister Mitchell Sharp said in the House of Commons that cabinet favoured quick approval of Arctic Gas's application and, he admitted, was prepared to give it the nod prior to receiving Berger's recommendation. Energy Minister Donald MacDonald and other prominent Liberals also spoke openly of the government's pro-Arctic Gas stance, and Judd Buchanan, who had replaced Jean Chrétien as DIAND minister, announced that the "connecting lines to the main pipeline are not to be considered part of the Judge's hearings."

Buchanan's statements, suggesting as they did that the land claim issue could be circumvented through this interpretation of the terms of reference, caused an uproar. The Committee for Original People's Entitlement and the Inuit Tapirisat of Canada sent a telegram of protest to the prime minister, and support for the position of the native people came from citizens across the country.

As the clamour over conflicting government statements increased, Berger felt compelled to preserve the integrity of the hearings and went to Ottawa where he had a chat with Prime Minister Trudeau over lunch. Trudeau told him that he was well aware of his record when he appointed him. "In fact," he said, "I chose you because I wanted someone who wasn't a patsy."

In turn, Berger told him about the wonders he had seen in the North, about the thunder of the Porcupine caribou herd, about the snow geese and the white whales calving in the warm summer waters of the Mackenzie Delta. Trudeau was fascinated and perhaps a little envious, for he, too, had a sense of and love for the North; in 1955, he had canoed the Mackenzie River to the Beaufort Sea with the man both he and Berger admired, F. R. Scott.

Scott wrote a poem about that trip, in which he described a figure standing stripped and white in the rapids:

> Leaning south up the current
> To stem the downward rush,
> A man testing his strength
> Against the strength of his country.

"That was me!" Trudeau confided.

Following this meeting, public grumbling by Liberals about the length and breadth of the Mackenzie inquiry ceased.

By this time another company, Foothills Pipe Lines Limited, had finally entered the game with their application. Foothills was a partnership of western utility companies under Chief Executive Officer Bob Blair, a man whom journalists called "a colourful nationalist." After several false starts, Foothills put forward their Alcan proposal, so named because their pipeline would roughly follow the Alaska Highway through the Yukon and northern British Columbia.

Berger invited Blair and Vern Horte of Arctic Gas to join the inquiry's community hearings. Blair accepted and was greeted in Fort Good Hope by Chief Frank T'Seleie who, in a much-quoted

incident, called him a "20th-century General Custer." But Blair
also had the ability to listen, and he soon admitted that while he
did not foresee violence if the pipeline were to be jammed down
the throats of the native people, sabotage was possible.

As the hearings continued, the inquiry and the native people developed what Bregha termed a symbiotic relationship. Berger
needed to learn from the natives of the North and, "To the Dene
and the Inuit, Berger represented perhaps the last chance to gain
some measure of control over their future."

This was precisely what Jean Chrétien had hoped they could
achieve. But he maintained then, as he does now, that the pipeline
itself was the "bargaining chip" that would propel native people
into a position of control over their social and economic future.
The pipeline right of way was slated to pass over Crown land in
which, in Chrétien's view, the native people might have had an
interest, similar to a mortgage interest, but which they did not
own in the proprietary sense of the term. When Chrétien was the
DIAND minister he was briefed by his staff that Berger,

> whilst recognizing the law of (Canada's) sovereignty as basic to
> native or aboriginal rights, appears to recognize the possibility of
> native ownership of lands within the law of sovereignty in the same
> way as other Canadians own land. Whilst other Canadians have ac-
> quired title to lands from the Crown, the native groups have not
> done so through failure of the Crown to recognize their entitle-
> ment. . . . This difference in view becomes important in light of
> . . . the Pipeline Guidelines which state "Where the construction,
> operation or abandonment of a pipeline results in loss or damage to
> the undertaking or property of Territorial residents—and native
> people in particular—then the Applicant shall deal promptly and
> equitably with all reasonable claims." We interpret this to be rele-
> vant to traplines, cabins, etc. whereas we believe Justice Berger may
> be regarding it as having much wider application to include lands in
> which native groups have an interest.

There was an obvious collision between the DIAND position that
cabins and traplines were at stake, and Berger's view that ownership of vast tracts of land was at issue. For northern natives, the
DIAND position was too narrow, and for bureaucrats, Berger's was
far too wide. He drew the ire of technocrats when he said publicly
that he was going to the people "because there is as much wisdom

in Old Crow as there is in Ottawa." As he had expected, the formal hearings were dominated by experts, whose testimony was essential, but it was the insight of northerners that brought to light many technical shortcomings in the Arctic Gas plan. The two most serious problems were refrigerated gas and snow roads, because the climate and terrain of the pipeline route varies drastically and the permafrost is discontinuous. Unless the gas was refrigerated, heat from the parts of the line buried in permafrost would turn the soil to rivers of mud; but where the refrigerated pipeline ran through soil that was not frozen, it would surround itself with a frost bulb that could cause frost heaves capable of rupturing the line. The industry planned to cope with frost heave by piling dirt and gravel on top of the pipeline—a primitive solution for people who prided themselves on their sophisticated technology. Eventually, Arctic Gas admitted it had miscalculated the height of the berm, or mound, required to control the heave. A veritable mountain of gravel would be needed in a land where there was not even gravel enough to build access roads, a fact that was part of the second problem. With no gravel available, service roads over the ice to the pipeline would have to be built of snow, but it was uncertain that such roads could be built as planned. Neither the snow road nor the frost heave problems were ever satisfactorily resolved.

Journalists labelled the inquiry process which elicited so much information a "cultural catharsis," as it changed the North by means of what journalist Martin O'Malley described as a "strange alchemy and internal logic." Fotheringham and other journalists called Berger the "therapist of the north," and Suzanne Zwarun wrote in *Maclean's* on 25 July 1977 that Berger was "a tundra-striding Solomon, adjudicating between cruel technological forces and harassed native people on Canada's last frontier."

"People feel uncomfortable at some of the things that are said at these hearings," Berger remarked. "Native people speak their minds quite openly and others don't like what they say. But my only client is truth."

Truth came in mysterious ways as Berger's entourage wound through the North. In Hay River, Fort Franklin, Fort Norman and in every settlement, people came out of the bush, in from the traplines and down rivers to tell Berger about broken promises and lost faith.

It was in Old Crow that eleven-year-old Harvey Kassie gave his statement to the judge: "I am against the pipeline. My mother's a trapper. She goes to Crow Flats every year. I go with her every spring and I would like to do the same thing when I grow up."

"Alcohol. Did we ever ask for that? How many more times and how much louder do we have to scream before we are heard? We have nowhere else to go," said Alistine Andre, the daughter of a chief. Berger heard her.

And John Goddard, writing in *Saturday Night* in April 1985, described how Berger listened to Dolphus Shae in Fort Good Hope, who told how at the age of eight he had been taken six hundred kilometres north to the mission school at Aklavik, where Indian children were threatened with beatings if they spoke in the native tongue. Despite his later mechanics training, he had struggled throughout his life to achieve "some kind of success," lost in "a sort of oblivion for people inadequately tutored in trapping life and inadequately trained for jobs in industry." And Berger remembered Dolphus when he read about his death: Dolphus Shae had been drinking heavily when he lost control of his snowmobile and was killed.

Nelson Small Legs Jr., a Blackfoot who was the 23-year-old director of the southern Alberta cell of the American Indian Movement, hinted of violence as he testified before the inquiry in Calgary: "My nation will stop this pipeline. . . . We will take up anything to defend outselves, our children, our wives, our culture, our spirits." Two days later, on 16 May 1976, Small Legs wrote a note demanding the resignation of Judd Buchanan and claiming that DIAND was incompetent and corrupt. In another note, he said, "I give my life in protest to the present conditions concerning the Indian people." Then, wearing scarlet ceremonial regalia, he performed the sacred rites of his sweat lodge, picked up his rifle and shot himself in the heart.

Months later, another witness invoked the name of Nelson Small Legs and his plea to prevent the pipeline. "I read about why he killed himself. He's showing us we should fight for ourselves even if it means death."

At Lac la Martre, Jim Green, a white man who used to wish he were Indian, told Berger: "They are thinking about their children. They are thinking about the future of the people. In this they cannot be wrong. It is not the money or oil or gas we should be thinking about. We should be thinking about our children. I am thinking about my children as I ask you, the government, the people of this country to slow down. . . . Listen to them while there is still time."

Berger was listening, and the native people knew he was. He had not come to them with an agenda, saying, "This is what we're going to talk about today." That was never his way. He kept quiet. He allowed people to say what they had on their minds, and they believed that somehow his limitless patience would prevail over political and industrial forces. For more than two years the people of the North talked, and Berger listened.

Whenever he could, Berger kept flying home to visit his family. On one of his trips home, Berger, a lifelong movie fan, took his son David to see *Little Big Man,* in which B.C. Indian chief Dan George had a major role. Authorship was credited to the well-known American writer Thomas Berger. "Gee, Dad," David whispered, "I didn't know you did that, too." Bev Berger came to the North from time to time, and David and Erin each came for separate visits to travel with their father. Still, they all felt the time and distance between them.

Although Tom Berger's inquiry travels separated him from family, friends and Vancouver, and he missed them terribly, the wide landscape and the people of the North gave him what many people never achieve. He became comfortable with who he is. Never a chatty man and never glib, he has been accused of being a cold fish. Even Essa Horswill, his secretary for a decade, found it a strain to pass hours in the office or an entire meal together without Tom saying a word. "If he was thinking about a case, that's what he did and it didn't occur to him that his silence hurt his companion. When he realized that other people found it unnerving, he tried to improve, but that was his way." In the North, however, he encountered people of his ilk—not just one or two, but entire communities of people who were content to sit together and think or to just enjoy the day without feeling compelled to make small talk. For Tom it was a revelation and a relief.

The Indians' refutation to the Gemini North report on country food use came serendipitously with the arrival of Scott Rushforth, who had come from New Mexico to study the relevance of housing arrangements among aboriginal people for his Ph.D. thesis in anthropology. Instead, Rushforth turned to field work that confirmed country food use was twenty times greater than the Gemini North estimate, and the report he made on this fulfilled his thesis requirement.

There were numerous submissions in favour of the pipeline project, of course, and at every hearing the industry applicants had the opportunity to answer the opposition. Oilmen were fond of using one vivid description of the impact of the pipeline on the North, likening it to running a thread across a football field. To this, George Manuel of the National Indian Brotherhood said, "Well, if that is right, then the aboriginal rights of the Indian people are like a football being kicked around by the same oil companies and politicians. Perhaps we Indians need to pick up the ball and simply go home." Environmentalists also turned the analogy against the pipeline, saying it would be more like a razor slash across the Mona Lisa.

A final brief that best presented the pro-development position was given by energy lawyer and author John Bishop Ballem, counsel for Gulf Oil Canada, Imperial Oil and Shell Canada. His submission built lucidly and logically to a rejection of the notion that construction of the pipeline prior to settlement of the land claims could prejudice them. That was a power play tactic, Ballem said, which if accepted might influence the government to settle at any cost. In his opinion, it was at odds with the concept of Canada as one nation and with what native groups desired. The pipeline and spin-offs from it would bring greater economic independence and higher living standards, and these benefits would outweigh any negative impact, or at worst, merely "accelerate a process that is already underway and already accelerating. . . . Social dynamics are at work and the natives' cause cannot be well served by ignoring these trends."

Through all of this, journalists tried to explain Berger. On 3 July 1976 Peter Gzowski wrote in *The Canadian* magazine that Berger "is one of the great Canadians of our time" and that the Mackenzie Inquiry is in the hands of "a man of fathomless integrity who . . . refuses to be badgered or shaken . . . and who has guts, wisdom and charm." Another reporter saw Berger as a "new Sergeant Preston to guard the true north strong and free." He was called a "morose beagle of a man," "a symbol of perhaps an intolerable burden of hope," and was compared to his friend, U.S. consumer advocate Ralph Nader.

In Alberta, where even God was known to be on the side of energy resource development, journalist J. P. O'Callaghan of the Edmonton *Journal* wrote on 20 May 1976 of his belief in the energy crisis to the extent that "our civilization is in peril. Our way of life is in doubt." But he also looked thoughtfully at the expectations placed on Berger: "Canada is in the throes of an apparently irreconcilable dilemma, but Mr. Justice Berger, from the vast loneliness of his own conscience and intellect, has to come up with a recommendation of one sort or another that might well decide for centuries how we are to live. . . . Whatever he recommends will earn the opprobrium of a great number of his fellow Canadians. He just cannot win."

By the time the inquiry had toured the rest of Canada, receiving four hundred briefs from individuals and groups in ten cities from Vancouver to Charlottetown, the process had succeeded in eliciting the consensus of the nation. Canadians had serious reservations about the pipeline project. Public opinion and circumstances were changing, and cabinet ministers, sensing a shift, were backing away from wholehearted support of the scheme. On 17 April 1977, Minister of Fisheries and Environment Canada Romeo LeBlanc, in a lengthy and thoughtful confidential letter to his prime minister on the pending northern gas pipeline decision, wrote:

The complex intermixture of energy needs, northern development, major capital investment (foreign and Canadian), environmental impact and native claims is rendered even more difficult and delicate by the critical importance of the subject to Canadian-U.S. relations and the deadline in decision-making facing President Carter . . .

I find myself disturbed by the prospect that the Government could find itself in a position where there seemed really to be no alternatives but to accept the Arctic Gas proposal.

I must inform you that, from the point of view of this Department, I have grave doubts about any Mackenzie Valley route, especially one with a Northern Yukon link. It is far more susceptible to environmental damage than a route along the Alaska Highway to northern British Columbia.

Even earlier than this, and unbeknownst to the public or the commission, DIAND staff had drafted an interim report on the background and status of native claims in the Yukon and Northwest Territories, the implications of making pipeline decisions, and the socioeconomic impact of northern pipelines on native people and northern regions. The report concluded that "in the absence of a clear national interest, any northern pipeline through undeveloped regions of the north is clearly indefensible in terms of the interests of the region because of the social problems it would create."

These concerns were echoing what Berger had all along been saying: "If Canada can't take time to make an informed decision about what is going to happen to our northland, then what has Canada got time for?"

On 15 October 1976, after 283 days of testimony, 1700 witnesses and over 40,000 pages of transcripts, the hearings concluded. The final phase of commission work, that of making decisions, was underway. For Berger's report to have the greatest efficacy, he and his commission team thought it should be submitted prior to the report of the National Energy Board, whose mandatory hearings had been taking place simultaneously. Ian Scott recalls the reason for the race with the NEB. "If there were two reports going two different ways, both of them would be wasted. Our game plan was to do a credible job on native rights, native people, environmental stuff and social issues. So if we got our report out in time, we thought the NEB might simply adopt it because they wouldn't be able to match it effectively or attack it. It was essential to get the NEB on our side so that if the two reports were essentially negative, then the pipeline would not go ahead."

Berger went home to Vancouver to crystallize his thoughts in a more comfortable environment and worked there alone with only the help of secretary Val Chapman. Then he rejoined his staff in the commission's Ottawa office and kept them working from November 1976 to May 1977, compiling evidence and brainstorming to render complex issues into language that everyone, including high school students and politicians, could easily grasp. Until Berger offered them the first draft of his recommendations, no member of the inquiry had any idea what he was planning to say. All those reports, the testimony, data and controversy, he boiled down to eight points:

1. No pipeline for the northern Yukon.
2. Creation of a national wilderness park in the northern Yukon to protect the Porcupine caribou herd.
3. Establishment of a whale sanctuary in Mackenzie Bay.
4. No pipeline along the Mackenzie Valley for ten years.
5. Settle native land claims in the Mackenzie Valley.

6. Development of the northern economy with the emphasis on renewable resources.
7. Preservation of native culture.
8. Bird sanctuaries in the Mackenzie Valley.

Berger gave his staff members the Table of Contents and asked for ideas, but they, unaware of the changing attitude in Ottawa, were stunned. Although from the start Berger had said "there are going to have to be some very hard choices made here," his staff had never expected him to go so far. Initially, and officially still, the momentum for a go-ahead on the pipeline had been so great that to the staff, acceptance of any of these propositions seemed improbable. His points were not antidevelopment; rather, they favoured rational, orderly development and stood for the responsibility to do it right.

As the work went on and as the staff neared completion of volume one of the report, the full implication of saying, "No pipeline now, and no pipeline across the northern Yukon ever," sank in. Staff consensus was that there should be another chapter to volume one. It should say, they decided, "If you decide to build a pipeline anyway, here are the minimum conditions for its construction."

The staff thought as they did because they had seen the trust of the people who had offered their testimony to the commission. Small acts of faith had been repeated over and over again as witnesses shared their thoughts, fears and experiences with Berger, opening up in a way that was without precedent. The staff thought that Berger could meet his obligation to these people only by writing an additional chapter, one that would specify terms and conditions if the "ideal world" recommendations were not met. Convinced of the logic of their argument, they tried to persuade him.

They were not successful.

Finally, Don Gamble says, they put it to him straight, pressing as hard as they dared. They were impassioned and had even drafted a version of the extra chapter while Berger was out playing tennis. When he returned, he tried tenaciously to brush off their demand. He strode around the room swinging his tennis racquet, saying, "No. Damn it, no. That's not what the people said. That's not what the evidence indicates. If we betray the people that way—if we give the politicians an out—they'll take it! I don't want them to do it on my recommendation. They'll have to do it on their own."

His staff returned to work. They all wrote hundreds of pages and Berger took the verbiage they thought was wonderful and went through it paragraph by paragraph, saying, "This doesn't fit. This does." In the end, all of the words were Berger's, but to reach that point all the members of his team worked together seven days a week for months. It was exhausting, exhilarating and intellectually challenging.

This group engendered an esprit de corps of such confidence and cohesiveness that there were absolutely no leaks, though the pressures in gossip-laced Ottawa were enormous. They were all certain that to some extent, at least, success depended upon a well-polished report being published at precisely the right time. The turbulence of the times was reflected in the fact that the report would be submitted to yet another new DIAND minister, Warren Allmand.

Northern Homeland, Northern Frontier, the first of the two-volume Report of the Mackenzie Valley Pipeline Inquiry, was released on 9 May 1977 at three o'clock when Allmand tabled it in the House of Commons.

Gamble had been despatched to Yellowknife with a box of reports, and he was so fearful about a foul-up that he booked a seat for them at his side rather than entrust them to baggage handlers. Other staffers were posted around the country to release the report as soon as Ottawa had the news.

Northern Homeland, Northern Frontier was a blockbuster from the start. Sensitively illustrated with photographs depicting the aching beauty of the North and its people, it was written in what Peter McCreath, in his book *Learning from the North: A Guide to the Berger Report,* called "a prose that flows as steadily as the Mackenzie itself. . . . The most definitive study of Canada's North." Journalist Martin O'Malley, who had been following and reporting on the inquiry, also wrote a book on the experience, *The Past and Future Land.*

Berger's report became the best-selling document ever published by the Canadian government. It was used across the country as a textbook and reference in high school, college and university classes in social studies, history, geography, political science and environmental studies. The report so distinctively bore the stamp of a pro-Native, pro-conservation, pro-environment philosophy that it killed any remaining chance that Tom Berger would ever be appointed to the Supreme Court of Canada or even to the British Columbia Court of Appeal. He had remained his own man throughout the course of the inquiry and could never again be a low-profile judge.

Politics, it is often said, is the allocation of resources: that is, who gets what, where and when. In this sense, the government had sat back and allowed Berger to politicize himself and northern issues because it was expedient for them to do so.

Some people argue to this day that the testimony of native people was skewed, that Berger only heard from people who had been persuaded to express opposition to the pipeline. Critics of the report say that upon hearing the inquiry's recommendations, certain native leaders were overheard to exclaim, "Oh, oh. Looks like we overdid it," but in each instance the person to whom these words were attributed has emphatically denied speaking them.

Jean Chrétien believes that matters did go awry. "All the hoopla, all the publicity, made it the popular thing not to build the pipeline. But the end result was negative for the Indians." Chrétien smiles sadly. "My point is this: Berger took away their bargaining chip. As long as they threatened to stop the pipeline, it was good. . . . I had already decided to negotiate these treaties in the Northwest Territories because there had been no selection of land by the Indians at that time. . . . It is very difficult for Indians to sign any agreement and I don't blame them. They remember their grandfathers signed treaties . . . so it's difficult to take the giant step because they know if they do, they take a hell of a responsibility on their shoulders and they have to live with it for generations to come."

The way Chrétien sees it, the Indians were a lobby group with speech bigger than their ambitions. "I warned Berger about it . . . but he got carried away with being a lawyer and a judge. He took it at face value each time an Indian would come to him and say, 'I am opposed.' And when they heard the report, they were shocked. They called me here in Ottawa and said, 'Everyone is leaving the village. Because there is no pipeline.' "

Berger responds to this version of the aftermath of his work with unshakable faith in what he heard and saw. Witnesses offered their testimony, and he called it truth.

Chrétien swivels slowly in his chair, his ambivalence apparent as he talks himself into taking the blame, and at the next turn, the credit. "Yes. I wanted someone from the west because it was the northwest and someone who knew Indians and I wanted a judge. But I told him what his mandate was to be. He listened to me and then he came back to me and says, 'I have to live with the evidence.' " Chrétien throws his hands high.

Yes. Tom Berger has to live with it.

"No doubt in our own time and in our own way," Berger said, "we *can* build a pipeline down the Mackenzie, and it can be built in an environmentally sensible way, but it can't be done now. That's not the issue now. More compelling is the need to put in place things which will allow it to happen."

The impact of Berger's report was so strong and it was so favourably received that, according to analyst Bregha, Arctic Gas realized that only an "unequivocal endorsement" from the National Energy Board could save the pipeline, and with cabinet support openly waning, even that might not be enough. In Bregha's opinion, "The Berger report cooled considerably the government's ardour for a Mackenzie pipeline." Nonetheless, it was the NEB, the official regulatory agency, that had the power to choose which, if any, pipeline should be built. The NEB report would deal with government and corporate participation in a natural gas pipeline; it would look at routes, transportation charges, costs, social and economic impacts, and environmental matters. When that report came down in July, two months after Berger's report, it recommended that the Arctic Gas proposal, on which the consortium had spent five years and $150 million, be rejected, and that preference be given to Bob Blair's Foothills Pipe Lines. Arctic Gas was devastated.

In due course, the government announced that *if* a pipeline were to be built, it would be along the Alcan route through the southern Yukon and northern British Columbia.

The NEB report vindicated Berger and complemented *Northern Homeland, Northern Frontier*. "People forget that it wasn't I who killed the Arctic Gas proposal," says Berger. "The National Energy Board said no. The NEB had a legal obligation to make the decision, and it was the Government of Canada that legislated the ultimate approval for the Alcan route."

Although confidential memoranda, documents and correspondence circulating in DIAND offices show that politicians and bureaucrats were monitoring Berger's popularity and the success of his report with an uneasy, sceptical eye, officially Tom Berger was the government's darling. On the other hand, by innuendo at least, Ottawa often blamed him for the death of a megaproject which, it was suggested, would have brought prosperity to the North. The fundamental criticism about Berger and the pipeline inquiry is that he did his job too well; he followed his terms of reference and did his work so thoroughly that many, many voices were heard. Perhaps Don Gamble is right. A man like Berger is dangerous because he insists people think for themselves; he wants them to think carefully and to stand up and say what they think. And he will listen.

For the benefits that came out of the inquiry and the report, Berger gives credit to the native people, though he admits that the way he planned the hearings helped them to make their voices heard. He is as certain now about the importance of that as he was then. He does not seek to "turn back the clock, to return in some way to nature or even to deplore, in a high-minded and sentimental manner, the real achievements of the industrial system." As he sees it, he was simply clarifying the northern situation so that Canadians, all Canadians, would be better equipped to choose what kind of country it would be.

"And," he warns, "it isn't an easy choice."

Only a year and a half after the completion of the Report of the Mackenzie Valley Pipeline Inquiry, Tom Berger, who had resumed his full bench duties, was again summoned by the government. This time it was the Honourable David Crombie, minister of National Health and Welfare for the Progressive Conservative government under the brief prime ministership of Joe Clark, who called upon him to undertake yet another commission of inquiry.

One of Berger's friends on the bench, Mr. Justice J. C. Bouck, expresses an opinion he says is shared by many of his brother judges. "There is nothing that obligates judges to accept a commission," he says. "And if a judge does one, he should have nothing to say about that work, once his report is done." The latter comment is in reference to Berger's frequent speaking engagements at which he talked about family law, native and environmental issues.

Nevertheless, when Berger received Crombie's request, he did not consider refusing because the subject was too dear to his heart and was a topic with which he had become well acquainted during his earlier work: Indian and Inuit health. Their health was so substandard to that of other Canadians as to be a crisis. Consequently,

Crombie couched the words of the assignment in advisory terms, an approach that moved it a step away from the investigative mode. This enabled Berger to act quickly and to rely upon existing material, knowledge and his own contacts in drawing up a plan of action and outlining methods of consultation that would ensure substantial participation by the Indians and Inuit themselves. Not only was Berger well informed about the topic before he began, he knew how to attract the participation of people who were affected.

Two months later, the Tory government toppled and Crombie suffered a heart attack. As Crombie and his staff attended to the sad task of cleaning out his office, Berger delivered to them his report. In it he expressed appreciation for the help received from the government, reviewed information gleaned from people whom he had consulted and made uncompromising recommendations, which were moral and practical:

> Consultation about the ways in which Indian people and Indian communities are to participate in planning, budgeting and delivering health programs cannot be severed from the participation in the actual planning, budgeting and delivery of these programs. The shape of the institutions which will be created to implement the new Indian Health Policy, will emerge from the consultations.

He went on to recommend that the management of the consultation process and the consultation funds be in the hands of the Indian people, and he made slightly different recommendations to meet the particular needs of the Inuit. As well, he advocated a federally sponsored native health conference, so that people could exchange ideas, problems and information. All of his recommendations, he said, were founded on the principles of the new Indian Health Policy that the federal government had adopted a few months before. It was an unassailable approach in which he praised the government for the far-reaching implications of that policy, which had the potential to ameliorate the underlying causes of Indian ill health in Canada.

On 30 November 1983, after three years of planning prompted by Berger's recommendations, delegates to the National Conference on Native Health packed the Hamilton Convention Centre in Ontario. The bleak statistics were much as they had been—Indian babies twice as likely as white infants to die before their first birthday, and young adults dying at two to four times the national average—but the mood was one of hope. "Dream a little," Roberta Jamieson, a prominent Ontario Indian lawyer, told the delegates from across the country. "Move on and create, for we owe nothing less to our children." She and other delegates agreed with Berger that the only route to a better life is self-government and native control of their own institutions.

In 1985 events came full circle as the Nishga Tribal Council, acting on Berger's recommendations, hired their first native health co-ordinator and moved into the first stages of native health autonomy.

Berger is, of course, pleased with the results of his work on commissions. Commissions have allowed him to accomplish what is often denied lawyers and politicians and judges—major changes to the social order. This happens, he says, partly because the "inquiry process itself creates receptive audiences which are themselves conducive to implementation of the recommendations."

Tom Berger proved himself to be a harbinger when in delivering the Corry Lecture at Queen's University on 25 November 1975 he said: "We know that Royal Commissions and Public Inquiries have brought new ideas into the public consciousness. They have expanded the vocabulary of politics, education and social science. They have added to the furniture that we now expect to find in Canada's storefront of ideas."

Commissions of inquiry were Berger's niche, his natural forum, and they enabled him to make his greatest contributions to society by offering a landscape broad enough for the scope of his vision.

CHAPTER 8

The Dissenter

The scope of Tom Berger's vision is broad. He not only admires but emulates F. R. Scott's protection of the rights of dissenters and has also been a vociferous opponent of injustice. After becoming a judge he remained a passionate civil libertarian, but one who functioned within an odd dichotomy—a dissenter obligated by his oath of office to uphold the laws of the land, be they ever so unjust or born of policies in conflict with his own deeply held philosophy.

A lover of books since boyhood, Berger calls himself an "omnivorous reader. I read the back of cereal boxes if there's nothing else around." The saving grace of his judicial position was that he was stimulated to read more and to look back in time for an understanding of contemporary problems. One day a friend browsing in a used book store found an old volume that he gave to Berger, saying: "You'll be interested in this. It's about a guy who was a lot like you."

The guy was Bartoleme de Las Casas, a conquistador who had accompanied Christopher Columbus on his fourth voyage to the New World, where the Spanish subjugated the Indians in the name of Jesus and forced them to work on their estates. Las Casas had his own enslaved Indians, but in time he began to question the right of the Spanish to take the land and to dominate the native people. He became a priest and made numerous trips home to Spain to implore King Charles V to bring an end to the forced labour of the Indians. Through the efforts of Las Casas, a great debate was held in 1550 in which a junta of learned men—lawyers, judges and philosophers—approached the question. In format and intent this was remarkably similar to a royal commission. One point of view was that as some men are superior, they have a divine mission to bring Indians to Jesus and to teach them to be manufacturers "for their own good," whereas Las Casas maintained that as all people of the world are human, none can be inferior. The debate was never settled, and the Spanish thought, as did other conquering peoples, that the original occupants of the new land would die or assimilate or otherwise cease to present a moral issue. When Berger mentions this still familiar theme there is a twinkle in his eye.

Las Casas was a pioneer in urging human rights and fundamental freedoms, and he captured Berger's imagination. Berger still harbours a dream of acquiring enough knowledge about Las Casas to write a book about him.

Now, nearly five hundred years after Las Casas took up the cause of native people in the New World, there is still pioneering in the law to be done. Tom Berger is carrying on Las Casas's message of the right to freedom, not just on behalf of Canadian aboriginal people but all people whose liberties have been lost or jeopardized. He carries on the message in the courts, in public forums, by teaching and through the written word. Instead of following his desire to chronicle the life and work of Las Casas, he turned his efforts to educating Canadians about freedom in Canada by writing a book he called *Fragile Freedoms: Human Rights and Dissent in Canada,* published in 1981. The book was but one way Mr. Justice Berger could reach beyond the limits of the bench. There was another, for the content of *Fragile Freedoms* had its origins in lectures Berger had been conducting in the Faculty of Law at the University of British Columbia and in the Canadian Studies program at Simon Fraser University. The book was soon published in paperback, and eventually a French translation by Marie-Cecile Brasseur, *Liberté fragile,* was published in Quebec.

Berger chose the words of F. R. Scott for the epigraph in *Fragile Freedoms:* "If human rights and harmonious relations between cultures are forms of the beautiful, then the state is a work of art that is never finished."

In his introduction, Berger writes:

> Freedom is a fragile commodity in the world today. Everywhere human rights are beset by ideology and orthodoxy, diversity is rejected, and dissent stifled . . .
>
> Canadian history has not been free of these injustices, although there is no reason to flagellate ourselves. We respect human rights and the rule of law. An intellectual tradition founded on the advantages of free inquiry and a long experience of the institutions of liberal democracy have equipped us to learn from our history. Canadians have, however, no justification for being smug. Sometimes we have upheld human rights, but sometimes we have succumbed to the temptations of intolerance. Sometimes we have listened to the voices of protest; at other times we have tried to stifle them. By examining our history, we can understand better what kind of world must be created to foster human rights and fundamental freedoms.

This was his reason for writing the book, but he knew that he would be criticized for it and that some people would ask why we should be reminded of these dark passages in the Canadian journey, that our only obligation, as President John F. Kennedy said, is to be just in our own time.

"But to be just in our own time requires an understanding of earlier times," argued Berger. "The world was not invented this morning, and we cannot comprehend what measures will supply justice in our own time unless we understand the history of times past."

The book, which is a walk through eight episodes in Canada's history, illustrates the different ways in which freedom has been denied to citizens of Canada. Berger starts with the eighteenth-century expulsion by the British of perhaps 8,000 Acadians from Nova Scotia, and moves on to the persecution of Louis Riel and the Métis during John A. Macdonald's time and of the Japanese Canadians in Mackenzie King's. He recreates the struggle for separate schools under Wilfrid Laurier and the struggle for recognition of aboriginal rights by the Nishga Indians. There is the now almost-forgotten animosity once shown to Jehovah's Witnesses in Quebec, and the hostility of the country towards the

Communist Party. When *Fragile Freedoms* was reviewed, Berger's tolerance of the Communist Party and his position on the FLQ crisis provoked the most response. Some critics said that he had gone too far, that some rights did not deserve protection. With respect to the former, he wrote:

> Ought we to concede freedom of speech to those who would deny that freedom to the rest of us, if they could?
>
> Communism is an internal challenge . . . to our attitudes, our institutions and to our ideas about the limits of dissent.
>
> The ways in which Canadian institutions—our Parliaments and police, our courts and lawyers, our industrial tribunals and trade unions—have dealt with the Communist Party show how far we have been prepared to accept, and to act on our professed belief in a free marketplace of ideas. In tracing the relations between our institutions and the Communist Party, we can learn something about the vital difference between autocracy and freedom, and between sedition and dissent.

Firm in his belief that Canadians should meet that internal challenge and meet it boldly, Berger asks, "How can we criticize the Soviet authorities for their refusal to allow dissent if we cannot abide dissent ourselves?"

A. Alan Borovoy has been a critic of Berger's position on this issue. In the April 1982 issue of *Canadian Forum,* Borovoy, then general counsel of the Canadian Civil Liberties Association, accused Berger of substituting faith for fact. He took issue with Berger's statement in *Fragile Freedoms* that: "It comes down to a question of evidence or of labels. If we say that simply joining the Communist Party is evidence of disloyalty to Canada, to the government, to a trade union, to a profession, or to a university, then we shall be told that for any citizen to join any group labelled extremist (whether of the left or right) disqualifies him or her from the ordinary rights of citizenship."

To this Borovoy asked whether "membership in the Communist Party couldn't be considered some evidence of less than requisite loyalty to such institutions . . . suffice at least to raise the issue of a person's eligibility for certain types of government employment."

Berger responded in the July issue, rejecting the idea that inferences can be drawn from any person's political affiliations.

"It seems to me that this is the hard choice that has to be made. Once you acknowledge that membership in a political organization constitutes some evidence of disloyalty, it raises all kinds of questions: is this an inference to be drawn against all Communists, no matter that they profess loyalty to their uniform, their university, their government?" This kind of reasoning, he said, had led to the Red hysteria of earlier decades, harming communists, noncommunists, and even anticommunists. "Once you admit that people are to be judged not by their overt acts, but by what they believe (or by what somebody says they believe or must be taken to believe), you get into this kind of trouble."

The debate continued with a rebuttal from Borovoy in the August issue, in which he remained adamant that an inference could be drawn from membership alone. "The inference need not be conclusive; it might merely be presumptive," he contended, reminding Berger of the commonly held belief that failure to face "the problem of communist-inspired espionage in the 1930s fostered later Red Scare repressions."

"Without the right to propagate error," Berger retorted, "there cannot be true freedom of speech, no real exchange of ideas. It is not the function of government to keep citizens from falling into error. Those chosen to watch over national security, whether they be members of the RCMP or of a civilian agency, should bear this constantly in mind."

Berger maintained that this principle had been articulated in his account in *Fragile Freedoms* about the Montreal newspaper *Le Devoir*'s response to the *Switzman* v. *Elbing* case challenging Quebec's "Padlock Act." That act, which had allowed government officials to padlock premises they suspected housed communist or revolutionary materials, was set aside by the Supreme Court of Canada in the *Switzman* case. The influential *Le Devoir* asked if "defence of freedom must go so far as to defend and to respect an alleged right to propagate error." Berger still maintains that it does because of the danger that "labels pasted on those on either side may stick, and no one will notice what the combatants' beliefs really are. This may virtually disarm persons who have a right to be heard." He warns that "patience and courage are required to reject insistent demands for repressive action against political dissenters."

On the issue of the arrest and incarceration of suspected FLQ members during the October 1970 crisis in Quebec, Berger and

F. R. Scott parted ideological company: Berger opposed Prime Minister Trudeau's proclamation of the War Measures Act, and Scott supported it. "If the FLQ had constituted a treasonous conspiracy to overthrow the government by force, its members could still have been charged and proceeded against under the Criminal Code," says Berger. "Arguments for the necessity to expand police power were spurious in 1970 and they are spurious today."

That is one reason why Berger was a strong proponent of the new Canadian constitutional package, including the Charter of Rights that Pierre Trudeau was attempting to bequeath to the nation. Berger said then: "The enactment of the Charter of Rights, the symbolic value it will have for the nation, the extent to which Canadians perceive that it embodies the ideals of citizenship —all of these will be more meaningful than the pure legal effect of the Charter in securing the protection of fundamental freedoms even when the gravest cause is thought to be seen for their attenuation."

Surprisingly, before long these sentiments and the content of the proposed Canadian Charter of Rights and Freedoms clashed, thrusting Tom Berger into the role of dissenter. With no charter in place, his right to speak and write were questioned. It was not only surprising, it was sad; for the dissent of Tom Berger was born of similarities of heart and mind which he shared with the jurists he most admired.

There is a strain of liberalism in Canadian legal thinking that does not spring from or run parallel to British or American jurisprudence. It is epitomized by the ideas of F. R. Scott, Bora Laskin, Emmett Hall, Pierre Trudeau and Tom Berger. Of these five, Trudeau and Berger share a remarkably similar centralist view of Canada; not only do they have little time for petty provincial ambitions and jealousies but they see Canada merely as one country functioning in a much larger and interrelated world. As Tom Berger said to a reporter from the Trent University newspaper:

I'm skeptical of nationalism. Canada is a fortunate country. We are constantly berating ourselves for not being nationalistic. It's a good thing that we're not. It's a disease that's caused untold damage and misery in the world. We don't have any brutal ideology and we're not subject to fits of mindless patriotism and that means we can get

along with other people and that's the kind of world we're going to
have to build . . .

Flags are for the birds. Anything promoting a bogus patriotism is
a mistake. What's wrong with being a country without a flag or
anthem? There are 150 countries with flags and anthems. Where has
it got them?"

Trudeau has expressed similar views. His experience before he
entered political life persuaded him that fervid nationalism is
dangerous. As well, both men are humanists who honed their
practice and theory of politics and justice on the intellectual
whetstones of the other three.

Syndicated columnist Richard Gwyn, reflecting on a decade of
political journalism spanning the 1970s, wrote about two events
of that era in which he had seen both men, Trudeau and Berger,
striving for the same kind of Canada: a country of diversity,
cherishing the rights of both founding linguistic communities, a
Canada having no single notion of her national identity, but with
the heart to accommodate minorities. The first event embedded
deep in Gwyn's memory was:

> Being in Inuvik and Tuktoyaktuk and Aklavik and Arctic Red
> River in the spring of 1975 to watch Judge Thomas Berger listening
> to the Inuit and the Cree and the Slavey Indians describe what the
> 20th century had done to them. There wasn't much he could do for
> them, other than to delay the gas pipeline, which he did. That, and
> to listen with respect, as few other white Canadians with his kind of
> authority have done before or since. It was a magical, beautiful,
> moment.

The other occasion was Trudeau's speech in the Paul Sauvé Arena
in Montreal in the spring of 1980, at the close of the referendum
campaign. Gwyn wrote: "It was, I think, his finest hour. He
turned our history around, not so much by winning the referendum as by winning for himself a mandate from English Canada to
change our constitution in the interest of his Quebeckers."

Gwyn was right to connect the two scenes, for in both the men
were celebrating the absence of what Berger calls "the curse of a
triumphant ideology . . . and mindless xenophobia. . . . Diversity," he says, "is what freedom is all about."

Ironically, it was Berger's protection of the position of

Trudeau's Quebeckers and of Maisie's people within the context of the Charter of Rights and Freedoms that was to cast the men as adversaries and to test, once more, the limits of dissent.

Pierre Trudeau wanted to accomplish what no other prime minister of Canada had come close to doing: he wanted to bring Canada's Constitution home. The confrontation that ensued between the two men changed not only the content of the Constitution but the course of Tom Berger's career.

The British North America Act, passed in 1867 by the British parliament, united the three colonies of British North America and created the Dominion of Canada. The BNA Act forms the basis of Canada's Constitution, and from the act there has developed a body of rules, legislation, interpretations and conventions. The act made no provision for its amendment, but on the rare occasions in Canada's history when an amendment was made to the Constitution, the federal parliament obtained the consent of the provinces before requesting that the British parliament implement the change.

This was an unwieldy process, and federal-provincial conferences—at which a formula for amendment was sought—became a Canadian rite of spring. Under Trudeau as prime minister, these sessions had a new vigour. In 1971 success came tantalizingly close but failed when Quebec did not ratify the formula within the prescribed ten days. In 1976 Trudeau announced that unless an accord was reached within four years, the federal parliament would request approval of an amending formula unilaterally: that is, without the consent of the provinces. When the time came, however, the government deflected some of the responsibility for the decision by referring the question to the Supreme Court of Canada. The court was asked for an opinion on whether the Canadian parliament, without the consent of the provinces, could request that the British parliament amend the BNA Act.

While the Supreme Court was considering its decision, Berger gave his opinion in a speech entitled "Into a New Canada," delivered to the annual meeting of the Canadian Bar Association: "I favour the patriation of the new Constitution and the Charter of Rights which is an essential part of it," he said and went on to note that the word "patriation" was a misnomer; in reality, the BNA Act would be repatriated, as it had always been a Canadian document. He approved of the proposed amending formula that gave veto power to Quebec, Ontario, the West and the Atlantic provinces. Berger also lauded the package as being the "logical outcome of our history," containing as it did French-English minority language rights, as well as a special status for native people and recognition of their aboriginal and treaty rights.

Berger agreed with Trudeau that the protection of freedoms took paramountcy over the participation of the provinces in the process, and he warned that

> an attack on the periphery is as serious as an attack on the heartland. F. R. Scott has said, "No citizen's right can be greater than that of the least protected group." It is, I believe, the obligation of every citizen to see that the rights of the least protected groups are given the same protection that he himself enjoys . . .
>
> This great exercise in Constitution-making should enable us to know ourselves; to discover who we are and what we may become; to realize the advantage of diversity and dissent. This is what the Canadian experience is all about: to see if people who are different can live together and work together; to regard diversity not with suspicion, but as a cause for celebration; to enshrine Wilfrid Laurier's idea of a regime of tolerance in the life of a nation.

Berger's remarks were reported in the popular press and in legal publications, and an edited version of his speech was included in the paperback edition of *Fragile Freedoms,* published in the same month.

Others, however, widely and noisily criticized the proposal to unilaterally repatriate the Constitution, and the provinces, but for Ontario and New Brunswick, also opposed the idea.

At the end of September 1981, five months after hearing the arguments, the Supreme Court of Canada handed down its judgment: the majority held that although from a strictly legal point of view Ottawa could proceed unilaterally, convention dictated that the consent of the provinces should be obtained. As a result, and in the interest of federal-provincial harmony, discussions resumed. On 5 November 1981, the prime minister and the premiers of the provinces finally reached an accord that repudiated two key elements of the previous proposal: there would be no entrenchment of aboriginal rights and no veto for Quebec. The Canada envisioned by Berger in his Mackenzie Valley Pipeline Inquiry Report and in his address to the Canadian Bar Association

—and as promised by Trudeau during his "finest hour"—had rolled away from the station. Vanished.

Berger was appalled, and the news darkened his thoughts all of that day, which should have been a happy one. "It was our twenty-sixth wedding anniversary," he says ruefully.

The couple's celebration was marked by a long discussion about the implications of the accord. Tom knew he had an obligation to oppose it and to draw attention to its shortcomings. Bev, though not surprised at his determination to set matters straight, told him, "There's going to be a lot of flak, Tom." Then she shrugged, yielding to the inevitable. "What else can you do?"

Tom framed his thoughts in a few hundred words, which Bev typed. When she did so, she realized how right she was: there was bound to be a lot of flak.

Berger planned to make his views known within a few days at the University of Guelph where he was slated to speak as part of its Distinguished Lecturer Series. The talk was entitled "Towards a Regime of Tolerance" after a quote from Laurier, and Berger's thoughts on the constitutional accord fit neatly into the text of his prepared speech, right after he cited Justice Emmett Hall's words that the Nishgas had their own concept of aboriginal title before the coming of the white man and were still entitled to assert it:

> Now the federal government has, in order to obtain a constitutional agreement, surrendered on the issue of Native rights. I confess that I never did believe they would . . .
>
> It is true that the Prime Minister and the premiers have promised to hold another conference to discuss Native rights. But, of course, then the urgency will be gone, and in any event the opting out formula in the new Constitution—the right of the provinces to opt out and the threat to opt out—will make it impossible to reach a meaningful amendment defining Native rights and applying throughout Canada. Native rights will be defined according to the constitutional checkerboard that Canadian statesmen have given us.
>
> In the end, no matter what ideology they profess, our leaders share one firm conviction: that Native rights should not be inviolable, the power of the state must encompass them. Their treatment of Native peoples reveals how essential it is to entrench minority rights, without qualification. In the agreement of November 5th, notwithstanding . . . that Native rights had been affirmed by all parties in the House of Commons, our leaders

repudiated that provision of the draft constitution. Why? Because they believed it was for the greater good of the nation. They believed there were compelling reasons to override the rights of this particular minority. It may, then, happen to other minorities in the future, whenever a political majority decides that their rights must be sacrificed in the interests of the nation or the province.

And then, as he had in his speech before the Canadian Bar Association, Berger called up F. R. Scott's words on the rights of the least protected group.

Berger could not have chosen a harsher criticism against his prime minister. In one blow he had assaulted Trudeau with the thinking of Hall, Scott and Laurier. Trudeau's respect for Emmett Hall was a long-standing one that predated the Nishga case. Frank Scott, "the lawyer's poet and the poet's lawyer," had been both friend and mentor to Trudeau and had been an openly steadfast supporter of the much-criticized use of the War Measures Act. And Wilfrid Laurier's record was exemplary: a Liberal statesman, he had striven for French-English equality, protested Riel's execution, supported the Nishgas and lived a life that epitomized his own plea for a "regime of tolerance." And finally, it was Berger who castigated Trudeau. Berger, sounding eerily like a young and idealistic Pierre Trudeau, had the audacity to shout no.

A few days later Berger had dinner with Martin O'Malley, who since the Mackenzie Valley Inquiry had been following and writing about Berger's career. O'Malley suggested Berger enlarge on his views for *The Globe and Mail*. This he did, and an article under Berger's name was published on 18 November.

Fragile Freedoms was newly on the market and his publishers wanted Berger to promote it, but, as he was a judge and not an ordinary author, he sought and followed the advice of Chief Justice Bora Laskin. Given the nature of the book, Laskin did not object. "Just don't go on any rock-and-roll stations," he admonished. However, interviewers often asked Berger's opinion of the agreement to delete aboriginal rights from the resolution slated to be sent to the British parliament.

Tom's mother was watching him on a television program called "Canada A.M." when hostess Gail Scott made the predictable leap from the book to current events. When Perle Berger heard Tom say precisely what he thought of the constitutional proposal, her heart sank. He seemed to be standing dangerously close to the edge of the bench.

As important as it was that Canada reclaim her Constitution, the quest had always been foiled by obdurate premiers. Trudeau gave his prime years in pursuit of his idea of Canada, and he continued to strive for it while his sons were born and growing into adolescence, as his marriage crumbled and as his adversaries hammered at the gates. He fought on until the ultimate prize, though tarnished, came within reach. He grabbed it, appeasing the national conscience with a promise to discuss native rights at an annual conference, even though the provinces, particularly western ones with land to lose, were notorious for their denial of aboriginal rights. It had also been agreed that there would be a clause to allow provincial governments to opt out of "guaranteed rights." Canadians were told that political accountability would preclude any government from ever using this opting out, or *non obstante,* clause to override any rights. But it was less than Canada could be. And it was wrong.

Public opinion on the issue ranged from disappointment to vehement opposition. Although some premiers showed signs of wavering as protest mounted, British Columbia's Premier Bill Bennett maintained that he would allow the aboriginal rights clause back in only if it did not cost B.C. a cent.

Jean Chrétien, who was minister of justice at the time, laboured long and hard to attain and maintain agreement. He says at that stage, "the provinces were scared to death. Alberta told me, 'We can't back away. We will look bad.' Then it came to me, what to do, like a flash in my head; I thought to put in that word, 'existing.' That was not cynical on my part. It was to permit B.C. and Alberta to save face—to make it acceptable for them. But it was a symbolic change. I was not in the position to rub salt in the wounds of the provinces."

"If you've got a right, you've got a right," Chrétien assured everyone. "If it exists, it exists. No one can take it away. Not even the politicians."

The problem was that nobody was exactly sure what those rights were.

"No problem. No change," says Chrétien. "The word 'existing' makes it clear that we didn't intend to create any new rights. But the word doesn't limit them. It can't. We leave it for the courts to decide what those rights are."

And so aboriginal rights, now characterized as "existing aboriginal rights," were returned to the constitutional package, and if Berger and some native people were not fully satisfied with that, at least those rights had a place in the Constitution. "And I did it all on the phone," Chrétien boasts. 'I'm proud of that. I negotiated and negotiated. I'm a conciliator, but I'm getting old. I don't need Berger or any other Monday morning quarterback making it harder for me."

From that point on, progress on the full package resumed; the plan won approval in the House of Commons, the Senate and finally the British parliament. The Constitution of Canada came home.

That was not the end of the story for Tom Berger, however.

Less than a week after Berger's *Globe* article, Prime Minister Trudeau was interviewed by Jack Webster on a Vancouver television talk show. Webster, in feigned innocence, asked Trudeau what he thought about Berger's blowing the whistle on the first ministers and their diluted "package." The full text of the prime minister's reply bears repeating because it is so inconsistent with the facts, with Trudeau's personality and in its logic:

> I'm not sure what permitted Berger to enter the public debate on a resolution which is before parliament. The judges are very sensitive when politicians criticize them. I think it's not the purpose of judges to get in and discuss an accord that was reached, or a bill before parliament, and I take strong exception to that. If he had wanted to do this I wonder why he didn't support us then. He saw fit to get off the bench and enter into the political arena at a very inopportune time. I just regard this as the judiciary getting mixed into politics and I hope the judges will do something about it.

One judge already had. Mr. Justice George Addy of the Federal Court of Canada had written a letter of complaint to Bora Laskin, chief justice of Canada, on the very day that Berger's article had been published in *The Globe and Mail*. Addy elaborated on his complaints in a second letter, written the following day.

Trudeau's response, of course, reveals his isolation, an isolation so great that he was unaware of Berger's publicly announced support for the original constitutional package. It was an odd response, too, in that Trudeau said in one breath that he took "strong exception" to a judge discussing a resolution still before parliament, while in the next he wondered why Berger had not supported the earlier proposal, implying that it would have been acceptable to have done so. And most strikingly, Trudeau's words are not in his trademark pellucid style, an indication of his vulnerability and frustration.

Justice Addy had written to Chief Justice Laskin in his capacity as head of the Canadian Judicial Council, which had been created under John Turner when he was justice minister. The council, comprised of twenty-seven federally-appointed provincial chief justices, is headed by the chief justice of Canada. Until what came to be known as "l'affaire Berger," few people were aware of the council's existence.

Addy alleged that Berger's comments were a threat "to the independence of the judiciary, the administration of justice and the maintenance of the principle of the separation of powers."

Strong words. They were ominous, too. A politician who interferes with the course of justice is in contempt and may be forced to resign. Justice Addy seemed to be implying that, conversely, a judge who interferes with the political process may be cited for contempt and forced to step down.

Addy's complaint seems really to be that Judge Berger was too independent, but that is surely neither contempt nor reason to force a resignation. The closing paragraph of his second letter reveals that he is not opposed to Berger's thinking: "I wish to emphasize that my complaint is not based on any divergence of views on the substance of the article. On the contrary, I feel that the views expressed therein are quite logical and acceptable and are also very relevant to the serious political problems currently facing our country."

British Columbia Supreme Court Chief Justice Allan McEachern thinks that what Addy meant was the independence of individual judges from "superintendence and discipline by the council over matters not arising from discharge of their duties." But McEachern disputes that the council has that jurisdiction and says that council members have a duty to "protect the historic personal independence . . . of all superior court judges in Canada. . . . They are not a profession . . . or independent guardians of the law."

In response to the brouhaha, Berger also wrote to Chief Justice Bora Laskin to explain what he thought would have been obvious:

why he did what he did. Bora Laskin, with the appearance, reputation and nickname of "Moses," had been perceived for decades as a protector of civil liberties, and Berger thought that philosophically and privately the chief justice of Canada would support him. He was wrong. And so, Berger was forced to explain that while his behaviour might have been unconventional, he did not see it as a "venture into politics in any ordinary sense." He continued:

This was, after all, a moment of constitutional renewal, unique in our country's history. . . . While these are questions that rise above narrow partisanship, they are nevertheless political questions in the broad sense. Indeed, they bear directly on the question of how we are to be governed for the next 100 years. It was for this reason that I felt obliged to speak out publicly . . .

What I did was done after considering carefully what I should do, and with the best interests of my country in mind. I do not believe anything I have done has impaired the independence of the judiciary. . . . I believe it is a mistake to think it is possible to place fences around a judge's conscience. These are matters that no tidy scheme of rules and regulations can encompass, for all judges are not cast from the same mould . . .

It is a question of principle. Should the Judicial Council issue edicts on matters of conscience? If you and your colleagues agree with Mr. Justice Addy, there is nothing more to be said. I believe, however, that these are matters that individual judges must decide for themselves.

After the historic vote that assured the Constitution's repatriation, tempers cooled. During the celebrations that evening, NDP Member of Parliament Ian Waddell mentioned the Berger incident to Trudeau, and from their short conversation he "got the impression" that the prime minister was unaware Berger had openly and vigorously defended the original constitutional package. Although Trudeau is reputed to be a man of cool reason, Waddell and others suspected he had snipped at Berger impetuously in a bit of a pique. On 15 December 1981, Waddell wrote to Trudeau enclosing a copy of Berger's speech to the Canadian Bar Association and a letter that said:

You may be right that, as a judge, Justice Berger should not have made comments on native matters during the constitutional debate but you must remember the absolute place Justice Berger has in the hearts of our native people. Your government had the foresight—as it turns out—to appoint him to the Mackenzie Valley Pipeline Inquiry which now has given Canada a worldwide reputation as a country that honestly tried to struggle with the implications of development on the frontier.

Who knows what the future holds for the eventual settlement on matters concerning our native people, but I remain convinced that your initiative in putting the guarantees in the Constitution (no matter how much criticized now) will be seen as a statesmanlike act. Judge Berger takes that view and said so. He also defended your Charter of Rights. Considering his position of trust among native people, Canada may need him in the future to work with our native people.

Your remarks could potentially undercut his position and I hope that, at some time, somewhere, in your future public remarks you might take the opportunity to temper your criticism with some positive comments. Otherwise, I feel an injustice may be done.

Trudeau, in reply, wrote:

You are right: I was unaware of Justice Berger's statement to the Canadian Bar, on September 2, 1981. It was a superb statement, and I am thankful that you brought it to my attention.

But it was made late in the game, and in a forum scarcely designed to get wide coverage. Whereas Berger's attack on the accord was made in *The Globe and Mail,* at a time when even your party was not certain of supporting the accord so painfully reached.

The paradox remains. Berger supports us in an esoteric forum, perhaps as might befit a member of the Judiciary. But Berger attacks us in a hostile "national" political newspaper, as hardly befits a judge.

But have no fear. I have no lasting grudges, nor have I the disposition to pursue them. And Berger will suffer no injustice on my account!

Trudeau must have forgotten that securing for himself the speaker's position at the 1967 Canadian Bar Association annual meeting had been a strategic move in his bid for the Liberal leadership. Interestingly, his handlers thought that the publicity and prestige of what he dismisses as an "esoteric forum" would thrust him into prominence. And, in time, Bora Laskin would choose the same forum to speak his mind.

Exactly a week after Trudeau wrote his conciliatory letter, the Judicial Council executive took their first steps into the spotlight by striking a committee to investigate Berger's behaviour. Whether they chose to pursue the matter of their own volition, or on Trudeau's account, or Addy's, or even upon the wishes of Bora Laskin, the fact remains that in the minds of the public, the judges, at the instigation of the chief justice of Canada, were avenging the prime minister by engaging in a witch hunt against Berger. The Committee of Investigation was directed to examine the conduct of the Honourable Thomas R. Berger "in private at such time and place and under such procedures, in conformity with the Judges Act, as the Committee may prescribe." Ironically, this behaviour, more than Berger's, seemed designed to bring the reputation and independence of the judiciary into disrepute.

This time was an exceedingly stressful one for the Berger family. Although Tom was heartened and sustained by the steadfast friendship of numerous people, he found it unnerving to know that judges and other members of the legal community were being questioned and canvassed for their opinions about his actions. He also knew that while many people harboured strong feelings on the issue, some of his peers simply resented his drawing attention to them in a way that might cause their lives as judges to be monitored even more stringently in the future, further increasing their isolation.

Berger refused to attend a hearing before the Committee of Investigation because he thought his actions and words were clear, unequivocal and spoke for themselves; participating in the fiasco would only serve to perpetuate the controversy.

If he was unwilling to say anything further in his own defence, the chief justice of his own court was eager to champion him. Allan McEachern, who believed that the reaction of the Judicial Council threatened to discredit the judiciary, wrote a letter on 29 March 1982 to the Committee of Investigation urging them to

proceed with utmost caution. Is not the procedure fraught with danger for the independence of the judiciary? Is it the role of the Council to impose its will upon the conscience of a judge who went unnoticed when he spoke up for the constitutional package, but who when he speaks critically of later developments in the process, feels the full weight of the judicial establishment coming down on him—possibly destroying his career?

As McEachern saw it, the council lacked the authority to issue reprimands, the more so as they did not even have a definition of misconduct. Could judges be independent, he asked, if they laboured under the threat of reprimand for displeasing a majority of the council through some undefined breach? And he warned that "Council is entering dangerous territory." He said that they had no venue for officially expressing disapproval for conduct which fell short of an actual breach of the statutory condition of "good behaviour," and he told them that Berger "considers it demeaning to him as an independent judge to participate in your proceedings. . . . I also wish you to consider whether a private inquiry is the appropriate way to reach conclusions of such consequences to the Judiciary." McEachern also argued the merits of Berger's position and told the committee that once he had discussed the matter with him, Berger had refrained from any further extrajudicial activism.

Berger and McEachern share a friendship and respect going back to their days as barristers. Tom was the first of the two to go to the bench; their professional relationship changed when McEachern also stepped up to the bench, and again when McEachern became chief justice. But nothing changed the respect the men had for each other.

When Berger saw the letter McEachern had written on his behalf, he was deeply moved. "You're acting like a lawyer, rushing to my defence," he said.

"Perhaps I was," McEachern concedes now with a trace of a smile, "but I was defending the office as much as I was the man. Preservation of the independence of the judiciary is of the utmost importance."

Despite growing public opposition, the investigation ground on with relentless thoroughness. When Berger realized the breadth and gravity of the probe, he felt that his personal independence and integrity, as well as that of the judiciary as a whole, were being undermined. To counteract this, he issued a press statement on 6 April 1982, though to "go public" was an audacious act for any judge, even Berger, who now had thrown professional protocol and reticence to the winds.

> I believe that a judge has the right—a duty in fact to speak out on an appropriate occasion, on questions of human rights and fundamental freedoms, particularly minority rights. . . . They are questions

of fundamental fairness. They are the foundations of Canada's claim
that it is a plural democracy. If we fail to acknowledge the rights of
one of Canada's founding peoples, and of native peoples, the rights
of all of our cultural and ethnic minorities may be at risk . . .

    I have no regrets.

The statement also mentioned several highly publicized instances
in which prominent jurists had spoken out on issues within the
political realm.

    At this juncture Chief Justice MacKinnon, on behalf of the
Committee of Investigation, sought the opinion of the eminent
lawyer John J. Robinette on three points raised by McEachern:

1. Does the Canadian Judicial Council have the power to investigate
    the extra-judicial conduct of a Judge without his consent?
2. Must there first be a *prima facie* case for removal of a Judge from
    office before the Council or an Inquiry Committee appointed by
    the Council can commence an inquiry as to whether the Judge
    should be removed from office?
3. Does the Canadian Judicial Council have the power to reprimand
    or impose some lesser penalty than to recommend removal of a
    Judge?

Robinette's reply of 27 April 1982 was delivered by hand. On the
first question, he thought the Judges Act wide enough to em-
power the council to investigate the extrajudicial conduct of a
judge without his consent. On the second question he found nothing in the act to indicate that a *prima facie* (or obvious) case need be
established prior to an inquiry. The third question, he said, was
more difficult. The act states that after an investigation the council
shall report its conclusions and submit the record of the inquiry to
the minister of justice of Canada. If the council's opinion is that
the judge's conduct placed him in a position incompatible with the
due execution of his office, the council may recommend that he be
removed from office. They do not, said Robinette, have the
power to recommend any disciplinary action other than removal
from office. "It follows, in my opinion, therefore, that the Council has no power to recommend a formal reprimand of the judge
to the Minister of Justice."

    That was how Berger saw the situation, too. If Robinette's
opinion had stopped there, that would have been the end of it. But

he went on to remind the council of its mandate to report its conclusions to the justice minister. In Robinette's opinion:

> Having regard to the objects of the Canadian Judicial Council I do not think that a narrow interpretation should be given to the word 'conclusions' in Section 41(1). The word 'conclusions' does not exclude an expression of Council's view as to the conduct of a judge. . .
>
> In my view in its report to the Minister of Justice the Council can . . . express its concluded opinion as to the conduct of the judge . . . [and] also express its reasons.

It was a small wedge but it had the potential to break open the wall protecting judicial independence. Through a "concluded opinion" and reasons, the council could accomplish something equivalent to a reprimand. This twist would confuse Jean Chrétien who, as justice minister, was to play yet another role in Berger's life.

The report of the council's investigation committee, tabled in the House of Commons in early June of 1982, was a hundred pages long and came down harshly on Berger. The notion that he had threatened the separation of powers was now refined to read:

> The principle that emerges from legal history is that the political and judicial spheres of action must remain clearly separate and apart if the fundamental premise of parliamentary democracy is not to be violated . . .
>
> Judges, of necessity, must be divorced from all politics. That does not prevent them from holding strong views on matters of great national importance but they are gagged by the very nature of their independent office, difficult as that may seem.
>
> We are prepared to believe that he had the best interests of Canada in mind when he spoke, but a judge's conscience is not an acceptable excuse for contravening a fundamental rule so important to the existence of a parliamentary democracy and judicial independence.
>
> If a judge wants to speak out on matters of great importance on which there are conflicting views, it should not be from the platform of a judge. Instead, the judge should resign and enter the arena, to become both an exponent and a target of those who oppose those views . . . we view his conduct seriously and are of the view that it would support a recommendation for removal from office.

The Judicial Council executive did not intend that Berger be provided with a copy of the investigators' report, and if Chief Justice McEachern had not given him a copy, he would have been denied any chance to reply to their attack on his integrity and fitness to sit as a judge. Berger still could scarcely believe that the council had proceeded with Judge Addy's complaint and was saddened by the knowledge that it could not have been without Laskin's consent. His only recourse was to write once more to Chief Justice Laskin, and he argued his own case in a tightly worded seven-page letter. In circulating the same letter to the secretary and members of the Judicial Council, Berger did nothing to lessen growing antagonism towards himself, but he wanted to be certain that all aspects of the important principle of judicial independence were considered. He berated the investigation committee for alleging his guilt while not asking parliament to remove him from office:

> The Committee may think this is a satisfactory outcome, but a moment's reflection will show that it is untenable. . . . You cannot have a judiciary where such breaches are excused. You cannot have judges continuing in office on probation, so to speak. Parliament is the final arbiter of good behaviour. The Committee is, in effect, urging the Council to arrogate to itself the right to determine what is or what is not a breach of the condition of good behaviour, and, by not recommending removal, to withhold its judgment from Parliamentary review, thereby denying me the opportunity for exoneration.

Berger went on to say the committee had ignored precedents, both American and Canadian, and found the former omission most surprising, because, as he pointed out, "the doctrine of the separation of powers is an American doctrine." He called this an "enterprising selectivity." As for Canadian precedents, he said, a member of the Judicial Council, Chief Justice Freedman, was well known for his public support of the invocation of the War Measures Act in 1970. And Berger asked about *The Sword and the Scales,* a published collection of Chief Justice Deschênes's speeches, with a foreword by the Right Honourable Bora Laskin, which contained a piece pleading "the rights of the unborn child, a subject of perennial controversy." Berger continued:

Suppose we take it that the gravamen of my offence lies in using my office "as a platform from which to express [my] views publicly on a matter of great political sensitivity." If this is the standard, I can follow the Committee's reasoning. I spoke at a time when the proposals agreed to by the First Ministers were about to come before Parliament. It was my hope that it might be possible to influence the course that Parliament was to take. I did not wish to disparage the policy of Parliament; rather I wanted to urge Parliament to reinstate the rights of minorities.

What if I had waited until Parliament had acted; and then criticized what they had done? Perhaps that would have been all right. If so, this would explain why Chief Justice Deschênes, who sits on the Judicial Council, would second the motion to have me investigated and then travel to Vancouver in the same month to give a speech denouncing the failure of Parliament to entrench the independence of the judiciary in the new Constitution: to intervene when one may be effective is apparently an offence, but to paw the air in exasperation after the event is not. I fear the public will not see the usefulness of the distinction. What is, after all, the singular aspect of my case? That my intervention aroused the resentment of the Prime Minister? I should think it unwise to make a finding based on such a distinction . . .

During my ten years as a judge . . . there has never in all that time been a complaint to the Judicial Council from a member of the public—not even by an unsuccessful litigant—that I have not properly discharged the duties of my office. Nor have there, as far as I know, been any complaints to the Council by members of the public about my intervention in the constitutional debate. The complaint was laid by a judge . . .

Public confidence in the judiciary has survived generations of political appointments, unconscionable delays by judges in getting their judgments down, and various kinds of criminal and otherwise scandalous activity by judges. The notion that it will be impaired because a judge urged our leaders to reconsider their rejection of the rights of minorities is fantastic.

I do not accept the council's authority to censure me—for this is what the Committee wants the Council to do. The Council has no statutory power to do so . . .

. . . But the question can now be resolved only by Parliament. It is too important to be left to judges. Certainly the Judicial Council has no mandate to deal with it; under no circumstances should it be dealt with behind closed doors. The views of the bar, of scholars, of the Conference of Judges of Canada and, of course, the public, should be considered.

The council did not rise to this challenge, but as copies of the full report and correspondence were circulated, a feeling of uneasiness about the implications of the proceedings began to be articulated more openly by the legal community. At the May meeting of the Criminal Justice subsection of the British Columbia Bar in Vancouver, this motion was unanimously passed: "RESOLVED that the section expresses its respect and admiration for the Honourable Mr. Justice Thomas Berger."

Similarly, the B.C. Branch of the Canadian Bar Association approved this motion, with nearly half of those present abstaining from voting: "THAT the branch record its support for Justice Berger's position in the current issues involving the Judicial Council." Subsequently, the Canadian Bar Association struck a committee to report on the independence of the judiciary.

The Investigation Committee Report was only one of many documents that the Judicial Council presented to Minister of Justice Jean Chrétien. The resolution they formulated and submitted with their own report adopted a submission received earlier from the Canadian Civil Liberties Association deploring the absence of clear rules to guide judges. The resolution said that while the Honourable Mr. Justice Berger's actions were "indiscreet," they did not constitute a basis for removing him from office.

At first, Chrétien interpreted the decision to mean that "The guidelines in the report of the three judges are, in my judgment, accepted by the Judicial Council. . . . Any guys who will become judges will be well advised to read that report because they will know that if they do not follow it, their fellow judges will ask them why they didn't read it, because most of the judges feel very strongly that the separation of powers is extremely important to our system."

This is not what the council's report and resolution indicated, but in light of the volume of material given to Chrétien, all in English (not his mother tongue) and the brief time he was given to respond to it, there is no reason at all to believe that he deliberately misrepresented the contents. It is more likely that he relied on Robinette's opinion letter, which was appended to the report.

The media reports, unfortunately, gave full coverage to his initial assessment, and it was commonly perceived that Chrétien was fishing for Berger's resignation. When asked at a 4 June press conference whether he would like Judge Berger to find another job, the justice minister replied carefully: "It's up to him to make up his own mind—just like any other person who is being criticized publicly."

Many of Berger's friends also held the same view: that resignation was in order. Nancy Morrison, who rates her friendship with Tom Berger as one of the great privileges of her life, is quick to say, "Of course he had to speak out. He was incapable of placing the consequences—if he even thought about them—before his moral obligation. But a judgeship carries a given. If you want to take a stance on a political issue, you have to resign. With Tom, it was only a question of when." Morrison was a Vancouver Provincial Court judge when she resigned in order that she could speak freely on abortion.

Berger was watching a televised version of *Hamlet* with his son David when he heard that the Judicial Council had decided he had been "indiscreet." There arose handily from this circumstance an analogy with which he responded to the press. "Council should remember what Hamlet said," he told reporters. " 'Our indiscretions sometimes serve us well, when our deep plots do pall.' "

Later, when he had a chance to read the investigation committee's report, he said it expressed a conventional wisdom in deeming his remarks "indiscreet." "But," he asked, concisely summarizing what he has always known, "how often has conventional wisdom been right about anything that truly matters?" In applying this credo throughout his life he has avoided passive acceptance of the status quo. He looks at each situation without the burden of preconceived notions, and it is this intellectual rigour that is the essence of Tom Berger.

Popular belief, if not conventional wisdom, wanted to attribute his speaking out to political ambitions or allegiances, and many people are to this day unwilling to concede that private conscience and decency moved Berger to jeopardize his career.

Jean Chrétien, a totally pragmatic politician, continues to be incredulous. "I like Berger. I like outspoken guys. This was a political arena. Berger knew the risk; he's no fool. You can fly 20 or 20,000 times but only crash once. He was putting me in a tough spot; that was very obvious. The reason, I would think, would be so he could run in the next election. But he didn't." Chrétien shakes his head, mystified by this lost opportunity. "If you are a judge, you are secure, but you can't be political. I could have been a judge ten times in my life, but I would rather be insecure and have fun."

The Bergers were not having fun; for them that summer was marked by weariness and disappointment. "My Dad has such respect for the law," Erin Berger explains. "For all of it—the courts, the police, the system by which we get laws. He's always taught us that, and he lives and believes it. He's never been cynical. I think he got that from his Dad—my Grandpa Berger who died when I was little. He was a policeman. Nana Berger is the same way. You know, respect and value what we have and if we see problems, we have a duty to do what we can to improve it."

But that summer, Tom Berger suffered a certain loss of faith. His confidence in the justice system faltered a bit.

"There was no getting away from it," Bev recalls. "We were constantly aware that Tom had been discussed and picked apart by his colleagues. It's always lonely being a judge, but this was worse, and it went on for a long, long time."

At last Tom and Bev slipped away for a week of tennis with good friends in Arizona. Tennis and the warm companionship of long walks have always been their antidote for tension, but this time the remedy did not work. The toll proved to be physical as well as emotional: Bev developed water on the knee, and Tom was hampered in his game by an increasingly touchy back. Unable to enjoy themselves, they came home early.

From time to time they discussed Tom's options, which were limited by two important considerations. Subsequent to his becoming a judge, the Law Society had passed a regulation preventing former judges from returning to practice before courts of the same or lower levels so that former judges would not be considered to have an unfair advantage. Although his strength is as a barrister, he would not be able to appear before his Supreme Court brethren. So, for courtroom work, that left the appeal courts; and as appeals flow from cases heard at the lower level, appearances in higher courts such as the Supreme Court of Canada, or the B.C. or federal courts of appeal would only come to him by way of referrals from other lawyers' clients. More important was Berger's reluctance to be separated from the law itself for which he harboured a love; for its promises, intricacies and truths.

It was in this context that Tom and Bev Berger tried to put the trauma behind them so that Tom could continue his judicial duties with some measure of normality. On Labour Day weekend, they spent the holiday in Victoria on Vancouver Island. On a soft, late summer evening, they were strolling back to their hotel after a visit with friends, when they came upon a late edition paper. The headline announced: LASKIN CALLS BERGER IGNORANT.

This headline stemmed from, yes, that esoteric forum again, the annual meeting of the Canadian Bar Association. This time, 2 September 1982, Chief Justice Bora Laskin was the keynote speaker. He began in a forthright fashion to say that he was impelled to speak on a matter of fundamental importance:

> The subject is the meaning and scope of judicial independence. I would have thought that its meaning would have been well understood . . . that there was a clear public understanding that Judges cannot be measured in the same way as other holders of public office. . . . In my understanding . . . Judges are expected to abstain from participation in political controversy. Obviously, considering the storm that has brewed early this year on the Berger affair, I was somewhat mistaken . . .
>
> . . . To a large degree, Judge Berger was reactivating his Mackenzie Valley Pipeline Inquiry, a matter which was years behind him and should properly be left dormant for a political decision, if any, and not for his initiative in the midst of a sensitive political controversy.

Royal commissions, Laskin said, once completed, do not permit a judge to make further comment. He warned that judicial commissioners were not intended to be protagonists, however enamoured they may become of their work, nor were they to make a career of the special assignment.

Laskin regretted that the controversy had reflected badly and incorrectly on the Judicial Council, and he blamed not only Berger but the media for failing to do adequate homework about the role of the council. The council deserved, he asserted, to have its record cleared, and that was what he hoped to accomplish in making his speech. However, in so doing, he placed his focus on the fact that judges have "no freedom of speech," and one who feels compelled to speak out "is best advised to resign from the bench."

Laskin relentlessly lashed out a second time, at Lakehead University, where he repeated his admonishment of judges who speak about their royal commissions.

Berger agrees that Laskin's position would be correct if the chief justice was speaking of a commissioner who had investigated allegations of wrongdoing, but Berger's commissions had been inquiries on public policy. Berger maintained that a judge is right to look to the example of Emmett Hall, who after his 1964 royal commission on health services made numerous speeches on behalf of medicare.

Minority rights in the Constitution are of singular importance to Berger, and he thumps his fist on the table to vow, "You bet your life I would do it again."

Christmas of 1982 was less than joyful at the Bergers' home. Clearly, it was time to take stock and for Tom to prepare himself for a major career change. At a holiday season meeting with his chief justice, Berger advised McEachern that he was prepared to take the only reasonable course left to him and leave the bench. A judge's salary would normally continue to age seventy-five when a judge can expect to retire with a pension, but there would be no pension for Berger, a fact that dismayed his friend Dennis Cocke, who is a pension consultant. Nor was there a thriving practice awaiting his return. He was fifty years old. With McEachern's agreement, Berger decided to leave the bench during the coming summer, giving him enough time to complete his workload, write his judgments and to hear the trials for which he was scheduled.

Perle Berger says that it had been perfectly obvious to her that Tom could not carry on. For reasons inherent in a loving relationship between a grown son and his elderly mother, Tom thought he had to shield her from the truth. Essa Horswill, whose fondness for Mrs. Berger arose from their years of working together in Tom's law office, was in the habit of calling the retired Perle to keep her up to date. During these chats, Mrs. Berger prodded Essa for tidbits of information, all the while accepting that Tom would tell her when he was ready. Finally, he and Bev asked her to dinner at a favourite restaurant, and after the meal, when they judged her ready to hear it, they gently broke the news.

"I'm a good actress and I knew my lines," Perle Berger chuckles. "Tom was relieved that I could handle it."

The next day, 25 April 1983, he wrote his letter of resignation:

My years on the Court have been altogether worthwhile. I have had the friendliest relations with my colleagues and with members of the bar; as well, I have received every consideration from Chief Justice Allan McEachern and his predecessors. I think the Supreme Court of British Columbia is a fine bench and serves our province well.

It used to be thought that an appointment to the bench was for a lifetime. But the judiciary, like all of our institutions, is changing. When I went on the bench I was 38. I am 50 now, a good time of life to consider a change.

Within a day or two of his writing that graceful letter, the newspapers began to call, pursuing the rumour of his resignation. "I called Don Rosenbloom. He came and helped me prepare a statement for the reporters. By May first it was in all the papers." His resignation struck a chord of regret in many hearts, and there was a sadness akin to a sense of shame. Something fine and upstanding in Canadian life had been rejected.

Alan Borovoy of the Canadian Civil Liberties Association, the same man who had spiritedly attacked Berger's *Fragile Freedoms,* went on record to urge that the resignation not be accepted until there was a full inquiry on the propriety of judges speaking out on public issues. But the damage had been done, and it was, to use Berger's words, only another example of "pawing the air in frustration when it's too late."

Later that summer Berger's chronic back pain became intolerable, and he underwent disk surgery. By the time he had finished convalescing, his time on the bench was over. Twenty-two months after he first deplored "the true limits of the Canadian conscience and the Canadian imagination," a great era in his life, and in the life of Canada, was over.

Two days after his resignation took effect, Maisie's people lured Tom Berger to Alaska.

CHAPTER 9

The Outsider

"Choices, sometimes hard choices, must be made." In October 1984 Tom Berger, the victor and victim of hard choices, was speaking at the Alaska Center for the Environment in Anchorage. His presentation was a masterly illumination of the problems that arise when native peoples and conservationists struggle to preserve land and sea resources for reasons which, at first, appear to conflict. He adopted a rational approach and, sharing his insights and experience, explored the common ground between the two groups, making it evident that if they recognized their shared goals and if they made the hard choices, they could mutually benefit.

The previous day, Berger had heard testimony in the tiny Kenai Peninsula community of English Bay, and the next day, he would take his Alaska Native Review Commission (ANRC) to the Aleutian Islands. In more than sixty towns, villages and fish camps, over the course of eighteen months, native Alaskans had told him what had been happening to them since the passing of the Alaska Native Claims Settlement Act (ANCSA) in 1971.

The events that transported Berger from a Canadian limbo to an international forum were complex and fortuitous. They had

begun years before with Eben Hopson's dream of bringing together for the first time Canadian, Greenlandic and Alaskan arctic
rim natives. As the busy mayor of the oil-rich North Slope
Borough, however, Hopson had too many responsibilities, so he
had recruited Dalee Sambo, an Inupiat high school girl, to help
organize the assembly. (The Inupiat are a polar people whose ancestors crossed the Bering Sea from Asia to Alaska many centuries
ago.) As a result, five to seven hundred native northerners had
come to Barrow, Alaska, in 1977 to discuss the conservation of
their common environment and to discover their similarities. This
had culminated in the founding of the Inuit Circumpolar Conference (ICC), and the expression of the intention to accomplish seven
goals involving Inuit solidarity and to promote the long-term
management and protection of arctic and subarctic wildlife and
environment.

To understand the ICC vision, remember that they look at their
land, ice and sea as these features would appear on a polar projec-
tion map. This circumpolar perspective of the world—where
100,000 Inuit live—emphasizes the artificiality of politically
drawn boundaries. For them, it is not logical to think that their
problems and values stop at unseen borders, and they are saddened by the "Ice Curtain" that blocks their kinship with Siberian
Inuit.

By July of 1982 Dalee Sambo had become an assistant to Jimmy
Stotts and Oscar Kawagley, Alaska's representatives on the ICC
Executive Council. Along with Archie Gottschalk, a native of the
Bristol Bay region, they had begun tossing around the idea of the
ICC undertaking a project that could benefit aboriginal peoples
around the world. Initially, the group had envisioned an arctic
review of global proportions, with a commissioner from each of
the three member countries, but they soon returned to reality and
thought of tackling the most pressing issue: the ANCSA legislation
in Alaska. And if they could not have three commissioners from
different countries, they wanted one person who had an international perspective. The obvious choice occurred to them all
almost simultaneously.

"Why the hell not get Tom Berger?"

They were electrified.

"I was familiar with who he was from the Mackenzie Valley
Report and his work for the Nishga tribe," says Dalee. "And I
knew he was a world-renowned jurist. Archie was so excited he

could barely speak straight. He paced around the office wondering, if he could speak to him, what he should call him: Judge, Mr. Justice, or Mr. Berger?

"I said, 'Call him Tom. He's just a man, like any other guy.' "

Archie got the number from the telephone operator and placed the call.

"To his home, no less," Dalee laughs. "And he asked for the Honourable Mr. Tom Berger."

Berger remembers being mystified by the call. "I didn't know who Archie was. He was stammering and talking about corporations and land settlements. I knew about the existence of the ICC and that it was carrying on after Eben Hopson's death, but I wasn't clear who wanted what of me."

Later that spring Jimmy Stotts and Archie Gottschalk flew to Vancouver to explain what they had in mind. Berger suggested that the time had surely passed when it was appropriate for a white man to come poking into native affairs, but that, they insisted, was exactly their point. Because Berger had absolutely no involvement in Alaska and because he had no financial, political or corporate stake in ANCSA, his findings and recommendations would be beyond reproach. Issues had become so intricate and convoluted that the two men doubted that a native commissioner could generate the necessary degree of co-operation, support, participation and trust. At last, despite grave doubts, Berger relented to the extent of suggesting that they write a letter to him, outlining their expectations.

The five-page, single-spaced letter Stotts sent to Berger included a reminder that Eben Hopson, before his death, had submitted testimony to the Mackenzie Valley Pipeline Inquiry. The proposed Alaska Native Review Commission, Stotts pointed out,

> is an extension of the process you initiated. It is a test of the basic premises from which you developed your report . . . premises I myself accept.
>
> ANCSA was intended to improve the quality of Alaska Native life, yet it has now come to threaten the very people that it was intended to help. How? Why? And by whom? What must be done to prevent our dreams from becoming social nightmares?

It was an invitation designed to entice Berger, piquing his interest with issues he deeply cared about and flattering him.

"And it worked," Berger laughingly admits. He flew to Alaska, where Dalee Sambo met him for the first time. She was escorting him to his room in the Inlet Towers, the only hotel in Anchorage to withstand the 1964 earthquake, when Berger commented on the large cracks along the corridor. "Well, as long as there's no earthquake tonight," Dalee said brightly, "you'll be fine."

Then they got to work, identifying the issues and planning how a commission could be set up. Here, Berger's Mackenzie inquiry experience came into play. He told them that the money would have to be "up front" in a trust and that he would have to be completely independent—both to protect him and the ANRC from interference or pressures from government, private or native agencies, and to ensure that financing would not become an issue. The ICC representatives were talking about a million dollars while Dalee was thinking: "This organization doesn't have a million dollars. Let's be realistic, guys."

When Berger said that the inquiry might cost two million, Archie popped off the couch and assured him, "We've got some artists who want to donate their work."

Dalee shook her head ruefully. "Even though I told Archie we were talking big money, millions, it hadn't sunk in. Now we were mesmerized. All we could think was, the man is right here. We've got the judge in this very room. It was like we were groupies or something."

If Berger thought the situation was bizarre, he did not let on, but he did tell them that he would have to have Don Gamble, who had been one of his mainstays in the Mackenzie inquiry, work some numbers and get a budget together before they talked about a contract.

Nothing cooled their ardour. Jimmy Stotts was buzzing. He kept pushing. "Will you do it," he asked Berger, "will you?" Finally, Tom said that he would and got out some hotel stationery, wrote a few paragraphs and signed his name. The "document" disappeared into Jimmy Stotts's pocket. Archie began drafting a resolution, and Dalee typed, for the first time, the words: Alaska Native Review Commission. It was 1:30 A.M. They were too tired and happy to imagine just how audacious they were. They agreed to rest and meet again at seven A.M.

At six o'clock an earth tremor shook Dalee out of her bed. Her first conscious thought was, "The judge! He's on the fourteenth floor!" She sped to the hotel, where, to her great relief, she found Berger unharmed. "Well, what do you think of earthquakes?" she asked casually.

Berger roared with laughter. "I thought it was a dream, until I went into the bathroom and saw my things on the floor. I looked out to the parking lot and when I saw there was no one scurrying around, I had my shower."

After that earth-shaking beginning, which demonstrated that Berger had the temperament needed for what lay ahead, there was only time for a brief chat before his plane left.

When Don Gamble came to Barrow a few weeks later, he drafted a budget that also ranked on the Richter scale. The ICC, as an international native association, is strong, serving a constituency of approximately 100,000. "But we're not the Chase-Manhattan Bank," Dalee laughs. "I thought it unrealistic to think we could come up with that amount of money, but it was not my place to say so. I was on staff, not on executive council. Still, I knew that ICC better have some grand scam plan under its wings or the commission was not going to fly."

Undaunted, the ICC was, if not flying, at least taxiing on the runway. The council met at its permanent secretariat in Nuuk, Greenland, to approve the terms of reference. On 29 July 1983, ICC President Hans-Pavia Rosing announced at the Third National Assembly in Frobisher Bay, Northwest Territories, Canada, that the Honourable Thomas R. Berger had accepted their invitation to conduct the Alaska Native Review Commission. With that announcement, Berger was back in the news; he would be exploring the consequences of what American native rights lawyer Fred Paul calls "the largest transfer of property and wealth achieved without bloodshed in the history of civilization," a deal frequently compared with the Louisiana Purchase. Curiously, despite the magnitude of the settlement and its highly unusual structure, North Americans knew very little about ANCSA. Equally curious was that the same could be said about Alaska Natives.

Although the terms of reference initially contemplated investigating the Alaska Native Claims Settlement Act as it related to Inuit people, this was inappropriate because the settlement also applied to native Indians in Alaska. Consequently, the World Council of Indigenous People, representing Indian people throughout North and South America, became a cosponsor of the Alaska Native Review Commission, and the word "Native" was substituted for "Inuit" in the terms of reference that authorized Berger to inquire and report on the following:

1. The socioeconomic status of Alaska Natives
2. The history and intent of the Alaska Native Claims Settlement Act of 1971 (ANCSA)
3. The historic policies and practices of the United States in settling claims by Native Americans, placing ANCSA in political perspective
4. The functions of the various Native Corporations in fulfilling the "spirit" of ANCSA for Alaska Natives; and
5. The social, cultural, economic, political and environmental significance of ANCSA to indigenous peoples around the world.

Why was a review of ANCSA so important? Because it was legislation with built-in urgency. Well before Alaska had achieved statehood, native tribes had filed aboriginal claim to 380 million acres. After statehood in 1969, state government leaders had seen rapid changes looming as oil discoveries coincided with high demands for energy. Native people, both urban and rural, had begun meeting to seek ways to settle their land claims; at the same time government and industrial interests were realizing that planning the development of natural resources would be simplified if those claims were "dealt with." Native representatives had met in Washington, D.C., with government and business officials, and together they had hammered out the Alaska Native Claims Settlement Act under the pressures of time and politics, and subsequently persuaded native people and the United States Congress to accept it. The act was heralded as an innovative vehicle that would propel 80,000 aboriginals into the market economy.

ANCSA is unique. It worked like this: first, all aboriginal land claims were extinguished. In exchange, 44 million acres of land and $962.5 million were parcelled out to thirteen regional and two hundred village corporations. Aleuts, Eskimos and Indians who were alive in 1971 and who claimed to have at least one-quarter native blood were enrolled as stockholders of these new corporations. Members of the same family were not always enrolled in the same corporation, as shares were allocated according to place of residence at the time. Natives who did not live in a village but who were associated with a region were issued shares in a regional corporation, in which villagers also held shares. Natives who did not reside in Alaska on a year-round or permanent basis received shares in a regional corporation that did not hold any land. Natives born after 1971 (the after-borns) would not be given shares. A few corporations have resource-rich land, some have barren glaciers; others have not as yet had their land allocated or conveyed. In most cases, village corporations hold surface rights only, while the regional corporations control subsurface resources.

The oddest aspect of ANCSA was the arbitrary decision to impose corporations upon Alaska Natives as a means of propelling them from subsistence living to the mainstream of American life. It was the converse of the usual situation in which entrepreneurs see an economic opportunity and decide to incorporate. The Alaskan shareholders were expected to create viable businesses, and ANCSA directs Eskimo, Aleuts and Indians to disregard their lack of kinship or cultural bonding and to go forth unified as capitalists even if it means competing with family and friends. Most stockholders had never owned shares in a corporation before, nor had they any experience in business ventures. Some corporations hired experts —consultants and lawyers who, in many cases, charged unconscionably high fees, imparted little or no knowledge, and fled. Many native shareholders served on boards of directors and grappled with a new language and new concepts in order to make land selections, assess shareholder needs and develop an economic base that would employ Natives, pay dividends and satisfy members. For them, the mantle of responsibility to their people has been a heavy one. Despite heroic efforts, some corporations failed, and many others teetered on the brink of bankruptcy. As one man pointed out, the survival rate of entities incorporated in the "real" business community is only one per cent.

In 1991 the shares in the native corporations were to become transferrable, meaning they could be bought, transferred or otherwise acquired by non-Natives. Settlement lands were also to become taxable twenty years after they were conveyed. Land had been the key issue from the start: when ANCSA was pending, it had taken a federally imposed land freeze by Secretary of the Interior Stewart Udall to force the state to agree to a settlement of land claims. Fear, confusion and suspicion ran rampant as ANCSA turned out to be a disaster and 1991 drew nigh.

Berger immediately realized that he would have to travel to each region of Alaska to learn what the people's experiences and expectations were. Remembering the loneliness and rigours of his

Mackenzie Valley travels, he stipulated that he would take on the commission only if Bev could travel with him or join him as often as she wished. "I had them put that in the contract," he uncharacteristically confides, "because I wanted her to be with me."

Although the travel was not always easy and was in fact sometimes wild and rugged, Bev Berger was often there, bouncing around bush Alaska with Tom and the troupe. As well, she kept Tom in touch with life back home; family, friends and colleagues —all of whom had become more important to him each year.

But Tom Berger's travels were not limited to Alaska. Just as Dalee had feared, there were immediate funding problems, and she says that she would have given up but for Berger's dedication. He was so utterly convinced of the importance of the commission that he swore, "If I have to take a tape recorder and hitchhike around Alaska, I'm going to do it."

Tom and Dalee pared and whittled away at the budget, revising figures after a few "bare-bones" hearings gave them a better idea of the true cost of the work. When, at last, they got the cost down to $1.5 million, they hit the skies, touching down at New York, Washington, Minneapolis—any place where they might find money. Dalee quickly adapted to her role as a fund raiser and was able to say, "We're a good team. He's the older, more philosophical member and I'm the younger one who wants to talk money. Of course, he's the key person who is going out there to listen to every word that those native people have to say, but I am a native person with a stake in this. When you can show foundation staff your parents' village on a map, that's something they can grasp. We're no longer picture-book aboriginals dancing on the arctic ice. It brings it home."

It brought the money home, too. The Ford Foundation, the Alaska Humanities Forum, the Wilderness Society, the Rockefeller Brothers Fund, numerous church foundations and native groups agreed to help them.

"There's no reason why Tom should have to have done the fund raising for his wages and for his own staff," Dalee says, "but he has such a commitment—a very sincere and deeply-rooted one. He took it on himself to help in every way possible and it was his reputation that carried us."

However logical and irresistible, the fund-raising junkets were additions to an already gruelling pace, for the organizational work was always heaviest at the beginning of a project. Berger also continued to carry his responsibilities as a member of the United Steelworkers' of America campaign conduct committee in Washington, D.C., as a part-time teacher at the University of British Columbia law school, and as an Interpreter (a labour arbitrator) for the forest industry in the southern interior of British Columbia. Given the short duration of ANRC and its precarious funding, he could not risk abandoning these other paying activities.

Don Gamble, who served as ANRC's control central responsible for almost everything, thought this excerpt from Gandhi's writing was apropos, and he taped it to the door of Berger's office in Anchorage:

> My experience has taught me that no movement ever stops or languishes for want of funds. This does not mean that any . . . movement can go on without money, but it does mean that wherever it has good men and true at its helm, it is bound to attract to itself the requisite funds. On the other hand, I have also observed that a movement takes its downward course from the time it is afflicted with a plethora of funds.

As many problems as there were, a plethora of funds was not one of them.

After two hearings, Berger realized that the villages were beset by problems both petty and profound, and that these tangled issues wound through and often dominated community hearings. Although the village hearings were the backbone of the commission's work, he decided that they must be supplemented with preliminary "overview hearings" which, he said in a speech to the United Tribes of Alaska on 18 October 1983, would

> establish the state, national and international context for the Commission's work. Without this broad perspective, there is a danger that we will become too restrictive in our assessment; that we will forget that other people in other places have faced similar challenges and have developed their own special solutions. They have something to offer from their successes and failures. I think these people are anxious to come to Alaska to share their experiences.

These overview sessions, as well as four later round tables focussing on specific issues, were broadcast on several occasions by LAST (Learn Alaska Satellite Television). The transcripts and papers were placed in libraries and other accessible locations in ICC countries, and were also integrated into radio documentaries and articles. This meant that the first phase of ANRC, as envisioned by Berger, had been kicked into gear. A Berger-style commission is an educational process, and ANRC was based on continuous use and dissemination of information to the native people of Alaska.

Eighty people responded to Berger's invitation to participate in one or more of four round tables held in Anchorage during February and March of 1984. They came from rural and urban Alaska, the lower forty-eight states, Australia, Greenland, Norway and Canada. Among them were anthropologists, tribal leaders, law professors, participants in the original settlement struggle, native elders, attorneys, former public servants and political aides, corporate directors, authors and historians. An Inuit joke that made the rounds was: describe an Inuit family—mother, father, children, elders and anthropologists.

The next step was to go back into the villages, as Berger did not intend to remain cloistered in the Anchorage office surrounded by professionals. Initially, the native corporations were resentful and expressed doubts about the efficacy of an outsider probing their affairs, but Berger was quick to say he was not on a witch hunt to uncover frauds or misappropriation of funds. "I understand that the corporations are apprehensive, but I have no interest in any particular verdict," he reassured them. "Determining whether the corporations have made money is perfectly straightforward. You don't need a commission to do that. But whether they've provided employment in local communities, whether they've strengthened the stability of local communities—there, it seems to me, are the broad questions."

The broadest question of all, Berger knew, was 1991. That deadline was at the root of the resistance of the corporation executives to his probe, for with so many current issues to deal with and so much to learn about corporate operation, preparing for 1991 had not ranked as a high priority. Somewhat abashed that the ICC had anticipated the urgency and nervous that Berger was stepping in where they had failed and might possibly usurp their new power, the corporations were slow to welcome him. Board executives often stood with folded arms at the rear of tribal halls, listening to what Berger and their shareholders had to say. They soon learned that they had nothing to fear and that everyone had wisdom to share and a great deal to learn before they could prepare for the future. There was no time for petty jealousies over who had taken the initiative.

Each village meeting began the same way. Tom Berger sauntered to a table, placed a pad of yellow paper before him and sat quietly while, off to one side or in an inconspicuous corner, Jim Sykes set up his audio equipment. People settled in to see what the former judge from Canada was all about, and when everyone seemed ready, Berger began. His opening words were always the same: reassuring, spoken slowly, but straightforward and easy to understand. He was never formal, yet he was always respectful:

> Hello. My name is Tom Berger. I'm conducting the Alaska Native Review Commission and my job is to go around to every region of Alaska to find out from you, the native people of Alaska, what you think of the Alaska Native Claims Settlement Act of 1971; how you think it's worked out, the good points, the bad points, where you think it should all go from here.
>
> I was asked to do this by the Inuit Circumpolar Conference, which is an international organization of Eskimos from Alaska, Canada and Greenland, and by the World Council of Indigenous People, which is an organization of Indian people from North and South America.
>
> I've been travelling around Alaska since the beginning of the year to give people like yourselves the opportunity to express their view. Everywhere I've gone, people are talking about ANCSA, 1991, and the sale of shares in the corporations . . . I'd like to hear from you tonight; whether you think that in 1991 you should be able to sell your shares, get some money, and fix your houses up or buy a snow machine or whatever you need. Or whether you think that there should be no right for people to sell their shares, to make sure that the land held by the corporations remains always in native hands . . .
>
> And everywhere I've gone, people have asked why the children born since 1971 can't have shares. They have also raised the question of native sovereignty. Couldn't the problems be solved by restoring tribal governments, strengthening the IRA councils [formed under the Indian Re-organization Act] and the traditional councils, and having the corporations turn the land over to the tribal governments which would hold the land safe from takeovers? These are the big questions I've heard from more than 600 people in 31 villages . . .

You may be asking "Why is this guy going around Alaska listening to us? What's going to happen at the end of it all?" Well, I'll write a report and it will be made public at the end of 1985 and it will be on ANCSA, the good side, the bad side. I'll make recommendations about what ought to be done now to preserve native land if that's what you want and what ought to be done about native sovereignty—all of these questions. I'll base it on what you tell me. That's why Jim Sykes is here recording what you say. Transcripts will be made and I'll base my report on what you tell me and then it will be sent to you and Alaska Natives can use it to help them decide what they're going to do about all of these important issues.

. . . I hope you'll feel free to discuss any issues which are important to you, and your ideas about where we should go from here.

. . . Well, I've talked enough and we're open for business.

Now the room would sigh and shuffle; matches would be struck, pop cans opened. People would look at each other but not at Berger, and he did not look at them. Finally, a woman would leave her chair, saying, "Well, I might as well get it over with."

The corporation executives would be interested in what she had to say, but at first they doubted that this method could "solve" anything. However, as time passed, this woman and other people who spoke after her in this hall and in the next village and the last fish camp would touch on all the recurring themes. As Don Gamble often told doubting leaders, "even though this process sounds fanciful or theoretical, it works. The villagers themselves are 'experts' and, given the time and opportunity, they will establish the points of consensus and difference. Judge Berger acts as a catalyst."

Don Gamble, engineer and humanist, likes to cite the recognition given to the innovative Mackenzie Valley Inquiry by the American Association for the Advancement of Science, which said that Berger's process "has shown that it is possible to acquire and disseminate information about highly complex technological projects and it is possible to do so while maintaining a human balance, a concern for things non-technical."

They were right. In fact, even as the ANRC was happening, Brazilians were looking to it as a way of evaluating their 1973 Indian Statute, and Australian and Hawaiian aboriginal people were requesting information on the Berger method of review and the ANRC results.

Mary Kancewick, a young lawyer from Chicago who had transplanted herself to Fairbanks, and Eileen MacLean, an Inupiat trained as a teacher and expert in Inupiat linguistics, carefully designed the schedule of hearings. They made preliminary forays around the state to get a sense of each region: village populations, number of shareholders, transportation and communication links, details of the corporations. Just as important as any of these facts was information about the pattern of living in each village. If a village seemed to be representational of or accessible to enough people, a hearing had to be scheduled for a time that did not conflict with the hunting, fishing, gathering or paid employment that took people away from their homes.

To this maze of detail was added yet another variable to consider—the vagaries of the climate that dictates Alaskan patterns of life. Heavy fogs, harsh winds and biting cold cannot be ignored in a land where travel is by boat through iceberg-dotted waters and by small plane over glaciers and featureless muskeg. In a state that has only a handful of urban centres and a few hundred miles of roads, "weathered in" is part of the vocabulary and a way of life.

After recommending to Berger where and when a hearing should be held, and he had confirmed that he could attend, Mary and Eileen returned to the villages to explain the purpose of the commission and to urge residents to testify. They also arranged meeting places, food and accommodation. The hard-times budget proved to be beneficial in that it brought Berger closer to the people. Wherever possible, they shared their homes, tribal halls and meals with the commission, which, in turn was kept as small as possible, sometimes consisting only of Berger and his audio technician, Jim Sykes. On other occasions Bev was with them, and now and then they were joined by an ANRC staff member, commission counsel David Case, *Tundra Times* reporter-photographer Bill Hess, other journalists, or by myself, Berger's biographer. These extra passengers were allowed only when space on the small chartered planes permitted. Otherwise, hangers-on paid full fare, covered all of their own expenses and developed respect for Berger's stamina and steady nature. Alaskan travel is extraordinarily demanding. Hearings, though fascinating and altogether engrossing, are draining; and meeting day after day with people who are at once fearful and hopeful, and who, despite being agonizingly shy, must share their private thoughts, their homes and their hospitality, is wearying in the extreme. But

Berger would have journeyed farther. "They asked me to go to the Soviet Union. We tried to get in to find out about Soviet Eskimos. We can go to Moscow and even to Siberia, but not to the Inuit villages in Siberia—not since the Cold War."

After the hearings, potluck dinners, tours of villages and schools, Berger found time to sit in some quiet place—usually on a log or rock—to think about what people had told him. Before the end of each day, he made notes that would eventually form part of his report. There were also numerous engagements— speaking to students, Natives, Whites and special interest groups—to which he devoted a great deal of thought and preparation.

More frequent than major speeches were interviews for television, radio and newspapers, both Native and mainstream, all of which were part of the ongoing education process. These efforts quickly proved their worth, as people in the villages they visited, however isolated, were increasingly cognizant of the issues raised at previous hearings and better informed about ANRC and ANCSA than earlier participants. To some extent this ensured that each hearing was more productive and that the same questions were not asked repeatedly. However, one theme always emerged without fail wherever Berger went: "It is usually in the villages that the greatest concern about the land is expressed, and—make no mistake—the land is the main issue."

He explained that though 44 million acres had been conveyed, the subsurface rights to ANCSA lands are, with a few exceptions, held by regional corporations. The village corporations hold only surface rights. This was a basis of concern as he said in a speech to the Tanana Chiefs Conference on 12 March 1985:

> Thus, as individuals and as tribal entities, Alaska Natives received little money and no land. What they received were shares in the corporations. The point is a significant one; it is the basis for present concerns about the future of Native land and Native people . . . Non-Native Alaskans, mesmerized by the Native corporations and their financial saga, have only now begun to understand that, to Alaska Natives, the success or failure of the corporations is not the paramount issue, except as it bears on the question of land.

In the shadow of Mount Marathon by Prince William Sound, Esther Ronne spoke of the land in the incongruous corporate language of shareholder rights, proxy votes and annual reports. A member of a landless regional corporation, she is a native community leader who worked for many years on a local newspaper, and she is a driving force on the Mount Marathon nonprofit corporation that attempts to provide the social welfare and educational services supplied by the government prior to ANCSA. But for all of her sense of community, she craved a place, a tangible place to call her land. "I wouldn't care if it looked like nothing to other people or if it was ankle deep in water eight months of the year, I'd make it my home. There's a difference, living where you can see the land, or build on it." Her shares are no consolation.

"Land is our heritage," whispered an elderly woman in English Bay. "It is subsistence. It is picking cranberries and catching big silvers—silver salmon—where my grandmother did."

Vance Koasnikoff is the Aleut chief of a traditional village council, a system of government retained by only a few villages. He recalled how it came to be that only three hundred or so native people were involved in the settlement that now affects up to 80,000. When ANCSA was being discussed in 1970, at English Bay "There was no radio. No telephone," he says. He also confirms what several people have said: many elders could not read, and they used to throw the few pieces of mail they ever received in the fire, "to get rid of the bad news." Koasnikoff sighed. "We didn't know what was happening. Not here." *Here* stills the soul. A ribbon of land that serves as airstrip, pathway and meeting place runs between the bay and a lagoon too perfect to be real. The chief moved his blunt hands in slow circles over the smoothly worn surface of a massive table whose legs are peeled lodgepole pine. In the gully-creased green hills around the lagoon are four waterfalls, and above the falls are the lakes where the women catch trout and Dollys.

"If we can't subsist on the land, how are we to live?" asked a great-grandmother who was recently charged with fishing out of season. "Food stamps. Energy subsidies. The rich have become poor."

For these people their land is everything. For them, the spectre of corporate bankruptcy and corporate takeovers, tax sales and stock acquisitions by opportunists is haunting. They know that their devotion to ancestral lands cannot prevent impoverished urban, out-of-state or village stockholders from surrendering their shares.

The land pervades every facet of life in village Alaska. In Port Graham, a thirty-minute flight from English Bay, the village corporation holds 66,000 acres and also owns a fish cannery, which employs a few dozen of the 196 Port Graham shareholders. President Mary Malachoff said, "I wish I knew more. We're a small corporation; we have to hire auditors—that costs thousands. We hire outside consultants, too, at $80 to $100 an hour, so we can't pay our own people very much."

In this community hall, Eleanor McMullen also spoke about the fact that her heritage and identity as a Native is the land. "I love to hunt and fish. My native spirituality is gone. The Russian Orthodox Church changed that." Her voice quivered with passion. "Mother is in a nursing home. Her bills add up. The state won't help because she owns a piece of land. My heritage! Sell it they say." She apologized for her tears. "Emotions are taking over." If she cannot pay the bills by 1991, Eleanor McMullen thought the government would reclaim her land. She urged Berger, urged everyone in the room, begged that someone, somehow, protect that land.

Next, an intense young man took his place at the table. "The act was designed to fail," he said bitterly. "Divide and conquer still works real good."

It was not the first time nor the last that Berger heard accusations of social engineering, but he chose to look to the present and the future, not the past.

Much of the wilderness, which once provided food, clothing and the means to participate in a cash economy, has become parkland. In some regions, corporation land was granted in a checkerboard fashion, preventing any consolidation of power and impeding traditional patterns of use and movement. Access to water and land resources was also barred by a staggering network of federal and state legislation. The litany of complaint is long and troublesome.

An overlying complication is a rising desire for native self-government. Every statement commanded Berger's full attention as he allowed the expert testimony of those most affected by ANCSA to work its own definition of the problem and hence solutions. This was typically so in Port Graham, where ANCSA (section 14.c.iii) required the village to convey 1280 acres to a state-chartered city government. The city would then be able to subdivide and, as a source of funding, offer lots for sale to those who could afford them, but people feared that these lots would go to non-Natives. They want the after-borns to be able to stay in the community, but for them there may not be any land. They wondered aloud if the act could be amended. Berger asked them, "Would it be feasible to convey the 1280 acres to the traditional council, as the logical entity to hold it?"

As he had in the Mackenzie Valley Inquiry, he insisted on an entirely public process, and no testimony was ever received behind closed doors. He shared all that he heard with Alaskans, whether Native or White, with the media people and with federal and state governments. For people who had been listening for the past few years, there were no surprises when *Village Journey* was released. Dedicated to Beverley, "who made the journey with me," the report of the Alaska Native Review Commission was published as a book, first of all in a paperback edition that was distributed to all of the people who had participated in the review and then in hardcover and paperback for bookstores. Published by Hill & Wang, with royalties accruing to the ICC, *Village Journey* stood on its own as a book, as had *Northern Frontier, Northern Homeland,* and was a "best seller" in Alaska. Berger says that his Alaskan travels were for him "an inner journey." He did not issue his own report so much as pass on what he had learned from the people and their deep concerns about ANCSA and the future. Those concerns centred on land, self-government and subsistence. He spoke about these in the report he delivered to the Inuit Circumpolar Conference on 1 August 1986:

> My *first* and most important recommendation is my recommendation for retribalization of Native corporation land at the village level. I put this recommendation ahead of all others. . . . Deep structural flaws in ANCSA make it likely that, if nothing is done, Native people will lose their land.
>
> I found that Native people in the villages want to keep the 44 million acres received under ANCSA in Native ownership. They sense — quite rightly — that as long as it remains a corporate asset it will be vulnerable. The fact is that most of the village corporations are in financial difficulty. Many will be facing bankruptcy before 1991. So, long before 1991, Native lands may be lost to creditors . . .
>
> The great urgency lies in ensuring the village people retain control of their land. So I have urged that the village corporations

should transfer their land to the tribal governments (IRA councils and traditional councils). The land can be held by the tribal governments or can be placed in federal trust. Either way, this will keep the land in Native ownership; it will also solve the problem of the New Natives, or "after-borns", who would, as tribal members, have the same rights of access to and use of tribal lands as anybody else. To do this without having to cash out dissenting shareholders, Congress will have to pass enabling legislation.

This had already come to pass. At the end of July 1986, ten months after the publication of *Village Journey,* the House of Representatives had passed amendments to ANCSA, including a measure that enabled village corporations to transfer their land to tribal governments. The villagers made a real impression in Washington, D.C., on people such as members of the House of Representatives Morris Udall and John Seiberling. Udall had urged Prime Minister Trudeau to implement Berger's Mackenzie Valley Report recommendations on wilderness preservation. The Senate, however, was not prepared to go along. But in November 1986, control of the Senate returned to the Democrats, and the villagers feel that success in the Senate is now more likely.

Berger's second main recommendation to the ICC was for the assumption of a greater role in local government by tribal governments. They are, he said, "appropriate vehicles for delivery of municipal services in Alaska" and "would bring the practice in line with the Lower 48." He continued:

This entails state recognition of Native sovereignty. Native sovereignty is a well-recognized expression in United States law, denoting Native self-government . . .

It is a mistake to think that tribal ownership and tribal governments are anachronisms. The Congress of the United States is 200 years old, but no one says it is not a contemporary institution. Tribal institutions have been around for a long time, too. That doesn't mean that they have no relevance to our own times.

Native sovereignty—the idea of Native self-determination within the nation-state—is an American idea . . . that has been adopted in many countries as the legal basis for asserting Native rights.

The third recommendation involved subsistence:

For Native people in many of the villages in Alaska, subsistence is necessary for survival . . .

I have recommended tribal jurisdiction over Native subsistence on Native lands, guaranteed Native access to fish and wildlife resources on public lands used by Native people, and shared jurisdiction with state and federal authorities over those lands. This doesn't mean that non-Natives from Anchorage and Fairbanks can't go out and take a moose or go fishing. I'm not talking about *all* public lands—just the land that Native people use . . .

The land must continue in Native ownership, there must be increased Native access to fish and wildlife resources, and a measure of native self-government at the local level—these were the themes that were struck by Alaska Natives who testified in my journey to the villages. My report reflects what they told me. No one put the case for Native subsistence rights better than Teddy Coopchiak, Jr., of Togiak, who said to the Commission:

How should Natives give up their hunting rights? It is well hidden in our mind, and nobody could take it away, like a bird who flies, and nobody could take it or boss it around.

Congress should let the Natives boss themselves because they have survived during the past. Had to make their own laws then, make their own decisions. That is why they are known to be smart people. That's why they survived in the Arctic for so long.

When Berger finished reading this report, he was mobbed by throngs of native well-wishers. Just as he had warned them, there had been controversy over his recommendations, but he and ANRC had emerged from the two-year study unscathed, their credibility and objectivity intact. The reason: Berger did not choose sides among native advocates. "I've tried to keep my distance from native politics and, believe me, in Alaska that isn't easy." Easy or not, he did manage to avoid being drawn in by local issues and, as ever, kept his long-distance vision on the horizon of truth. He told the assembly:

All over the world we are witnessing a resurgence of Native culture, Native claims, and Native pride.

The expansion of the European powers, first Spain and Portugal, later France and England, into the New World raised the central

question: By what right did Europeans take the land and subjugate the indigenous peoples of the New World? By what right did the Russians and then the Americans lay claim to the lands of Alaska?
. . .

If governments continue in their efforts to force Native societies into moulds that they have cast, I believe they will continue to fail. No tidy bureaucratic plan of action for Native people can have any chance of success unless it takes into account the determination of Native peoples to remain themselves . . .

The indigenous peoples of the world are raising profound questions that cannot be answered by the conventional wisdom of science, material progress, or liberal democracy.

A famous Canadian poet, F. R. Scott, described the Arctic as

A land so bleak and bare
A single plume of smoke
Is a scroll of history.

In *Village Journey,* I wrote about the message in that plume of smoke. Out of this land, that to others seems bleak and bare, *you* at the ICC are writing a new scroll of history.

Epilogue

Tom Berger's return to the practice of law was contingent upon the approval of the benchers of the Law Society of British Columbia. The rules state that no judge shall return to practise before a court over which he presided or a lower one without first receiving the approval of the benchers, who are the elected guardians of the ethics of the legal profession. Bencher Gary Somers explains that the Law Society considers a judgeship to be a marriage for life and that a divorce can create a public misapprehension that a former judge, having seen the inside of the circle, may have an unfair advantage. And so, Berger was required to submit to the scrutiny of a committee of benchers. When Somers was a young, newly called lawyer, Berger had recruited him to work on the British Columbia Family and Children's Law Reform Commission. Events had come full circle and Somers was obliged to assess the fitness of his former boss to do what he does best.

"I asked two questions," Somers explains. "Is Tom Berger likely to be a credit to the profession? Yes. Is he likely to use his previous position to advantage? No. Berger's reputation is impeccable." The benchers decided that, as of September 1986, he could return to the unrestricted practice of law. However, the Law Society decreed that the Honourable Thomas R. Berger could no longer use that distinguished form of address, for fear that it might be misconstrued by clients or the public to mean that the former judge had special clout in the courts. Berger relinquished "The Honourable" without a qualm. More than anything else he wanted to return to where life for him had really begun: the practice of law. And he particularly wanted to resume his work on behalf of native people.

During the 1960s young Don Rosenbloom had persuaded Berger to take him on as an articling law student and afterwards they practised together. Subsequently, when Berger was appointed a judge, he persuaded Rosenbloom to stay with the law and assume his practice. Rosenbloom and Aldridge was a busy law firm with a reputation for civil liberties work when Berger was ready to return to his vocation in 1986. Although still a loner by nature, Berger joined Rosenbloom and Aldridge as associate counsel and convinced Val Chapman, who had come to his aid after he left the bench, to return to work. Sometimes a man is lucky. Sometimes he can come home again.

Of the cases and causes awaiting Berger's attention, the first involved Indians, the government and an individual who had lost his job because he had taken a stand on a matter of principle. This was Richard Price, an ordained United Church minister who was director of policy and program consultation for the Department of Indian Affairs and Northern Development in Ottawa when he gave to his former theology professor at the University of British Columbia federal cabinet documents revealing plans to cut back more than $300 million in native programs. These papers found their way to the hands of the Opposition. For that indiscretion Price was fired and criminal breach of trust charges were laid against him—in distant British Columbia where the leak had occurred. An ad hoc group of friends and church staff across Canada lobbied on his behalf and, though they could not have known about Sgt. Ted Berger's difficulties because of taking a stand on a matter of principle, they sought the counsel of Tom Berger, who agreed to coordinate Price's defence. Berger urged that the charge be dropped, on the ground that it violated the Charter of Rights, since the Conservative government had not laid charges against public servants who had leaked documents to the Conservatives when the party had been in opposition. "The charge should never have been laid," Berger told the press. "It was very clearly a case of selective prosecution."

Prime Minister Brian Mulroney, Justice Minister John Crosbie and B.C. Attorney General Brian Smith were taken aback by the storm of protest and support for Price. The charges against him were dropped.

Almost immediately Berger was once more front page news when he agreed to act as counsel for the Manitoba Métis Federation in connection with their claims under the Manitoba Act of 1870. Berger says this claim is firmly grounded in legal and constitutional propositions well known to courts of law. He will bring suits in the Manitoba Court of Queen's Bench and in the Federal Court of Canada against both the federal and provincial governments, as their responsibilities are mingled. Their failure to enforce the provisions of the Manitoba Act as it relates to Métis land, he explained in a letter of opinion to the Métis association on 30 October 1985,

> constitutes the unfinished business of Canadian history. . . . In this case we will be putting the conventional view of Canadian history on trial. . . . Some will say that the injustices the Métis allege in this case happened long ago, that their claims are specious and half-forgotten. We are a nation, however, that believes in the rule of law. Commitments were made, but were not kept. These commitments are not ancient history.

His work on this case may take five years and numerous trips to Ottawa and Manitoba, but those factors do not matter. "I'm going to win this one," he promises.

The third case, which was actually three native rights cases, had more immediate ramifications in British Columbia. In one case the Gitksan and Wet'suwet'en tribal councils claim aboriginal title to a vast tract of land of about 51 800 square kilometres in northwestern B.C. In a second suit, two bands, the Clayoquot and Ahousaht, claim aboriginal title to Meares Island and have obtained an injunction restraining MacMillan Bloedel from logging the island until the case is heard. And, finally, thirty-six bands with unresolved claims sought to prevent the CNR from building a second set of tracks in the canyons along the Thompson and Fraser rivers.

B.C. Supreme Court Chief Justice Allan McEachern ordered that these three disparate cases be heard together, though the three suits have in common only that they concern aboriginal claims to land and have been brought by Indians.

The plaintiffs turned to Tom Berger, who led them in argument before the B.C. Court of Appeal to have the cases heard separately on the grounds that each is unique. "The evidence supporting the claims in the three cases is very different. The cases involve native peoples from wholly different parts of the Province. Their histories, culture, institutions, spiritual beliefs, traditions, languages and resource management practices are distinct. They are as different as the Dutch, French and Belgians are from one another." The judges of the Court of Appeal overturned McEachern's decision, ruling that "aboriginal title cannot be determined on a global or province-wide basis, but must be determined on a case-by-case basis."

Within weeks, McEachern again ordered that the cases be heard together, varying his earlier order only to the extent of saying that the trial judge would have the discretion to decide whether evidence in one case would be admissible in another. Berger returned to the B.C. Court of Appeal, which ruled that while it is within the administrative discretion of the chief justice to designate one judge to hear three cases, a single judge cannot hear them at the same time.

Perhaps McEachern's orders were an expression of his frustration with the policies and politics that impinged on the Indians' cases, or perhaps they were an expression of his frustration with the limited number of judges and courtrooms he had available. In any case, the tactics of both courts and counsel emphasize the burden that unresolved native claims are placing on the legal system.

Berger deplores the government of British Columbia's unwillingness to discuss settlement. As he wrote in the Vancouver *Province* on 24 November 1985:

> In each case the problem can be solved only through resolution of land claims. These claims are not impediments to progress, but the means to progress. How can there be a settlement when one of the essential parties will not come to the table? . . . There is room for the accommodation of the interests of all concerned. Any government that, in the 1980s for political gain, seeks to turn the populace against the native people and their claims will occupy a lonely and unforgiving place in the history of our country.

Tom Berger's practice now extends well beyond native rights, for he has agreed to undertake a variety of cases involving constitutional and Charter questions. Don Rosenbloom has brought him back to another long-standing injustice that he had first learned of from his father who had told him about Angus MacInnis speaking out against the treatment of Japanese Canadians during the Second World War. Tom Berger became more involved with this issue when Don Rosenbloom undertook to represent the National Association of Japanese Canadians. They sought redress for their explusion and internment, and for the confiscation of their goods, lands, boats and businesses which resulted when a surge of racial paranoia followed the 1941 attack by the Japanese on Pearl Harbour. In 1986 at a testimonial dinner for Grace MacInnis (the widow of Angus and daughter of J. S. Woodsworth), given by the Vancouver Japanese Canadian Citizens Association Redress Committee, Berger reminded his audience:

> Redress means compensation. . . . An acknowledgement without compensation is not redress. If compensation for the survivors of internment during the Second World War will not help, then high-sounding language will not either. . . . But compensation is possible; that's how we make good the losses suffered in personal injury cases, including the loss of loved ones; we do it also in cases of wrongful imprisonment. Why imply that it is beneath the dignity of Japanese Canadians for them to seek compensation? . . .
>
> There is nothing to prevent the Government of Canada sitting down and negotiating compensation with the Japanese Canadians. . . . It is a question of accepting national responsibility. . . . If, however, we demonstrate that our concern is tangible by compensating the survivors, we are demonstrating that we believe it should never have happened, and we make it less likely that it will ever happen again.
>
> This is the best we can do; at the same time it is the least that we can do.

Berger's interest in the protection of human rights knows no national borders. He is president of International Defence and Aid, an organization that raises money to hire lawyers to defend political prisoners in South Africa.

He still harbours a concern for the environment and is serving on the Governing Council of the Wilderness Society. He is pleased that his Mackenzie Valley Report recommendation for the northern Yukon to be set aside as wilderness has been adopted to the extent of saving half the area he suggested as a new national park, the remainder being protected under territorial legislation. The object of his recommendations was to preserve the habitat of the Porcupine caribou herd, one of the last of two or three great caribou herds in North America. Now, an agreement has been signed providing for native participation in the management of the herd.

Another matter arising out of Berger's work in the Mackenzie involved his recommendation in *Northern Frontier, Northern Homeland* for the establishment of a whale sanctuary for belugas in Mackenzie Bay. In 1981 the United Nations Environmental Programme (UNEP) considered establishing a worldwide inquiry into whales and dolphins, and Berger agreed to head the inquiry because he thought it would prove a "worthwhile means of strengthening the legal basis for conservation of whales and dolphins and achieving a larger measure of co-operation by national and international institutions for this purpose." Unfortunately, the proposal was scuttled when another arm of the UN, the Food and Agriculture Organization, objected that the inquiry was an invasion into their jurisdiction—whales being categorized as "food" for some people.

Life has been rich and satisfying for Bev and Tom Berger, and though their children are grown and living away, their family is as important to them as it was for Ted and Perle Berger. Erin spent half of the summer of 1986 working for Tom and half working for John Baigent, and plans to article with another Vancouver lawyer, Harry Rankin. David completed a B.A. in history at the University of British Columbia before heading to Australia in search of adventure. He has been travelling the continent and working in the tourism and mining industries. "I'm very proud of Erin and David," Tom says. "They both have a social conscience, they are active politically, and I always enjoy their company."

In 1986 Tom and Bev moved to Trent University in Ontario for three months. There, Bev led several seminars on native art and education, and Berger occupied the Eben Hopson Chair on Northern Studies to deliver a series of lectures on the Arctic, its people, environment and future. He returned to Vancouver to develop these themes as the basis of a new book on the North and to pick up his part-time teaching duties at the University of British Columbia.

Looking back, Tom Berger must be satisfied by how fully his

early aspirations have been met, and how true to his nature were his early desires to be a teacher, writer and lawyer. Although he was for a time diverted by the lure of politics and the bench, he found their scope was too narrow and their constraints too rigid to contain his driving quest for justice, and he returned to a satisfying and challenging life in the law. He is able to teach—in classrooms, seminars and all manner of public gatherings—and finally, even to fulfill his early interest in writing. "Writing books is the hardest work there is," he says. "You've got to put your bum on a chair and keep it there until you've finished." His love of the language and respect for the power of words that are concise, telling and true have enabled him to write scholarly and popular articles, books and commission reports that have become best sellers.

In all of Tom Berger's endeavours and many careers there flows a steady integrity, an unwavering dedication to his belief in the equality, decency and dignity of all beings. It winds through his work in the courts, in politics, in teaching, in his commissions, his environmental and civil liberties work, his writing and his personal life. He regrets none of the hard choices he has made and some lines from Tennyson's "Ulysses" aptly express his life:

> I am a part of all that I have met;
> Yet all experience is an arch wherethro'
> Gleams that untravell'd world whose
> margin fades
> For ever and for ever when I move.

Notes on Sources

Published Material

Berger, Thomas R. "The Constitution, the Charter and Fragile Free-
doms," *Canadian Forum,* June/July, 1982.
————. "The Family, the Courts and the Community." Speech to the
B.C. Bar Association, 1 February 1975, published in 33 *The Advocate*
(1975) 122.
————. *Fragile Freedoms: Human Rights and Dissent in Canada.* Toronto:
Clarke, Irwin, 1981.
————. "The Mackenzie Valley Pipeline Inquiry," 16 *Osgoode Hall Law
Journal* (1978) 639.
————. "The Mackenzie Valley Pipeline Inquiry," 3 *Queen's Law Journal*
(1976–77) 5.
————. "Time to Settle Native Claims," Vancouver *Province,* 24 No-
vember 1985.
————. *Village Journey: The Report of the Alaska Native Review Commission.*
New York: Hill & Wang/Farrar, Straus & Giroux, 1985.
Borovoy, Alan. "The Plight of Minorities," *Canadian Forum,* April 1982.
Borovoy, Alan. "A Rejoinder to Mr. Justice Berger," *Canadian Forum,*
August 1982.
Bregha, François. *Bob Blair's Pipeline.* Toronto: James Lorimer, 1979.
Cruickshank, David A. "Alternatives to the Judicial Process: Court

Avoidance in Child Neglect Cases," 12 *University of British Columbia Law Review* (1978) 248.

Cruickshank, David A. "The Berger Commission Report on Child Protection: The Impact on Prevention of Child Abuse and Neglect." University of Calgary, 1983. Reprinted in *The Challenge of Child Welfare,* edited by Levitt and Wharf. Vancouver: University of British Columbia Press, 1985.

Duff, Wilson. *The Indian History of British Columbia.* Vol. 1, *The Impact of the White Man.* Memoir no. 5. Victoria: British Columbia Provincial Museum, 1964.

Fairley, Jim. *Vancouver Province,* 6 January 1972.

Fotheringham, Allan. *Vancouver Sun,* 1 March 1969 and others.

Goddard, John. "Limbo Country," *Saturday Night,* April 1985.

Gwyn, Richard. "Random Reflections on an Ego Trip," *Toronto Star,* 2 November 1983.

Gzowski, Peter. "Here's Looking at Me," *The Canadian,* 3 July 1976.

Hogg, Peter W. *Constitutional Law of Canada.* Toronto: Carswell, 1977.

Holt, Simma. *Vancouver Sun,* 1964.

Jackson, Michael. *Sentences that Never End: The Report on the Habitual Criminal Study.* Vancouver: University of British Columbia Faculty of Law, 1982.

Jamieson, Roberta. Speech at Indian and Inuit Health Conference, Hamilton, reported in *Victoria Times-Colonist,* 1 December 1982.

Lysyk, Kenneth. "Indian Hunting Rights: Constitutional Considerations and the Role of Indian Treaties in British Columbia," 2 *University of British Columbia Law Review* (1964–66) 401.

Lysyk, Kenneth. "The Indian Title Question in Canada: An Appraisal in Light of Calder," 5 *Canadian Bar Review* (1973) 450.

McCreath, Peter, ed. *Learning from the North: A Guide to the Berger Report.* Toronto: James Lorimer, 1978.

MacDonald, John A. "Family Court Reform in British Columbia," 18 *Reports of Family Law* (1975) 201.

McDonald, Marci. "The Riddle of Nelson Small Legs," *Maclean's* 18 October 1976, p. 38.

MacFarlane, George. *Globe Magazine,* 29 October 1966.

Metcalfe, Ben. *Vancouver Province,* 7 January 1960.

Nagle, Patrick. "Maisie Says B.C. Still Belongs to the Indians," *Weekend Magazine* no. 14, 1964, p. 14.

The Native Voice: Official Organ of the Native Brotherhood of British Columbia, Vancouver. Various issues.

Northern Frontier, Northern Homeland: The Report of the Mackenzie Valley Pipeline Inquiry, Toronto: James Lorimer, 1978.

O'Callaghan, J. P. *Edmonton Journal,* 20 May 1976.

O'Malley, Martin. *The Past and Future Land.* Toronto: Peter Martin and Associates, 1976.

Raunet, Daniel. *Without Surrender, Without Consent: A History of the Nishga Land Claims.* Vancouver: Douglas & McIntyre, 1984.

Rockett, Eve. *Vancouver Sun,* 21 December 1971.

Scott, F. R. *The Collected Poems of F. R. Scott.* Toronto, McClelland and Stewart, 1971.

Sherman, Paddy. *Vancouver Sun,* 7 January 1972.

Trent University newspaper, March 1986.

Zwarun, Suzanne. *Maclean's,* 25 July 1977.

Unpublished Material

Berger, Thomas R. Corry Lecture, Queen's University, Kingston, Ontario, 25 November 1975.

———. "Reflections on Redress," speech to Japanese Canadian Citizens Association, Vancouver, 15 February 1986.

———. Speech to Tanana Chiefs Conference, Fairbanks, Alaska, 12 March 1985.

———. "Towards a Regime of Tolerance," Distinguished Lecturer Series, University of Guelph, Guelph, Ontario, November 1981.

———. Speech to United Tribes of Alaska, 18 October 1983.

———. "Village Journey Report," speech to Inuit Circumpolar Conference, Kotzebue, Alaska, 1 August 1986.

Laskin, The Rt. Hon. Bora. Speech to Canadian Bar Association, 2 September 1982.

Trudeau, Pierre. Interview with Jack Webster on BCTV, Vancouver, 24 November 1981.

Trudeau, Pierre. Speech aired by CBC radio, 8 August 1969.

Public Documents

British Columbia. "Report of the Commission of Inquiry, Workmen's Compensation Act," Chairman The Hon. Mr. Justice Charles W. Tysoe, 1966.

———. "Report of the Royal Commission on Family and Children's Law," Vols. 1 to 13, Chairman The Hon. Mr. Justice Thomas R. Berger, 1974–76.

———. *Sessional Papers,* 1888, p. vcii, "Papers relating to the commission appointed to enquire into the conditions of the Indians of the North-West coast" and p. 436, "Report of the Commissioners to the North-

West Coast Indians," as quoted in *Without Surrender, Without Consent* by Daniel Raunet. Vancouver: Douglas & McIntyre, 1984.

Canada. Dept. of Justice. News release, "Royal Prerogative of Mercy Extended to Remove Habitual Criminal Status," 23 May 1984.

———. Dept. of Justice. "Report of the Canadian Committee on Corrections," Chairman The Hon. Mr. Justice Ouimet, 1969.

———. Dept. of Justice. "Report of the Inquiry into Habitual Criminals in Canada," Chairman The Hon. Mr. Justice Stuart M. Leggatt, 1984.

———. Dept. of Justice. "Report of the Investigation Committee to the Canadian Judicial Council," released at a press conference in Ottawa, 4 June 1982.

———. Dept. of National Health and Welfare. "Report of the Advisory Commission on Indian and Inuit Health Consultation," Chairman The Hon. Mr. Justice Thomas R. Berger, 1980.

———. House of Commons. *Expanded Guidelines for Northern Pipelines,* Environmental-Social Committee, Northern Pipelines, Task Force on Northern Oil Development Report no. 72–73, 28 June 1972.

———. Mackenzie Valley Pipeline Inquiry. *Northern Frontier, Northern Homeland: The Report of the Mackenzie Valley Pipeline Inquiry,* vols. I and II, Chairman The Hon. Mr. Justice Thomas R. Berger, 1977.

———. Mackenzie Valley Pipeline Inquiry, Summaries of Proceedings, 6 vols., 1976.

Public Archives of Canada. Dept. of Indian Affairs and Northern Development Records.

———. Mackenzie Valley Pipeline Inquiry, Transcripts.

Legal References

Re Battaglia and the Workmen's Compensation Board (1960), 22 DLR (2d) 446 (BCSC); (1960), 24 DLR (2d) 21 (BCCA).

Bowlay Logging Ltd. v. *Domtar Ltd.* (1978), 87 DLR (3d) 325 (BCSC).

Calder v. *Attorney General of British Columbia* (1969), 8 DLR (3d) 59 (BCSC); (1970) 13 DLR (3d) 64 (BCCA); (1973), 34 DLR (3d) 145 (SCC).

Canadian Pacific Railway v. *United Transportation Union, Local 144* (1970), 14 DLR (3d) 497 (BCSC).

Dominion Bridge Co. Ltd. v. *International Association of Bridge, Structural and Ornamental Ironworkers, Local 97 and Attorney General of British Columbia* (1959), 20 DLR (2d) 621 (BCCA).

Farrell v. *Workmen's Compensation Board* (1960), 24 DLR (2d) 272 (BCSC); (1960), 26 DLR (2d) 185 (BCCA).

Farrell v. *Workmen's Compensation Board and Attorney General of British Columbia* (1961), 31 DLR (2d) 177 (SCC).

Gee v. *Freeman* et al (1958), 16 DLR (2d) 65 (BCSC); BCCA unreported.

Guerin v. *The Queen* (1984), 13 DLR (4d) 321 (SCC).

Hadden (John) v. *The Queen* [1968] 64 WWR 143 (SCC); (1968), 67 DLR (2d) 469 (SCC).

Jones v. *Bennett* (1966), 56 DLR (2d) 553 (BCSC); (1966), 58 DLR (2d) 603 (BCCA); (1968), 66 DLR (2d) 497 (BCCA); (1968), 2 DLR (3d) 291 (SCC).

Re Kinnaird and the Workmen's Compensation Board (1961), 28 DLR (2d) 771 (BCSC); (1962), 34 DLR (2d) 110 (BCCA); (1963), 38 DLR (2d) 245 (SCC).

Koss v. *Konn* (1961), 28 DLR (2d) 319 (BCSC); (1961), 30 DLR (2d) 242 (BCCA).

MacLennan v. *Workmen's Compensation Board.* Unreported.

McCrea v. *City of White Rock* (1972), 34 DLR (3d) 227 (BCSC).

Re O'Brien and The Queen (1981), 64 CCC (2d) 285 (BCSC).

Oil, Chemical and Atomic Workers International Union, Local No. 16-601 v. *Imperial Oil Ltd.* (1961), 30 DLR (2d) 657 (BCSC); (1962), 33 DLR (2d) 732 (BCCA); (1963), 41 DLR (2d) 732 (BCCA); (1963), 41 DLR (2d) 1 (SCC).

Paton v. *The Queen* [1968] 63 WWR 713; (1968), 68 DLR (2d) 304 (SCC).

Regina v. *Bengert* (1978), 47 CCC (2d) 457 (BCSC).

Regina v. *Bengert (No. 2)* (1979), 47 CCC (2d) 552 (BCSC).

Regina v. *Bengert (No. 3)* (1979), 48 CCC (2d) 413 (BCSC).

Regina v. *Bengert (No. 4)* (1979), 52 CCC (2d) 100 (BCSC).

Regina v. *Cappello.* Unreported.

Regina v. *Gilbert.* Unreported.

Regina v. *Hadden* (Danny) [1970] 73 WWR 542 (BCCA).

Regina v. *McNeil.* Unreported.

Regina v. *McNight* (1960) 34 Criminal Reports 37 (BCCA).

Regina v. *Mason.* Unreported.

Regina v. *Paton.* Unreported.

Regina v. *Neale, Clarke, O'Keefe and Power* (1966), 60 DLR (2d) 619 (BCCA).

Regina v. *White and Bob* (1964), 50 DLR (2d) 613 (BCCA); (1965), 50 DLR (2d) 481 (SCC).

Teck Corporation Ltd. v. *Millar* (1972), 33 DLR (3d) 288 (BCSC).

Re Ursaki (1960), 24 DLR (2d) 761 (BCSC).

Correspondence

All letters to and from Thomas R. Berger are from his files.

Addy, Mr. Justice George. Letters to the Canadian Judicial Council, 18 and 19 November 1981, Appendixes "B" and "D" to the Report of the Investigation Committee to the Canadian Judicial Council. *See* Public Documents, Canada, Dept. of Justice.

McEachern, Chief Justice Allan. Letter to the Canadian Judicial Council,

29 March 1982, Appendix "M" to the Report of the Investigation Committee of the Canadian Judicial Council. *See* Public Documents, Canada, Dept. of Justice.

Robinette, John J. Letter to the Canadian Judicial Council, 27 April 1982, Appendix "P" to the Report of the Investigation Committee to the Canadian Judicial Council. *See* Public Documents, Canada, Dept. of Justice.

Trudeau, Pierre E. Letter to Ian Waddell, 18 January 1982.

Waddell, Ian. Letter to Pierre E. Trudeau, 15 December 1981.

Interviews with Author

Baigent, John. Vancouver, 16 October 1985.

Barrett, Dave. Vancouver, 13 January 1986.

Berger, Beverley. Vancouver and Alaska, 1985–86.

Berger, Erin. Vancouver, August 1986.

Berger, Perle. Vancouver, various dates 1985–86.

Berger, Thomas R. Vancouver, Victoria and Alaska: various dates 1983–86.

Birrell, Gordon. Richmond (telephone), 1985.

Bouck, The Hon. Mr. Justice John C. Vancouver, 1986.

Bregha, François. Ottawa (telephone), 1984.

Bruk, John. Vancouver, 29 January 1986.

Burnett, Allison. White Rock, 9 July 1985.

Chapman, Val. Vancouver, various dates 1984–86.

Chrétien, Jean. Ottawa, 12 February 1985.

Cocke, Yvonne and Dennis. New Westminster, 18 December 1985.

Gamble, Don. Anchorage, Alaska, 19 and 20 September 1984.

Getz, Leon. Vancouver (letter), 25 October 1985.

Halliday, Amber. Victoria (telephone), 1986.

Harvey, James Teetzel. Prince Rupert (telephone), 21 June 1985.

Horswill, Essa. Vancouver, 1985–86.

Hubbard, Percy and Sidney. Clearbrook, 1985.

Hunter, Michael. Vancouver (telephone), 6 August 1985.

Jackson, Michael. Vancouver, 4 February 1985.

Kirkness, Verna. Vancouver (telephone), 1986.

McEachern, The Hon. Mr. Justice Allan. Vancouver, 27 March 1985.

Marchand, Senator Len. Kamloops (telephone), 3 October 1984 and Vancouver, 29 November 1984.

Mechau, Dorik. Anchorage, Alaska, 20 September 1984.

Morrison, Nancy. Vancouver, 23 May 1985.

O'Malley, Martin. Toronto, 14 May 1985.

Rosenbloom, Don. Vancouver, various dates 1984–85.

Sambo, Dalee. Anchorage, Alaska, 21 September 1984.
Sanders, Doug. Vancouver, 26 September 1984.
Scott, The Hon. Ian G. Toronto, 14 November 1985.
Somers, Gary. New Westminster (telephone), 31 January 1986.
Waddell, Ian. Ottawa, 9 January and 13 February 1985.

Acknowledgements

Care has been taken to trace ownership of copyright material contained in this book. The author will be glad to receive information that will enable her to rectify any reference or credit in subsequent editions.

Thomas R. Berger, *Fragile Freedoms: Human Rights and Dissent in Canada,* © 1981 Clarke, Irwin & Co. Ltd., excerpts reprinted by permission of Irwin Publishing Inc. A. Alan Borovoy and Thomas R. Berger, excerpts from reviews and letters published in various issues of *Canadian Forum* in 1982, reprinted by permission of the publisher and authors. François Bregha, *Bob Blair's Pipeline,* excerpts reprinted by permission of the author and James Lorimer & Co. Allan Fotheringham, excerpts from columns in the *Vancouver Sun,* reprinted by permission of the author and the publisher. Richard Gwyn, excerpts from "Random Reflections on an Ego Trip," published 2 November 1983 in the *Toronto Star,* reprinted by permission of the author. Peter W. Hogg, *Constitutional Law of Canada,* excerpts reprinted by permission of Carswell Co. Ltd. F. R. Scott, excerpts from "MacKenzie River" (A land so bleak and bare), "Flying to Fort Smith" (An arena) and "Fort Smith" (Leaning south up the current), all from "Letters from the Mackenzie River" in *The Collected Poems of F. R. Scott,* reprinted by permission of McClelland and Stewart.

Index